DAN-18   DANTES SUBJECT STANDARDIZED TESTS (DSST)

This is your
PASSBOOK for...

Geology (Physical)

Test Preparation Study Guide
Questions & Answers

COPYRIGHT NOTICE

This book is SOLELY intended for, is sold ONLY to, and its use is RESTRICTED to individual, bona fide applicants or candidates who qualify by virtue of having seriously filed applications for appropriate license, certificate, professional and/or promotional advancement, higher school matriculation, scholarship, or other legitimate requirements of education and/or governmental authorities.

This book is NOT intended for use, class instruction, tutoring, training, duplication, copying, reprinting, excerption, or adaptation, etc., by:

1) Other publishers
2) Proprietors and/or Instructors of "Coaching" and/or Preparatory Courses
3) Personnel and/or Training Divisions of commercial, industrial, and governmental organizations
4) Schools, colleges, or universities and/or their departments and staffs, including teachers and other personnel
5) Testing Agencies or Bureaus
6) Study groups which seek by the purchase of a single volume to copy and/or duplicate and/or adapt this material for use by the group as a whole without having purchased individual volumes for each of the members of the group
7) Et al.

Such persons would be in violation of appropriate Federal and State statutes.

PROVISION OF LICENSING AGREEMENTS – Recognized educational, commercial, industrial, and governmental institutions and organizations, and others legitimately engaged in educational pursuits, including training, testing, and measurement activities, may address request for a licensing agreement to the copyright owners, who will determine whether, and under what conditions, including fees and charges, the materials in this book may be used them. In other words, a licensing facility exists for the legitimate use of the material in this book on other than an individual basis. However, it is asseverated and affirmed here that the material in this book CANNOT be used without the receipt of the express permission of such a licensing agreement from the Publishers. Inquiries re licensing should be addressed to the company, attention rights and permissions department.

All rights reserved, including the right of reproduction in whole or in part, in any form or by any means, electronic or mechanical, including photocopying, recording, or by any information storage and retrieval system, without permission in writing from the Publisher.

Copyright © 2025 by
National Learning Corporation

212 Michael Drive, Syosset, NY 11791
(516) 921-8888 • www.passbooks.com
E-mail: info@passbooks.com

PASSBOOK® SERIES

THE *PASSBOOK® SERIES* has been created to prepare applicants and candidates for the ultimate academic battlefield – the examination room.

At some time in our lives, each and every one of us may be required to take an examination – for validation, matriculation, admission, qualification, registration, certification, or licensure.

Based on the assumption that every applicant or candidate has met the basic formal educational standards, has taken the required number of courses, and read the necessary texts, the *PASSBOOK® SERIES* furnishes the one special preparation which may assure passing with confidence, instead of failing with insecurity. Examination questions – together with answers – are furnished as the basic vehicle for study so that the mysteries of the examination and its compounding difficulties may be eliminated or diminished by a sure method.

This book is meant to help you pass your examination provided that you qualify and are serious in your objective.

The entire field is reviewed through the huge store of content information which is succinctly presented through a provocative and challenging approach – the question-and-answer method.

A climate of success is established by furnishing the correct answers at the end of each test.

You soon learn to recognize types of questions, forms of questions, and patterns of questioning. You may even begin to anticipate expected outcomes.

You perceive that many questions are repeated or adapted so that you can gain acute insights, which may enable you to score many sure points.

You learn how to confront new questions, or types of questions, and to attack them confidently and work out the correct answers.

You note objectives and emphases, and recognize pitfalls and dangers, so that you may make positive educational adjustments.

Moreover, you are kept fully informed in relation to new concepts, methods, practices, and directions in the field.

You discover that you are actually taking the examination all the time: you are preparing for the examination by "taking" an examination, not by reading extraneous and/or supererogatory textbooks.

In short, this PASSBOOK®, used directedly, should be an important factor in helping you to pass your test.

NONTRADITIONAL EDUCATION

Students returning to school as adults bring more varied experience to their studies than do the teenagers who begin college shortly after graduating from high school. As a result, there are numerous programs for students with nontraditional learning curves. Hundreds of colleges and universities grant degrees to people who cannot attend classes at a regular campus or have already learned what the college is supposed to teach.

You can earn nontraditional education credits in many ways:
- Passing standardized exams
- Demonstrating knowledge gained through experience
- Completing campus-based coursework, and
- Taking courses off campus

Some methods of assessing learning for credit are objective, such as standardized tests. Others are more subjective, such as a review of life experiences.

With some help from four hypothetical characters – Alice, Vin, Lynette, and Jorge – this article describes nontraditional ways of earning educational credit. It begins by describing programs in which you can earn a high school diploma without spending 4 years in a classroom. The college picture is more complicated, so it is presented in two parts: one on gaining credit for what you know through course work or experience, and a second on college degree programs. The final section lists resources for locating more information.

Earning High School Credit

People who were prevented from finishing high school as teenagers have several options if they want to do so as adults. Some major cities have back-to-school programs that allow adults to attend high school classes with current students. But the more practical alternatives for most adults are to take the General Educational Development (GED) tests or to earn a high school diploma by demonstrating their skills or taking correspondence classes.

Of course, these options do not match the experience of staying in high school and graduating with one's friends. But they are viable alternatives for adult learners committed to meeting and, often, continuing their educational goals.

GED Program

Alice quit high school her sophomore year and took a job to help support herself, her younger brother, and their newly widowed mother. Now an adult, she wants to earn her high school diploma – and then go on to college. Because her job as head cook and her family responsibilities keep her busy during the day, she plans to get a high school equivalency diploma. She will study for, and take, the GED tests. Every year, about half a million adults earn their high school credentials this way. A GED diploma is accepted in lieu of a high school one by more than 90 percent of employers, colleges, and universities, so it is a good choice for someone like Alice.

The GED testing program is sponsored by the American Council on Education and State and local education departments. It consists of examinations in five subject areas: Writing, science, mathematics, social studies, and literature and the arts. The tests also measure skills such as analytical ability, problem solving, reading comprehension, and ability to understand and apply information. Most of the questions are multiple choice; the writing test includes an essay section on a topic of general interest.

Eligibility rules for taking the exams vary, but some states require that you must be at least 18. Tests are given in English, Spanish, and French. In addition to standard print, versions in large print, Braille, and audiocassette are also available. Total time allotted for the tests is 7 1/2 hours.

The GED tests are not easy. About one-fourth of those who complete the exams every year do not pass. Passing scores are established by administering the tests to a sample of graduating high school seniors. The minimum standard score is set so that about one-third of graduating seniors would not pass the tests if they took them.

Because of the difficulty of the tests, people need to prepare themselves to take them. Often, they start by taking the Official GED Practice Tests, usually available through a local adult education center. Centers are listed in your phone book's blue pages under "Adult Education," "Continuing Education," or "GED." Adult education centers also have information about GED preparation classes and self-study materials. Classes are generally arranged to accommodate adults' work schedules. National Learning Corporation publishes several study guides that aim to thoroughly prepare test-takers for the GED.

School districts, colleges, adult education centers, and community organizations have information about GED testing schedules and practice tests. For more information, contact them, your nearest GED testing center, or:

GED Testing Service
One Dupont Circle, NW, Suite 250
Washington, DC 20036-1163
1(800) 62-MY GED (626-9433)
(202) 939-9490

Skills Demonstration

Adults who have acquired high school level skills through experience might be eligible for the National External Diploma Program. This alternative to the GED does not involve any direct instruction. Instead, adults seeking a high school diploma must demonstrate mastery of 65 competencies in 8 general areas: Communication; computation; occupational preparedness; and self, social, consumer, scientific, and technological awareness.

Mastery is shown through the completion of the tasks. For example, a participant could prove competency in computation by measuring a room for carpeting, figuring out the amount of carpet needed, and computing the cost.

Before being accepted for the program, adults undergo an evaluation. Tests taken at one of the program's offices measure reading, writing, and mathematics abilities. A take-home segment includes a self-assessment of current skills, an individual skill evaluation, and an occupational interest and aptitude test.

Adults accepted for the program have weekly meetings with an assessor. At the meeting, the assessor reviews the participant's work from the previous week. If the task has not been completed properly, the assessor explains the mistake. Participants continue to correct their errors until they master each competency. A high school diploma is awarded upon proven mastery of all 65 competencies.

Fourteen States and the District of Columbia now offer the External Diploma Program. For more information, contact:

External Diploma Program
One Dupont Circle, NW, Suite 250
Washington, DC 20036-1193
(202) 939-9475

Correspondence and Distance Study

Vin dropped out of high school during his junior year because his family's frequent moves made it difficult for him to continue his studies. He promised himself at the time he dropped out that he would someday finish the courses needed for his diploma. For people like Vin, who prefer to earn a traditional diploma in a nontraditional way, there are about a dozen accredited courses of study for earning a high school diploma by correspondence, or distance study. The programs are either privately run, affiliated with a university, or administered by a State education department.

Distance study diploma programs have no residency requirements, allowing students to continue their studies from almost any location. Depending on the course of study, students need not be enrolled full time and usually have more flexible schedules for finishing their work. Selection of courses ranges from vo-tech to college prep, and some programs place different emphasis on the types of diplomas offered. University affiliated schools, for example, allow qualified students to take college courses along with their high school ones. Students can then apply the college credits toward a degree at that university or transfer them to another institution.

Taking courses by distance study is often more challenging and time consuming than attending classes, especially for adults who have other obligations. Success depends on each student's motivation. Students usually do reading assignments on their own. Written exercises, which they complete and send to an instructor for grading, supplement their reading material.

A list of some accredited high schools that offer diplomas by distance study is available free from the Distance Education and Training Council, formerly known as the National Home Study Council. Request the "DETC Directory of Accredited Institutions" from:

The Distance Education and Training Council
1601 18th Street, NW.
Washington, DC 20009-2529
(202) 234-5100

Some publications profiling nontraditional college programs include addresses and descriptions of several high school correspondence ones. See the Resources section at the end of this article for more information.

Getting College Credit For What You Know

Adults can receive college credit for prior coursework, by passing examinations, and documenting experiential learning. With help from a college advisor, nontraditional students should assess their skills, establish their educational goals, and determine the number of college credits they might be eligible for.

Even before you meet with a college advisor, you should collect all your school and training records. Then, make a list of all knowledge and abilities acquired through experience, no matter how irrelevant they seem to your chosen field. Next, determine your educational goals: What specific field do you wish to study? What kind of a degree do you want? Finally, determine how your past work fits into the field of study. Later on, you will evaluate educational programs to find one that's right for you.

People who have complex educational or experiential learning histories might want to have their learning evaluated by the Regents Credit Bank. The Credit Bank, operated by Regents College of the University of the State of New York, allows people to consolidate credits earned through college, experience, or other methods. Special assessments are available for Regents College enrollees whose knowledge in a specific field cannot be adequately evaluated by standardized exams. For more information, contact the Regents Credit Bank at:

Regents College
7 Columbia Circle
Albany, NY 12203-5159
(518) 464-8500

Credit For Prior College Coursework

When Lynette was in college during the 1970s, she attended several different schools and took a variety of courses. She did well in some classes and poorly in others. Now that she is a successful business owner and has more focus, Lynette thinks she should forget about her previous coursework and start from scratch. Instead, she should start from where she is.

Lynette should have all her transcripts sent to the colleges or universities of her choice and let an admissions officer determine which classes are applicable toward a degree. A few credits here and there may not seem like much, but they add up. Even if the subjects do not seem relevant to any major, they might be counted as elective credits toward a degree. And comparing the cost of transcripts with the cost of college courses, it makes sense to spend a few dollars per transcript for a chance to save hundreds, and perhaps thousands, of dollars in books and tuition.

Rules for transferring credits apply to all prior coursework at accredited colleges and universities, whether done on campus or off. Courses completed off campus, often called extended learning, include those available to students through independent study and correspondence. Many schools have extended learning programs; Brigham Young University, for example, offers more than 300 courses through its Department of Independent Study. One type of extended learning is distance learning, a form of correspondence study by technological means such as television, video and audio, CD-ROM, electronic mail, and computer tutorials. See the Resources section at the end of this article for more information about publications available from the National University Continuing Education Association.

Any previously earned college credits should be considered for transfer, no matter what the subject or the grade received. Many schools do not accept the transfer of courses graded below a C or ones taken more than a designated number of years ago. Some colleges and universities also have limits on the number of credits that can be transferred and applied toward a degree. But not all do. For example, Thomas Edison State College, New Jersey's State college for adults, accepts the transfer of all 120 hours of credit required for a baccalaureate degree – provided all the credits are transferred from regionally accredited schools, no more than 80 are at the junior college level, and the student's grades overall and in the field of study average out to C.

To assign credit for prior coursework, most schools require original transcripts. This means you must complete a form or send a written, signed request to have your transcripts released directly to a college or university. Once you have chosen the schools you want to apply to, contact the schools you attended before. Find out how much each transcript costs, and ask them to send your transcripts to the ones you are applying to. Write a letter that includes your name (and names used during attendance, if different) and dates of attendance, along with the names and addresses of the schools to which your transcripts should be sent. Include payment and mail to the registrar at the schools you have attended. The registrar's office will process your request and send an official transcript of your coursework to the colleges or universities you have designated.

Credit For Noncollege Courses

Colleges and universities are not the only ones that offer classes. Volunteer organizations and employers often provide formal training worth college credit. The American Council on Education has two programs that assess thousands of specific courses and make recommendations on the amount of college credit they are worth. Colleges and universities accept the recommendations or use them as guidelines.

One program evaluates educational courses sponsored by government agencies, business and industry, labor unions, and professional and voluntary organizations. It is the Program on Noncollegiate Sponsored Instruction (PONSI). Some of the training seminars Alice has participated in covered topics such as food preparation, kitchen safety, and nutrition. Although she has not yet earned her GED, Alice can earn college credit because of her completion of these formal job-training seminars. The number of credits each seminar is worth does not hinge on Alice's current eligibility for college enrollment.

The other program evaluates courses offered by the Army, Navy, Air Force, Marines, Coast Guard, and Department of Defense. It is the Military Evaluations Program. Jorge has never attended college, but the engineering technology classes he completed as part of his military training are worth college credit. And as an Army veteran, Jorge is eligible for a service that takes the evaluations one step further. The Army/American Council on Education Registry Transcript System (AARTS) will provide Jorge with an individualized transcript of American Council on Education credit recommendations for all courses he completed, the military occupational specialties (MOS's) he held, and examinations he passed while in the Army. All Army and National Guard enlisted personnel and veterans who enlisted after October 1981 are eligible for the transcript. Similar services are being considered by the Navy and Marine Corps.

To obtain a free transcript, see your Army Education Center for a 5454R transcript request form. Include your name, Social Security number, basic active service date, and complete address where you want the transcript sent. Mail your request to:
AARTS Operations Center
415 McPherson Ave.
Fort Leavenworth, KS 66027-1373

Recommendations for PONSI are published in *The National Guide to Educational Credit for Training Programs;* military program recommendations are in *The Guide to the Evaluation of Educational Experiences in the Armed Forces.* See the Resources section at the end of this article for more information about these publications.

Former military personnel who took a foreign language course through the Defense Language Institute may request course transcripts by sending their name, Social Security number, course title, duration of the course, and graduation date to:

Commandant, Defense Language Institute
Attn: ATFL-DAA-AR
Transcripts
Presidio of Monterey
Monterey, CA 93944-5006

Not all of Jorge's and Alice's courses have been assessed by the American Council on Education. Training courses that have no Council credit recommendation should still be assessed by an advisor at the schools they want to attend. Course descriptions, class notes, test scores, and other documentation may be helpful for comparing training courses to their college equivalents. An oral examination or other demonstration of competency might also be required.

There is no guarantee you will receive all the credits you are seeking – but you certainly won't if you make no attempt.

Credit By Examination

Standardized tests are the best-known method of receiving college credit without taking courses. These exams are often taken by high school students seeking advanced placement for college, but they are also available to adult learners. Testing programs and colleges and universities offer exams in a number of subjects. Two U.S. Government institutes have foreign language exams for employees that also may be worth college credit.

It is important to understand that receiving a passing score on these exams does not mean you get college credit automatically. Each school determines which test results it will accept, minimum scores required, how scores are converted for credit, and the amount of credit, if any, to be assigned. Most colleges and universities accept the American Council on Education credit recommendations, published every other year in the 250-page *Guide to Educational Credit by Examination*. For more information, contact:

The American Council on Education
Credit by Examination Program
One Dupont Circle, Suite 250
Washington, DC 20036-1193
(202) 939-9434

Testing programs:

You might know some of the five national testing programs by their acronyms or initials: CLEP, ACT PEP: RCE, DANTES, AP, and NOCTI. (The meanings of these initialisms are explained below.) There is some overlap among programs; for example, four of them have introductory accounting exams. Since you will not be awarded credit more than once for a specific subject, you should carefully evaluate each program for the subject exams you wish to take. And before taking an exam, make sure you will be awarded credit by the college or university you plan to attend.

CLEP (College-Level Examination Program), administered by the College Board, is the most widely accepted of the national testing programs; more than 2,800 accredited schools award credit for passing exam scores. Each test covers material taught in basic undergraduate courses. There are five general exams – English composition, humanities, college mathematics, natural sciences, and social sciences and history – and many subject exams. Most exams are entirely multiple-choice, but English composition exams may include an essay section. For more information, contact:

    CLEP
    P.O. Box 6600
    Princeton, NJ 08541-6600
    (609) 771-7865

ACT PEP: RCE (American College Testing Proficiency Exam Program: Regents College Examinations) tests are given in 38 subjects within arts and sciences, business, education, and nursing. Each exam is recommended for either lower- or upper-level credit. Exams contain either objective or extended response questions, and are graded according to a standard score, letter grade, or pass/fail. Fees vary, depending on the subject and type of exam. For more information or to request free study guides, contact:

    ACT PEP: Regents College Examinations
    P.O. Box 4014
    Iowa City, IA 52243
    (319) 337-1387
    (New York State residents must contact Regents College directly.)

DANTES (Defense Activity for Nontraditional Education Support) standardized tests are developed by the Educational Testing Service for the Department of Defense. Originally administered only to military personnel, the exams have been available to the public since 1983. About 50 subject tests cover business, mathematics, social science, physical science, humanities, foreign languages, and applied technology. Most of the tests consist entirely of multiple-choice questions. Schools determine their own administering fees and testing schedules. For more information or to request free study sheets, contact:

    DANTES Program Office
    Mail Stop 31-X
    Educational Testing Service
    Princeton, NJ 08541
    1(800) 257-9484

The AP (Advanced Placement) Program is a cooperative effort between secondary schools and colleges and universities. AP exams are developed each year by committees of college and high school faculty appointed by the College Board and assisted by consultants from the Educational Testing Service. Subjects include arts and languages, natural sciences, computer science, social sciences, history, and mathematics. Most tests are 2 or 3 hours long and include both multiple-choice and essay questions. AP courses are available to help students prepare for exams, which are offered in the spring. For more information about the Advanced Placement Program, contact:

    Advanced Placement Services
    P.O. Box 6671
    Princeton, NJ 08541-6671
    (609) 771-7300

NOCTI (National Occupational Competency Testing Institute) assessments are designed for people like Alice, who have vocational-technical skills that cannot be evaluated by other tests. NOCTI assesses competency at two levels: Student/job ready and teacher/experienced worker. Standardized evaluations are available for occupations such as auto-body repair, electronics, mechanical drafting, quantity food preparation, and upholstering. The tests consist of multiple-choice questions and a performance component. Other services include workshops, customized assessments, and pre-testing. For more information, contact:

NOCTI
500 N. Bronson Ave.
Ferris State University
Big Rapids, MI 49307
(616) 796-4699

Colleges and universities:

Many colleges and universities have credit-by-exam programs, through which students earn credit by passing a comprehensive exam for a course offered by the institution. Among the most widely recognized are the programs at Ohio University, the University of North Carolina, Thomas Edison State College, and New York University.

Ohio University offers about 150 examinations for credit. In addition, you may sometimes arrange to take special examinations in non-laboratory courses offered at Ohio University. To take a test for credit, you must enroll in the course. If you plan to transfer the credit earned, you also need written permission from an official at your school. Books and study materials are available, for a cost, through the university. Exams must be taken within 6 months of the enrollment date; most last 3 hours. You may arrange to take the exam off campus if you do not live near the university.

Ohio University is on the quarter-hour system; most courses are worth 4 quarter hours, the equivalent of 3 semester hours. For more information, contact:

Independent Study
Tupper Hall 302
Ohio University
Athens, OH 45701-2979
1(800) 444-2910
(614) 593-2910

The University of North Carolina offers a credit-by-examination option for 140 independent study (correspondence) courses in foreign languages, humanities, social sciences, mathematics, business administration, education, electrical and computer engineering, health administration, and natural sciences. To take an exam, you must request and receive approval from both the course instructor and the independent studies department. Exams must be taken within six months of enrollment, and you may register for no more than two at a time. If you are not near the University's Chapel Hill campus, you may take your exam under supervision at an accredited college, university, community college, or technical institute. For more information, contact:

Independent Studies
CB #1020, The Friday Center
UNC-Chapel Hill
Chapel Hill, NC 27599-1020
1(800) 862-5669 / (919) 962-1134

The Thomas Edison College Examination Program offers more than 50 exams in liberal arts, business, and professional areas. Thomas Edison State College administers tests twice a month in Trenton, New Jersey; however, students may arrange to take their tests with a proctor at any accredited American college or university or U.S. military base. Most of the tests are multiple choice; some also include short answer or essay questions. Time limits range from 90 minutes to 4 hours, depending on the exam. For more information, contact:

Thomas Edison State College
TECEP, Office of Testing and Assessment
101 W. State Street
Trenton, NJ 08608-1176
(609) 633-2844

New York University's Foreign Language Program offers proficiency exams in more than 40 languages, from Albanian to Yiddish. Two exams are available in each language: The 12-point test is equivalent to 4 undergraduate semesters, and the 16-point exam may lead to upper level credit. The tests are given at the university's Foreign Language Department throughout the year.

Proof of foreign language proficiency does not guarantee college credit. Some colleges and universities accept transcripts only for languages commonly taught, such as French and Spanish. Nontraditional programs are more likely than traditional ones to grant credit for proficiency in other languages.

For an informational brochure and registration form for NYU's foreign language proficiency exams, contact:

New York University
Foreign Language Department
48 Cooper Square, Room 107
New York, NY 10003
(212) 998-7030

Government institutes:

The Defense Language Institute and Foreign Service Institute administer foreign language proficiency exams for personnel stationed abroad. Usually, the tests are given at the end of intensive language courses or upon completion of service overseas. But some people – like Jorge, who knows Spanish – speak another language fluently and may be allowed to take a proficiency exam in that language before completing their tour of duty. Contact one of the offices listed below to obtain transcripts of those scores. Proof of proficiency does not guarantee college credit, however, as discussed above.

To request score reports from the Defense Language Institute for Defense Language Proficiency Tests, send your name, Social Security number, language for which you were tested, and, most importantly, when and where you took the exam to:

Commandant, Defense Language Institute
Attn: ATFL-ES-T
DLPT Score Report Request
Presidio of Monterey
Monterey, CA 93944-5006

To request transcripts of scores for Foreign Service Institute exams, send your name, Social Security number, language for which you were tested, and dates or year of exams to:

Foreign Service Institute
Arlington Hall
4020 Arlington Boulevard
Rosslyn, VA 22204-1500
Attn: Testing Office (Send your request to the attention of the testing office of the foreign language in which you were tested)

Credit For Experience

Experiential learning credit may be given for knowledge gained through job responsibilities, personal hobbies, volunteer opportunities, homemaking, and other experiences. Colleges and universities base credit awards on the knowledge you have attained, not for the experience alone. In addition, the knowledge must be college level; not just any learning will do. Throwing horseshoes as a hobby is not likely to be worth college credit. But if you've done research on how and where the sport originated, visited blacksmiths, organized tournaments, and written a column for a trade journal – well, that's a horseshoe of a different color.

Adults attempting to get credit for their experience should be forewarned: Having your experience evaluated for college credit is time-consuming, tedious work – not an easy shortcut for people who want quick-fix college credits. And not all experience, no matter how valuable, is the equivalent of college courses.

Requesting college credit for your experiential learning can be tricky. You should get assistance from a credit evaluations officer at the school you plan to attend, but you should also have a general idea of what your knowledge is worth. A common method for converting knowledge into credit is to use a college catalog. Find course titles and descriptions that match what you have learned through experience, and request the number of credits offered for those courses.

Once you know what credit to ask for, you must usually present your case in writing to officials at the college you plan to attend. The most common form of presenting experiential learning for credit is the portfolio. A portfolio is a written record of your knowledge along with a request for equivalent college credit. It includes an identification and description of the knowledge for which you are requesting credit, an explanatory essay of how the knowledge was gained and how it fits into your educational plans, documentation that you have acquired such knowledge, and a request for college credit. Required elements of a portfolio vary by schools but generally follow those guidelines.

In identifying knowledge you have gained, be specific about exactly what you have learned. For example, it is not enough for Lynette to say she runs a business. She must identify the knowledge she has gained from running it, such as personnel management, tax law, marketing strategy, and inventory review. She must also include brief descriptions about her knowledge of each to support her claims of having those skills.

The essay gives you a chance to relay something about who you are. It should address your educational goals, include relevant autobiographical details, and be well organized, neat, and convey confidence. In his essay, Jorge might first state his goal of becoming an engineer. Then he would explain why he joined the Army, where he got hands-on training and experience in developing and servicing electronic equipment.

This, he would say, led to his hobby of creating remote-controlled model cars, of which he has built 20. His conclusion would highlight his accomplishments and tie them to his desire to become an electronic engineer.

Documentation is evidence that you've learned what you claim to have learned. You can show proof of knowledge in a variety of ways, including audio or video recordings, letters from current or former employers describing your specific duties and job performance, blueprints, photographs or artwork, and transcripts of certifying exams for professional licenses and certification – such as Alice's certification from the American Culinary Federation. Although documentation can take many forms, written proof alone is not always enough. If it is impossible to document your knowledge in writing, find out if your experiential learning can be assessed through supplemental oral exams by a faculty expert.

Earning a College Degree

Nontraditional students often have work, family, and financial obligations that prevent them from quitting their jobs to attend school full time. Can they still meet their educational goals? Yes.

More than 150 accredited colleges and universities have nontraditional bachelor's degree programs that require students to spend little or no time on campus; over 300 others have nontraditional campus-based degree programs. Some of those schools, as well as most junior and community colleges, offer associate's degrees nontraditionally. Each school with a nontraditional course of study determines its own rules for awarding credit for prior coursework, exams, or experience, as discussed previously. Most have charges on top of tuition for providing these special services.

Several publications profile nontraditional degree programs; see the Resources section at the end of this article for more information. To determine which school best fits your academic profile and educational goals, first list your criteria. Then, evaluate nontraditional programs based on their accreditation, features, residency requirements, and expenses. Once you have chosen several schools to explore further, write to them for more information. Detailed explanations of school policies should help you decide which ones you want to apply to.

Get beyond the printed word – especially the glowing words each school writes about itself. Check out the schools you are considering with higher education authorities, alumni, employers, family members, and friends. If possible, visit the campus to talk to students and instructors and sit in on a few classes, even if you will be completing most or all of your work off campus. Ask school officials questions about such things as enrollment numbers, graduation rate, faculty qualifications, and confusing details about the application process or academic policies. After you have thoroughly investigated each prospective college or university, you can make an informed decision about which is right for you.

Accreditation

Accreditation is a process colleges and universities submit to voluntarily for getting their credentials. An accredited school has been investigated and visited by teams of observers and has periodic inspections by a private accrediting agency. The initial review can take two years or more.

Regional agencies accredit entire schools, and professional agencies accredit either specialized schools or departments within schools. Although there are no national accrediting standards, not just any accreditation will do. Countless "accreditation associations" have been invented by schools, many of which have no academic programs and sell phony degrees, to accredit themselves. But 6 regional and about 80 professional accrediting associations in the United States are recognized by the U.S. Department of Education or the Commission on Recognition of Postsecondary Accreditation. When checking accreditation, these are the names to look for. For more information about accreditation and accrediting agencies, contact:

> Institutional Participation Oversight Service Accreditation and State Liaison Division
> U.S. Department of Education
> ROB 3, Room 3915
> 600 Independence Ave., SW
> Washington, DC 20202-5244
> (202) 708-7417

Because accreditation is not mandatory, lack of accreditation does not necessarily mean a school or program is bad. Some schools choose not to apply for accreditation, are in the process of applying, or have educational methods too unconventional for an accrediting association's standards. For the nontraditional student, however, earning a degree from a college or university with recognized accreditation is an especially important consideration. Although nontraditional education is becoming more widely accepted, it is not yet mainstream. Employers skeptical of a degree earned in a nontraditional manner are likely to be even less accepting of one from an unaccredited school.

Program Features

Because nontraditional students have diverse educational objectives, nontraditional schools are diverse in what they offer. Some programs are geared toward helping students organize their scattered educational credits to get a degree as quickly as possible. Others cater to those who may have specific credits or experience but need assistance in completing requirements. Whatever your educational profile, you should look for a program that works with you in obtaining your educational goals.

A few nontraditional programs have special admissions policies for adult learners like Alice, who plan to earn their GEDs but want to enroll in college in the meantime. Other features of nontraditional programs include individualized learning agreements, intensive academic counseling, cooperative learning and internship placement, and waiver of some prerequisites or other requirements – as well as college credit for prior coursework, examinations, and experiential learning, all discussed previously.

Lynette, whose primary goal is to finish her degree, wants to earn maximum credits for her business experience. She will look for programs that do not limit the number of credits awarded for equivalency exams and experiential learning. And since well-documented proof of knowledge is essential for earning experiential learning credits, Lynette should make sure the program she chooses provides assistance to students submitting a portfolio.

Jorge, on the other hand, has more credits than he needs in certain areas and is willing to forego some. To become an engineer, he must have a bachelor's degree; but because he is accustomed to hands-on learning, Jorge is interested in getting experience as he gains more technical skills. He will concentrate on finding schools with strong cooperative education, supervised fieldwork, or internship programs.

Residency Requirements

Programs are sometimes deemed nontraditional because of their residency requirements. Many people think of residency for colleges and universities in terms of tuition, with in-state students paying less than out-of-state ones. Residency also may refer to where a student lives, either on or off campus, while attending school.

But in nontraditional education, residency usually refers to how much time students must spend on campus, regardless of whether they attend classes there. In some nontraditional programs, students need not ever step foot on campus. Others require only a very short residency, such as one day or a few weeks. Many schools have standard residency requirements of several semesters but schedule classes for evenings or weekends to accommodate working adults.

Lynette, who previously took courses by independent study, prefers to earn credits by distance study. She will focus on schools that have no residency requirement. Several colleges and universities have nonresident degree completion programs for adults with some college credit. Under the direction of a faculty advisor, students devise a plan for earning their remaining credits. Methods for earning credits include independent study, distance learning, seminars, supervised fieldwork, and group study at arranged sites. Students may have to earn a certain number of credits through the degree-granting institution. But many programs allow students to take courses at accredited schools of their choice for transfer toward their degree.

Alice wants to attend lectures but has an unpredictable schedule. Her best course of action will be to seek out short residency programs that require students to attend seminars once or twice a semester. She can take courses that are televised and videotape them to watch when her schedule permits, with the seminars helping to ensure that she properly completes her coursework. Many colleges and universities with short residency requirements also permit students to earn some credits elsewhere, by whatever means the student chooses.

Some fields of study require classroom instruction. As Jorge will discover, few colleges and universities allow students to earn a bachelor's degree in engineering entirely through independent study. Nontraditional residency programs are designed to accommodate adults' daytime work schedules. Jorge should look for programs offering evening, weekend, summer, and accelerated courses.

Tuition and Other Expenses

The final decisions about which schools Alice, Jorge, and Lynette attend may hinge in large part on a single issue: Cost. And rising tuition is only part of the equation. Beginning with application fees and continuing through graduation fees, college expenses add up.

Traditional and nontraditional students have some expenses in common, such as the cost of books and other materials. Tuition might even be the same for some courses, especially for colleges and universities offering standard ones at unusual times. But for nontraditional programs, students may also pay fees for services such as credit or transcript review, evaluation, advisement, and portfolio assessment.

Students are also responsible for postage and handling or setup expenses for independent study courses, as well as for all examination and transcript fees for transferring credits. Usually, the more nontraditional the program, the more detailed the fees. Some schools charge a yearly enrollment fee rather than tuition for degree completion candidates who want their files to remain active.

Although tuition and fees might seem expensive, most educators tell you not to let money come between you and your educational goals. Talk to someone in the financial aid department of the school you plan to attend or check your library for publications about financial aid sources. The U.S. Department of Education publishes a guide to Federal aid programs such as Pell Grants, student loans, and work-study. To order the free 74-page booklet, *The Student Guide: Financial Aid from the U.S. Department of Education,* contact:

Federal Student Aid Information Center
P.O. Box 84
Washington, DC 20044
1 (800) 4FED-AID (433-3243)

Resources

Information on how to earn a high school diploma or college degree without following the usual routes is available from several organizations and in numerous publications. Information on nontraditional graduate degree programs, available for master's through doctoral level, though not discussed in this article, can usually be obtained from the same resources that detail bachelor's degree programs.

National Learning Corporation publishes study guides for all of these exams, for both general examinations and tests in specific subject areas. To order study guides, or to browse their catalog featuring more than 5,000 titles, visit NLC online at www.passbooks.com, or contact them by phone at (800) 632-8888.

Organizations

Adult learners should always contact their local school system, community college, or university to learn about programs that are readily available. The following national organizations can also supply information:

American Council on Education
One Dupont Circle
Washington, DC 20036-1193
(202) 939-9300

Within the American Council on Education, the Center for Adult Learning and Educational Credentials administers the National External Diploma Program, the GED Program, the Program on Noncollegiate Sponsored Instruction, the Credit by Examination Program, and the Military Evaluations Program.

DANTES Subject Standardized Tests

INTRODUCTION

The DANTES (Defense Activity for Non-Traditional Education Support) subject standardized tests are comprehensive college and graduate level examinations given by the Armed Forces, colleges and graduate schools as end-of-subject course evaluation final examinations or to obtain college equivalency credits in the various subject areas tested.

The DANTES Examination Program enables students to obtain college credit for what they have learned on the job, through self-study, personal interest, correspondence courses or by any other means. It is used by colleges and universities to award college credit to students who demonstrate that they know as much as students completing an equivalent college course. It is a cost-efficient, time-saving way for students to use their knowledge to accomplish their educational goals.

Most schools accept the American Council on Education (ACE) recommendations for the minimum score required and the amount of credit awarded, but not all schools do. Be sure to check the policy regarding the score level required for credit and the number of credits to be awarded.

Not all tests are accepted by all institutions. Even when a test is accepted by an institution, it may not be acceptable for every program at that institution. Before considering testing, ascertain the acceptability of a specific test for a particular course.

Colleges and universities that administer DANTES tests may administer them to any applicant – or they may administer the tests only to students registered at their institution. Decisions about who will be allowed to test are made by the school. Students should contact the test center to determine current policies and schedules for DANTES testing.

Colleges and universities authorized to administer DANTES tests usually do so throughout the calendar year. Each school sets its own fee for test administration and establishes its own testing schedule. Contact the representative at the administering school directly to make arrangements for testing.

Checklist
For Students

- ✓ Visit **www.getcollegecredit.com** to obtain a list of tests, fact sheets, test preparation materials, participating colleges and universities, and much more.

- ✓ Contact your school advisor to confirm that the DSST you selected will fit into your curriculum.

- ✓ Consult the *DSST Candidate Information Bulletin* for answers to specific questions.

- ✓ Contact the test site to schedule your test.

- ✓ Prepare for your examination by using the fact sheet as a guide.

- ✓ Take the test.

If you would like a score report sent to your college or university, it is a good idea to bring the four-digit code with you. You must write the DSST Test Center Code for that institution on your answer sheet at the time of testing. DSST Test Center Codes are noted in the DSST Participating Colleges and Universities listing on the Web site.

If you prefer to send a score report to an institution at a later date, there is a transcript fee of $20 for each transcript ordered.

Thomson Prometric
DSST Program
2000 Lenox Drive, Third Floor
Lawrenceville, NJ 08648

Toll-free: 877-471-9860
609-895-5011

E-mail: pnj-dsst@thomson.com

parts of this introduction excerpted for educational purposes from the official announcement ©2006 Thompson Prometric

MAKING A COLLEGE DEGREE WITHIN YOUR REACH

Today, there are many educational alternatives to the classroom—you can learn from your job, your reading, your independent study, and special interests you pursue. You may already have learned the subject matter covered by some college-level courses.

The DSST Program is a nationally recognized testing program that gives you the opportunity to receive college credit for learning acquired outside the traditional college classroom. Colleges and universities throughout the United States administer the program, developed by Thomson Prometric, year-round. Annually, over 90,000 DSSTs are administered to individuals who are interested in continuing their education. Take advantage of the DSST testing program; it speeds the educational process and provides the flexibility adults need, making earning a degree more feasible.

Since requirements differ from college to college, please check with the credit-awarding institution before taking a DSST. More than 1,800 colleges and universities currently award credit for DSSTs, and the number is growing every day. You can choose from 37 test titles in the areas of Social Science, Business, Mathematics, Applied Technology, Humanities, and Physical Science. A brief description of each examination is found on the pages that follow.

Reach Your Career Goals Through DSSTs

Use DSSTs to help you earn your degree, get a promotion, or simply demonstrate that you have college-level knowledge in subjects relevant to your work.

Save Time...

You don't have to sit through classes when you have previously acquired the knowledge or experience for most of what is being taught and can learn the rest yourself. You might be able to bypass introductory-level courses in subject areas you already know.

Save Money...

DSSTs save you money because the classes you bypass by earning credit through the DSST Program are classes you won't have to pay for on your way to earning your degree. You can use the money instead to take more advanced courses that can be more challenging and rewarding.

Improve Your Chances for Admission to College

Each college has its own admission policies; however, having passing scores for DSSTs on your transcript can provide strong evidence of how well you can perform at the college level.

Gain Confidence Performing at a College Level

Many adults returning to college find that lack of confidence is often the greatest hurdle to overcome. Passing a DSST demonstrates your ability to perform on a college level.

Make Up for Courses You May Have Missed

You may be ready to graduate from college and find that you are a few credits short of earning your degree. By using semester breaks, vacation time, or leisure time to study independently, you can prepare to take one or more DSSTs, fulfill your academic requirements, and graduate on time.

If You Cannot Attend Regularly Scheduled Classes...

If your lifestyle or responsibilities prevent you from attending regularly scheduled classes, you can earn your college degree from a college offering an external degree program. The DSST Program allows you to earn your degree by study and experience outside the traditional classroom.

Many colleges and universities offer external degree or distance learning programs. For additional information, contact the college you plan to attend or:

Center for Lifelong Learning
American Council on Education
One DuPont Circle NW, Suite 250
Washington, DC 20036
202-939-9475
www.acenet.edu
(Select "Center for Lifelong Learning" under "Programs & Services"
for more information)

Fact Sheets

For each test, there is a Fact Sheet that outlines the topics covered by each test and includes a list of sample questions, a list of recommended references of books that would be useful for review, and the number of credits awarded for a passing score as recommended by the American Council on Education (ACE). *Please note that some schools require scores that are higher than the minimum ACE-recommended passing score.* It is suggested that you check with your college or university to determine what score they require in order to earn credit. You can obtain Fact Sheets by:
- Downloading them from www.getcollegecredit.com
- E-mailing a request to pnj-dsst@thomson.com
- Completing a Candidate Publications Order Form

DSST Online Practice Tests

DSST online practice tests contain items that reflect a *partial range of difficulty* identified in the Content Outline section on each Fact Sheet. There is an online DSST Practice Test in the following categories:
- Mathematics
- Social Science
- Business
- Physical Science
- Applied Technology
- Humanities

Although the online DSST Practice Test questions do not indicate the full range of difficulty you would find in an actual DSST test, they will help you assess your knowledge level. Each online DSST Practice Test can be purchased by visiting www.getcollegecredit.com and clicking on DSST Practice Exams.

TAKING DSST EXAMINATIONS

Earning College Credit for DSST Examinations

To find out if the college of your choice awards credit for passing DSST scores, contact the admissions office or counseling and testing office. The college can also provide information on the scores required for awarding credit, the number of credit hours awarded, and any courses that can be bypassed with satisfactory scores.

It is important that you contact the institution of your choice as early as possible since credit-awarding policies differ among colleges and universities.

Where to Take DSSTs

DSSTs are administered at colleges and universities nationwide. Each location determines the frequency and scheduling of test administrations. To obtain the most current list of participating DSST colleges and universities:
- Visit and download the information from www.getcollegecredit.com
- E-mail pnj-dsst@thomson.com

Scheduling Your Examination

Please be aware that some colleges and universities provide DSST testing services to enrolled students only. After you have selected a college or university that administers DSSTs, you will need to contact them to schedule your test date.

The fee to take a DSST is $60 per test. This fee entitles you to two score reports after the test is scored. One will be sent directly to you and the other will be sent to the college or university that you designate on your answer sheet. You may pay the test fee with a certified check or U.S. money order made payable to Thomson Prometric or you may charge the test fee to your Visa, MasterCard or American Express credit card. Note: The credit card statement will reflect a charge from Thomson Prometric for all DSST examinations. *(Declined credit card charges will be assessed an additional $25 processing fee.)*

In addition, the test site may also require a test administration fee for each examination, to be paid directly to the institution. Contact the test site to determine its administration fee and payment policy.

Other Testing Arrangements

If you are unable to find a participating DSST college or university in your area, you may want to contact the testing office of a local accredited college or university to determine whether a representative from that office will agree to administer the test(s) for you.

The school's representative should then contact the DSST Program at 866-794-3497 to arrange for this administration. If you are unable to locate a test site, contact Thomson Prometric for assistance at pnj-dsst@thomson.com or 866-794-3497.

Testing Accommodations for Students with Disabilities

Thomson Prometric is committed to serving test takers with disabilities by providing services and reasonable testing accommodations as set forth in the provisions of the *Americans with Disabilities Act* (ADA). If you have a disability, as prescribed by the ADA, and require special testing services or arrangements, please contact the test administrator at the test site. You will be asked to submit to the test administrator documentation of your disability and your request for special accommodations. The test administrator will then forward your documentation along with your request for testing accommodations to Thomson Prometric for approval.

Please submit your request as far in advance of your test date as possible so that the necessary accommodations can be made. Only test takers with documented disabilities are eligible for special accommodations.

On the Day of the Examination

It is important to review this information and to have the correct identification present on the day of the examination:
- Arrive on time as a courtesy to the test administrator.
- Bring a valid form of government-issued identification that includes a current photo and your signature (acceptable documents include a driver's license, passport, state-issued identification card or military identification). *Anyone who fails to present valid identification will not be allowed to test.*
- Bring several No. 2 (soft-lead) sharpened pencils with good erasers, a watch, and a black pen if you will be writing an essay.
- Do not bring books or papers.
- Do not bring an alarm watch that beeps, a telephone, or a phone beeper into the testing room.
- The use of nonprogrammable calculators, slide rules, scratch paper and/or other materials is permitted for some of the tests.

DSST SCORING POLICIES

Your DSST examination scores are reported only to you, unless you request that they be sent elsewhere. If you want your scores sent to your college, you must provide the correct DSST code number of the school on your answer sheet at the time you take the test. See the *DSST Directory of Colleges and Universities* on the Web site www.getcollegecredit.com.

If your institution is not listed, contact Thomson Prometric at 866-794-3497 to establish a code number. (Some schools may require a student to be enrolled prior to receiving a score report.)

Receiving Your Score Report

Allow approximately four weeks after testing to receive your score report.

Calling DSST Customer Service before the required four-week score processing time has elapsed will not expedite the processing of your scores. Due to privacy and security requirements, scores will not be reported to students over the telephone under any circumstance.

Scoring of Principles of Public Speaking Speeches

The speech portion of the *Principles of Public Speaking* examination will be sent to speech raters who are faculty members at accredited colleges that currently teach or have previously taught the course. Scores for the *Principles of Public Speaking* examination are available six to eight weeks from receipt by Thomson Prometric. If you take the *Principles of Public Speaking* examination and fail (either the objective, speech portion, or both), you must follow the retesting policy waiting period of six months (180 days) before retaking the entire exam.

Essays
      The essays for *Ethics in America* and *Technical Writing* are <u>optional</u> and thus are not scored by raters. The essays are forwarded to the college or university that you designate, along with your score report, for their use in determining the award of credit. <u>Before taking the *Ethics in America* or *Technical Writing* examinations, check with your college or university to determine whether the essay is required.</u>
      NOTE: *Principles of Public Speaking* speech topic cassette tapes and essays are kept on file at Thomson Prometric for one year from the date of administration.

How to Get Transcripts
      There is a $20 fee for each transcript you request. Payment must be in the form of a certified check, U.S. money order payable to Thomson Prometric, or credit card. Personal checks and debit cards are NOT an acceptable method of payment. One transcript may include scores for one or more examinations taken. To request a transcript, download the Transcript Order Form from www.getcollegecredit.com.

DESCRIPTION OF THE DSST EXAMINATIONS

Mathematics
• **Fundamentals of College Algebra** covers mathematical concepts such as fundamental algebraic operations; linear, absolute value; quadratic equations, inequalities, radials, exponents and logarithms, factoring polynomials and graphing. The use of a nonprogrammable, handheld calculator is permitted.

• **Principles of Statistics** tests the understanding of the various topics of statistics, both qualitatively and quantitatively, and the ability to apply statistical methods to solve a variety of problems. The topics included in this test are descriptive statistics; correlation and regression; probability; chance models and sampling and tests of significance. The use of a nonprogrammable, handheld calculator is permitted.

Social Science
• **Art of the Western World** deals with the history of art during the following periods: classical; Romanesque and Gothic; early Renaissance; high Renaissance, Baroque; rococo; neoclassicism and romanticism; realism, impressionism and post-impressionism; early twentieth century; and post-World War II.

• **Western Europe Since 1945** tests the knowledge of basic facts and terms and the understanding of concepts and principles related to the areas of the historical background of the aftermath of the Second World War and rebuilding of Europe; national political systems; issues and policies in Western European societies; European institutions and processes; and Europe's relations with the rest of the world.

• **An Introduction to the Modern Middle East** emphasizes core knowledge (including geography, Judaism, Christianity, Islam, ethnicity); nineteenth-century European impact; twentieth-century Western influences; World Wars I and II; new nations; social and cultural changes (1900-1960) and the Middle East from 1960 to present.

• **Human/Cultural Geography** includes the Earth and basic facts (coordinate systems, maps, physiography, atmosphere, soils and vegetation, water); culture and environment, spatial processes (social processes, modern economic systems, settlement patterns, political geography); and regional geography.

- **Rise and Fall of the Soviet Union** covers Russia under the Old Regime; the Revolutionary Period; New Economic Policy; Pre-war Stalinism; The Second World War; Post-war Stalinism; The Khrushchev Years; The Brezhnev Era; and reform and collapse.

- **A History of the Vietnam War** covers the history of the roots of the Vietnam War; the First Vietnam War (1946-1954); pre-war developments (1954-1963); American involvement in the Vietnam War; Tet (1968); Vietnamizing the War (1968-1973); Cambodia and Laos; peace; legacies and lessons.

- **The Civil War and Reconstruction** covers the Civil War from presecession (1861) through Reconstruction. It includes causes of the war; secession; Fort Sumter; the war in the east and in the west; major battles; the political situation; assassination of Lincoln; end of the Confederacy; and Reconstruction.

- **Foundations of Education** includes topics such as contemporary issues in education; past and current influences on education (philosophies, democratic ideals, social/economic influences); and the interrelationships between contemporary issues and influences.

- **Life-span Developmental Psychology** covers models and theories; methods of study; ethical issues; biological development; perception, learning and memory; cognition and language; social, emotional, and personality development; social behaviors, family life cycle, extrafamilial settings; singlehood and cohabitation; occupational development and retirement; adjustment to life stresses; and bereavement and loss.

- **Drug and Alcohol Abuse** includes such topics as drug use in society; classification of drugs; pharmacological principles; alcohol (types, effects of, alcoholism); general principles and use of sedative hypnotics, narcotic analgesics, stimulants, and hallucinogens; other drugs (inhalants, steroids); and prevention/treatment.

- **General Anthropology** deals with anthropology as a discipline; theoretical perspectives; physical anthropology; archaeology; social organization; economic organization; political organization; religion; and modernization and application of anthropology.

- **Introduction to Law Enforcement** includes topics such as history and professional movement of law enforcement; overview of the U.S. criminal justice system; police systems in the U.S.; police organization, management, and issues; and U.S. law and precedents.

- **Criminal Justice** deals with criminal behavior (crime in the U.S., theories of crime, types of crime); the criminal justice system (historical origins, legal foundations, due process); police; the court system (history and organization, adult court system, juvenile court, pre-trial and post-trial processes); and corrections.

- **Fundamentals of Counseling** covers historical development (significant influences and people); counselor roles and functions; the counseling relationship; and theoretical approaches to counseling.

Business
- **Principles of Finance** deals with financial statements and planning; time value of money; working capital management; valuation and characteristics; capital budgeting; cost of capital; risk and return; and international financial management. The use of a nonprogrammable, handheld calculator is permitted.

- **Principles of Financial Accounting** includes topics such as general concepts and principles, accounting cycle and classification; transaction analysis; accruals and deferrals; cash and internal control; current accounts; long- and short-term liabilities; capital stock; and financial statements. The use of a nonprogrammable, handheld calculator is permitted.

- **Human Resource Management** covers general employment issues; job analysis; training and development; performance appraisals; compensation issues; security issues; personnel legislation and regulation; labor relations and current issues; an overview of the Human Resource Management Field; Human Resource Planning; Staffing; training and development; compensation issues; safety and health; employee rights and discipline; employment law; labor relations and current issues and trends.

- **Organizational Behavior** deals with the study of organizational behavior (scientific approaches, research designs, data collection methods); individual processes and characteristics; interpersonal and group processes and characteristics; organizational processes and characteristics; and change and development processes.

- **Principles of Supervision** deals with the roles and responsibilities of the supervisor; management functions (planning, organization and staffing, directing at the supervisory level); and other topics (legal issues, stress management, union environments, quality concerns).

- **Business Law II** covers topics such as sales of goods; debtor and creditor relations; business organizations; property; and commercial paper.

- **Introduction to Computing** includes topics such as history and technological generations; hardware/software; applications to information technology; program development; data management; communications and connectivity; and computing and society. The use of a nonprogrammable, handheld calculator is permitted.

- **Management Information Systems** covers systems theory, analysis and design of systems, hardware and software; database management; telecommunications; management of the MIS functional area and informational support.

- **Introduction to Business** deals with economic issues affecting business; international business; government and business; forms of business ownership; small business, entrepreneurship and franchise; management process; human resource management; production and operations; marketing management; financial management; risk management and insurance; and management and information systems.

- **Money and Banking** covers the role and kinds of money; commercial banks and other financial intermediaries; central banking and the Federal Reserve system; money and macroeconomics activity; monetary policy in the U.S.; and the international monetary system.

- **Personal Finance** includes topics such as financial goals and values; budgeting; credit and debt; major purchases; taxes; insurance; investments; and retirement and estate planning. The use of auxiliary materials, such as calculators and slide rules, is NOT permitted.

- **Business Mathematics** deals with basic operations with integers, fractions, and decimals; round numbers; ratios; averages; business graphs; simple interest; compound interest and annuities; net pay and deductions; discounts and markups; depreciation and net worth; corporate securities; distribution of ownership; and stock and asset turnover.

Physical Science
- **Astronomy** covers the history of astronomy, celestial mechanics; celestial systems; astronomical instruments; the solar system; nature and evolution; the galaxy; the universe; determining astronomical distances; and life in the universe.

- **Here's to Your Health** covers mental health and behavior; human development and relationships; substance abuse; fitness and nutrition; risk factors, disease, and disease prevention; and safety, consumer awareness, and environmental concerns.

- **Environment and Humanity** deals with topics such as ecological concepts (ecosystems, global ecology, food chains and webs); environmental impacts; environmental management and conservation; and political processes and the future.

- **Principles of Physical Science I** includes physics: Newton's Laws of Motion; energy and momentum; thermodynamics; wave and optics; electricity and magnetism; chemistry: properties of matter; atomic theory and structure; and chemical reactions.

- **Physical Geology** covers Earth materials; igneous, sedimentary, and metamorphic rocks; surface processes (weathering, groundwater, glaciers, oceanic systems, deserts and winds, hydrologic cycle); internal Earth processes; and applications (mineral and energy resources, environmental geology).

Applied Technology
- **Technical Writing** covers topics such as theory and practice of technical writing; purpose, content, and organizational patterns of common types of technical documents; elements of various technical reports; and technical editing. Students have the option to write a short essay on one of the technical topics provided. Thomson Prometric will not score the essay; however, for determining the award of credit, a copy of the essay will be forwarded to the college or university you've designated along with the score report or transcript.

Humanities
- **Ethics in America** deals with ethical traditions (Greek views, Biblical traditions, moral law, consequential ethics, feminist ethics); ethical analysis of issues arising in interpersonal and personal-societal relationships and in professional and occupational roles; and relationships between ethical traditions and the ethical analysis of situations. Students have the option to write an essay to analyze a morally problematic situation in terms of issues relevant to a decision and arguments for alternative positions. Thomson Prometric will not score the essay; however, for determining the award of credit, a copy of the essay will be forwarded to the college or university you've designated along with the score report or transcript.

- **Introduction to World Religions** covers topics such as dimensions and approaches to religion; primal religions; Hinduism; Buddhism; Confucianism; Taoism; Judaism; Christianity; and Islam.

- **Principles of Public Speaking** consists of two parts: Part One consists of multiple-choice questions covering considerations of Principles of Public Speaking; audience analysis; purposes of speeches; structure/organization; content/supporting materials; research; language and style; delivery; communication apprehension; listening and feedback; and criticism and evaluation. Part Two requires the student to record an impromptu persuasive speech that will be scored.

FREQUENTLY ASKED QUESTIONS ABOUT DSSTs

In order to pass the test, must I study from one of the recommended references?
The recommended references are a listing of books that were being used as textbooks in college courses of the same or similar title at the time the test was developed. Appropriate textbooks for study are not limited to those listed in the fact sheet. If you wish to obtain study resources to prepare for the examination, you may reference either the current edition of the listed titles or textbooks currently used at a local college or university for the same class title. It is recommended that you reference more than one textbook on the topics outlined in the fact sheet. You should begin by checking textbook content against the content outline included on the front page of the DSST fact sheet before selecting textbooks that cover the text content from which to study. Textbooks may be found at the campus bookstore of a local college or university offering a course on the subject.

Is there a penalty for guessing on the tests?
There is no penalty for guessing on DSSTs, so you should mark an answer for each question.

How much time will I have to complete the test?
Many DSSTs can be completed within 90 minutes; however, additional time can be allowed if necessary.

What should I do if I find a test question irregularity?
Continue testing and then report the irregularity to the test administrator after the test. This may be done by asking that the test administrator note the irregularity on the Supervisor's Irregularity Report or you can write to Thomson Prometric, DSST Program, 2000 Lenox Drive, Third Floor, Lawrenceville, NJ 08648, and indicate the form and question number(s) or circumstances as well as your name and address.

When will I receive my score report?
Allow approximately four weeks from the date of testing to receive your score report. Allow six to eight weeks to receive a score report for the *Principles of Public Speaking* examination.

Will my test scores be released without my permission?
Your test score will not be released to anyone other than the school you designate on your answer sheet unless you write to us and ask us to send a transcript elsewhere. Instructions about how to do this can be found on your score report. Your scores may be used for research purposes, but individual scores are never made public nor are individuals identified if research findings are made public.

If I do not achieve a passing score on the test, how long must I wait until I can take the test again?
If you do not receive a score on the test that will enable you to obtain credit for the course, you may take the test again after six months (180 days). Please do not attempt to take the test before six months (180 days) have passed because you will receive a score report marked *invalid* and your test fee will not be refunded.

Can my test scores be canceled?

The test administrator is required to report any irregularities to Thomson Prometric. <u>The consequence of bringing unauthorized materials into the testing room, or giving or receiving help, will be the forfeiture of your test fee and the invalidation of test scores.</u> The DSST Program reserves the right to cancel scores and not issue score reports in such situations.

What can I do if I feel that my test scores were not accurately reported?

Thomson Prometric recognizes the extreme importance of test results to candidates and has a multi-step quality-control procedure to help ensure that reported scores are accurate. If you have reason to believe that your score(s) were not accurately reported, you may request to have your answer sheet reviewed and hand scored.

The fees for this service are:
- $20 fee if requested within six months of the test date
- $30 fee if requested more than six months from the test date
- $30 fee if a re-evaluation of the *Principles of Public Speaking* speech is requested

The fee for this service can be paid by credit card or by certified check or U.S. money order payable to Thomson Prometric. Submit your request for score verification along with the appropriate fee or credit card information (credit card number and expiration date) to Thomson Prometric, DSST Program, 2000 Lenox Drive, Third Floor, Lawrenceville, NJ 08648. Include your full name, the test title, the date you took the test, and your Social Security number. Candidates will be notified if a scoring discrepancy is discovered within four weeks of receipt of the request.

What does ACE recommendation mean?

The ACE recommendation is the minimum passing score recommended by the American Council on Education for any given test. It is equivalent to the average score of students in the DSST norming sample who received a grade of C for the course. Some schools require a score higher than the ACE recommendation.

Who is NLC?

National Learning Corporation (NLC) has been successfully preparing candidates for 40 years for over 5,000 exams. NLC publishes Passbook® study guides to help candidates prepare for all DANTES and CLEP exams and almost every other type of exam from high school through adult career.

Go to our website — www.passbooks.com — or call (800) 632-8888 for information about ordering our Passbooks.

To get detailed information on the DSST program and DSST preparation materials, visit www.getcollegecredit.com.

If you are interested in taking the DSST exams, call 877-471-9860 or e-mail pnj-dsst@thomson.com.

HOW TO TAKE A TEST

You have studied long, hard and conscientiously.

With your official admission card in hand, and your heart pounding, you have been admitted to the examination room.

You note that there are several hundred other applicants in the examination room waiting to take the same test.

They all appear to be equally well prepared.

You know that nothing but your best effort will suffice. The "moment of truth" is at hand: you now have to demonstrate objectively, in writing, your knowledge of content and your understanding of subject matter.

You are fighting the most important battle of your life—to pass and/or score high on an examination which will determine your career and provide the economic basis for your livelihood.

What extra, special things should you know and should you do in taking the examination?

I. YOU MUST PASS AN EXAMINATION

A. WHAT EVERY CANDIDATE SHOULD KNOW
Examination applicants often ask us for help in preparing for the written test. What can I study in advance? What kinds of questions will be asked? How will the test be given? How will the papers be graded?

B. HOW ARE EXAMS DEVELOPED?
Examinations are carefully written by trained technicians who are specialists in the field known as "psychological measurement," in consultation with recognized authorities in the field of work that the test will cover. These experts recommend the subject matter areas or skills to be tested; only those knowledges or skills important to your success on the job are included. The most reliable books and source materials available are used as references. Together, the experts and technicians judge the difficulty level of the questions.
Test technicians know how to phrase questions so that the problem is clearly stated. Their ethics do not permit "trick" or "catch" questions. Questions may have been tried out on sample groups, or subjected to statistical analysis, to determine their usefulness.
Written tests are often used in combination with performance tests, ratings of training and experience, and oral interviews. All of these measures combine to form the best-known means of finding the right person for the right job.

II. HOW TO PASS THE WRITTEN TEST

A. BASIC STEPS

1) Study the announcement

How, then, can you know what subjects to study? Our best answer is: "Learn as much as possible about the class of positions for which you've applied." The exam will test the knowledge, skills and abilities needed to do the work.

Your most valuable source of information about the position you want is the official exam announcement. This announcement lists the training and experience qualifications. Check these standards and apply only if you come reasonably close to meeting them. Many jurisdictions preview the written test in the exam announcement by including a section called "Knowledge and Abilities Required," "Scope of the Examination," or some similar heading. Here you will find out specifically what fields will be tested.

2) Choose appropriate study materials

If the position for which you are applying is technical or advanced, you will read more advanced, specialized material. If you are already familiar with the basic principles of your field, elementary textbooks would waste your time. Concentrate on advanced textbooks and technical periodicals. Think through the concepts and review difficult problems in your field.

These are all general sources. You can get more ideas on your own initiative, following these leads. For example, training manuals and publications of the government agency which employs workers in your field can be useful, particularly for technical and professional positions. A letter or visit to the government department involved may result in more specific study suggestions, and certainly will provide you with a more definite idea of the exact nature of the position you are seeking.

3) Study this book!

III. KINDS OF TESTS

Tests are used for purposes other than measuring knowledge and ability to perform specified duties. For some positions, it is equally important to test ability to make adjustments to new situations or to profit from training. In others, basic mental abilities not dependent on information are essential. Questions which test these things may not appear as pertinent to the duties of the position as those which test for knowledge and information. Yet they are often highly important parts of a fair examination. For very general questions, it is almost impossible to help you direct your study efforts. What we can do is to point out some of the more common of these general abilities needed in public service positions and describe some typical questions.

1) General information

Broad, general information has been found useful for predicting job success in some kinds of work. This is tested in a variety of ways, from vocabulary lists to questions about current events. Basic background in some field of work, such as sociology or economics, may be sampled in a group of questions. Often these are principles which have become familiar to most persons through exposure rather than through formal training. It is difficult to advise you how to study for these questions; being alert to the world around you is our best suggestion.

2) Verbal ability

An example of an ability needed in many positions is verbal or language ability. Verbal ability is, in brief, the ability to use and understand words. Vocabulary and grammar tests are typical measures of this ability. Reading comprehension or paragraph interpretation questions are common in many kinds of civil service tests. You are given a paragraph of written material and asked to find its central meaning.

IV. KINDS OF QUESTIONS

1. Multiple-choice Questions

Most popular of the short-answer questions is the "multiple choice" or "best answer" question. It can be used, for example, to test for factual knowledge, ability to solve problems or judgment in meeting situations found at work.

A multiple-choice question is normally one of three types:
- It can begin with an incomplete statement followed by several possible endings. You are to find the one ending which best completes the statement, although some of the others may not be entirely wrong.
- It can also be a complete statement in the form of a question which is answered by choosing one of the statements listed.
- It can be in the form of a problem – again you select the best answer.

Here is an example of a multiple-choice question with a discussion which should give you some clues as to the method for choosing the right answer:

When an employee has a complaint about his assignment, the action which will best help him overcome his difficulty is to
- A. discuss his difficulty with his coworkers
- B. take the problem to the head of the organization
- C. take the problem to the person who gave him the assignment
- D. say nothing to anyone about his complaint

In answering this question, you should study each of the choices to find which is best. Consider choice "A" – Certainly an employee may discuss his complaint with fellow employees, but no change or improvement can result, and the complaint remains unresolved. Choice "B" is a poor choice since the head of the organization probably does not know what assignment you have been given, and taking your problem to him is known as "going over the head" of the supervisor. The supervisor, or person who made the assignment, is the person who can clarify it or correct any injustice. Choice "C" is, therefore, correct. To say nothing, as in choice "D," is unwise. Supervisors have and interest in knowing the problems employees are facing, and the employee is seeking a solution to his problem.

2. True/False

3. Matching Questions

Matching an answer from a column of choices within another column.

V. RECORDING YOUR ANSWERS

Computer terminals are used more and more today for many different kinds of exams.

For an examination with very few applicants, you may be told to record your answers in the test booklet itself. Separate answer sheets are much more common. If this separate answer sheet is to be scored by machine – and this is often the case – it is highly important that you mark your answers correctly in order to get credit.

VI. BEFORE THE TEST

YOUR PHYSICAL CONDITION IS IMPORTANT

If you are not well, you can't do your best work on tests. If you are half asleep, you can't do your best either. Here are some tips:

1) Get about the same amount of sleep you usually get. Don't stay up all night before the test, either partying or worrying—DON'T DO IT!
2) If you wear glasses, be sure to wear them when you go to take the test. This goes for hearing aids, too.
3) If you have any physical problems that may keep you from doing your best, be sure to tell the person giving the test. If you are sick or in poor health, you relay cannot do your best on any test. You can always come back and take the test some other time.

Common sense will help you find procedures to follow to get ready for an examination. Too many of us, however, overlook these sensible measures. Indeed, nervousness and fatigue have been found to be the most serious reasons why applicants fail to do their best on civil service tests. Here is a list of reminders:

- Begin your preparation early – Don't wait until the last minute to go scurrying around for books and materials or to find out what the position is all about.
- Prepare continuously – An hour a night for a week is better than an all-night cram session. This has been definitely established. What is more, a night a week for a month will return better dividends than crowding your study into a shorter period of time.
- Locate the place of the exam – You have been sent a notice telling you when and where to report for the examination. If the location is in a different town or otherwise unfamiliar to you, it would be well to inquire the best route and learn something about the building.
- Relax the night before the test – Allow your mind to rest. Do not study at all that night. Plan some mild recreation or diversion; then go to bed early and get a good night's sleep.
- Get up early enough to make a leisurely trip to the place for the test – This way unforeseen events, traffic snarls, unfamiliar buildings, etc. will not upset you.
- Dress comfortably – A written test is not a fashion show. You will be known by number and not by name, so wear something comfortable.
- Leave excess paraphernalia at home – Shopping bags and odd bundles will get in your way. You need bring only the items mentioned in the official notice you received; usually everything you need is provided. Do not bring reference books to the exam. They will only confuse those last minutes and be taken away from you when in the test room.

- Arrive somewhat ahead of time – If because of transportation schedules you must get there very early, bring a newspaper or magazine to take your mind off yourself while waiting.
- Locate the examination room – When you have found the proper room, you will be directed to the seat or part of the room where you will sit. Sometimes you are given a sheet of instructions to read while you are waiting. Do not fill out any forms until you are told to do so; just read them and be prepared.
- Relax and prepare to listen to the instructions
- If you have any physical problem that may keep you from doing your best, be sure to tell the test administrator. If you are sick or in poor health, you really cannot do your best on the exam. You can come back and take the test some other time.

VII. AT THE TEST

The day of the test is here and you have the test booklet in your hand. The temptation to get going is very strong. Caution! There is more to success than knowing the right answers. You must know how to identify your papers and understand variations in the type of short-answer question used in this particular examination. Follow these suggestions for maximum results from your efforts:

1) Cooperate with the monitor

The test administrator has a duty to create a situation in which you can be as much at ease as possible. He will give instructions, tell you when to begin, check to see that you are marking your answer sheet correctly, and so on. He is not there to guard you, although he will see that your competitors do not take unfair advantage. He wants to help you do your best.

2) Listen to all instructions

Don't jump the gun! Wait until you understand all directions. In most civil service tests you get more time than you need to answer the questions. So don't be in a hurry. Read each word of instructions until you clearly understand the meaning. Study the examples, listen to all announcements and follow directions. Ask questions if you do not understand what to do.

3) Identify your papers

Civil service exams are usually identified by number only. You will be assigned a number; you must not put your name on your test papers. Be sure to copy your number correctly. Since more than one exam may be given, copy your exact examination title.

4) Plan your time

Unless you are told that a test is a "speed" or "rate of work" test, speed itself is usually not important. Time enough to answer all the questions will be provided, but this does not mean that you have all day. An overall time limit has been set. Divide the total time (in minutes) by the number of questions to determine the approximate time you have for each question.

5) Do not linger over difficult questions

If you come across a difficult question, mark it with a paper clip (useful to have along) and come back to it when you have been through the booklet. One caution if you do this – be sure to skip a number on your answer sheet as well. Check often to be sure that you have not lost your place and that you are marking in the row numbered the same as the question you are answering.

6) Read the questions

Be sure you know what the question asks! Many capable people are unsuccessful because they failed to read the questions correctly.

7) Answer all questions

Unless you have been instructed that a penalty will be deducted for incorrect answers, it is better to guess than to omit a question.

8) Speed tests

It is often better NOT to guess on speed tests. It has been found that on timed tests people are tempted to spend the last few seconds before time is called in marking answers at random – without even reading them – in the hope of picking up a few extra points. To discourage this practice, the instructions may warn you that your score will be "corrected" for guessing. That is, a penalty will be applied. The incorrect answers will be deducted from the correct ones, or some other penalty formula will be used.

9) Review your answers

If you finish before time is called, go back to the questions you guessed or omitted to give them further thought. Review other answers if you have time.

10) Return your test materials

If you are ready to leave before others have finished or time is called, take ALL your materials to the monitor and leave quietly. Never take any test material with you. The monitor can discover whose papers are not complete, and taking a test booklet may be grounds for disqualification.

VIII. EXAMINATION TECHNIQUES

1) Read the general instructions carefully. These are usually printed on the first page of the exam booklet. As a rule, these instructions refer to the timing of the examination; the fact that you should not start work until the signal and must stop work at a signal, etc. If there are any special instructions, such as a choice of questions to be answered, make sure that you note this instruction carefully.

2) When you are ready to start work on the examination, that is as soon as the signal has been given, read the instructions to each question booklet, underline any key words or phrases, such as least, best, outline, describe and the like. In this way you will tend to answer as requested rather than discover on reviewing your paper that you listed without describing, that you selected the worst choice rather than the best choice, etc.

3) If the examination is of the objective or multiple-choice type – that is, each question will also give a series of possible answers: A, B, C or D, and you are called upon to select the best answer and write the letter next to that answer on your answer paper – it is advisable to start answering each question in turn. There may be anywhere from 50 to 100 such questions in the three or four hours allotted and you can see how much time would be taken if you read through all the questions before beginning to answer any. Furthermore, if you

come across a question or group of questions which you know would be difficult to answer, it would undoubtedly affect your handling of all the other questions.

4) If the examination is of the essay type and contains but a few questions, it is a moot point as to whether you should read all the questions before starting to answer any one. Of course, if you are given a choice – say five out of seven and the like – then it is essential to read all the questions so you can eliminate the two that are most difficult. If, however, you are asked to answer all the questions, there may be danger in trying to answer the easiest one first because you may find that you will spend too much time on it. The best technique is to answer the first question, then proceed to the second, etc.

5) Time your answers. Before the exam begins, write down the time it started, then add the time allowed for the examination and write down the time it must be completed, then divide the time available somewhat as follows:
   - If 3-1/2 hours are allowed, that would be 210 minutes. If you have 80 objective-type questions, that would be an average of 2-1/2 minutes per question. Allow yourself no more than 2 minutes per question, or a total of 160 minutes, which will permit about 50 minutes to review.
   - If for the time allotment of 210 minutes there are 7 essay questions to answer, that would average about 30 minutes a question. Give yourself only 25 minutes per question so that you have about 35 minutes to review.

6) The most important instruction is to read each question and make sure you know what is wanted. The second most important instruction is to time yourself properly so that you answer every question. The third most important instruction is to answer every question. Guess if you have to but include something for each question. Remember that you will receive no credit for a blank and will probably receive some credit if you write something in answer to an essay question. If you guess a letter – say "B" for a multiple-choice question – you may have guessed right. If you leave a blank as an answer to a multiple-choice question, the examiners may respect your feelings but it will not add a point to your score. Some exams may penalize you for wrong answers, so in such cases only, you may not want to guess unless you have some basis for your answer.

7) Suggestions
   a. Objective-type questions
      1. Examine the question booklet for proper sequence of pages and questions
      2. Read all instructions carefully
      3. Skip any question which seems too difficult; return to it after all other questions have been answered
      4. Apportion your time properly; do not spend too much time on any single question or group of questions
      5. Note and underline key words – all, most, fewest, least, best, worst, same, opposite, etc.
      6. Pay particular attention to negatives
      7. Note unusual option, e.g., unduly long, short, complex, different or similar in content to the body of the question
      8. Observe the use of "hedging" words – probably, may, most likely, etc.

9. Make sure that your answer is put next to the same number as the question
10. Do not second-guess unless you have good reason to believe the second answer is definitely more correct
11. Cross out original answer if you decide another answer is more accurate; do not erase until you are ready to hand your paper in
12. Answer all questions; guess unless instructed otherwise
13. Leave time for review

b. Essay questions
1. Read each question carefully
2. Determine exactly what is wanted. Underline key words or phrases.
3. Decide on outline or paragraph answer
4. Include many different points and elements unless asked to develop any one or two points or elements
5. Show impartiality by giving pros and cons unless directed to select one side only
6. Make and write down any assumptions you find necessary to answer the questions
7. Watch your English, grammar, punctuation and choice of words
8. Time your answers; don't crowd material

8) Answering the essay question

Most essay questions can be answered by framing the specific response around several key words or ideas. Here are a few such key words or ideas:

M's: manpower, materials, methods, money, management
P's: purpose, program, policy, plan, procedure, practice, problems, pitfalls, personnel, public relations

a. Six basic steps in handling problems:
1. Preliminary plan and background development
2. Collect information, data and facts
3. Analyze and interpret information, data and facts
4. Analyze and develop solutions as well as make recommendations
5. Prepare report and sell recommendations
6. Install recommendations and follow up effectiveness

b. Pitfalls to avoid
1. Taking things for granted – A statement of the situation does not necessarily imply that each of the elements is necessarily true; for example, a complaint may be invalid and biased so that all that can be taken for granted is that a complaint has been registered
2. Considering only one side of a situation – Wherever possible, indicate several alternatives and then point out the reasons you selected the best one
3. Failing to indicate follow up – Whenever your answer indicates action on your part, make certain that you will take proper follow-up action to see how successful your recommendations, procedures or actions turn out to be
4. Taking too long in answering any single question – Remember to time your answers properly

EXAMINATION SECTION

EXAMINATION SECTION
TEST 1

DIRECTIONS: Each question or incomplete statement is followed by several suggested answers or completions. Select the one that BEST answers the question or completes the statement. PRINT THE LETTER OF THE CORRECT ANSWER IN THE SPACE AT THE RIGHT.

1. Of the following, it is correct to say that as colder ocean water sinks to the ocean bottom it has a tendency to "creep"

    A. toward the equator
    B. toward the North and South Poles
    C. eastward
    D. westward

    1._____

2. Of the following, the one that is NOT a factor contributing to the origin and distribution of ocean currents is the

    A. prevailing winds
    B. changing tides
    C. rotation of the earth
    D. shape of continents

    2._____

3. Coral reefs have the best chance of becoming established in warm shallow waters where

    A. waves and currents are active
    B. there is little or no motion
    C. rocks on which they form are frequently exposed to air
    D. turbidity is great

    3._____

4. Of the following, it is correct to say that, if coral grows upward as fast as an island sinks, the reef will

    A. come closer to the sinking land
    B. get farther from the sinking land
    C. not change its size
    D. grow equally both toward the island and seaward

    4._____

5. Of the following locations, submarine canyons extending across a continental shelf may occur where

    A. rivers enter the ocean
    B. littoral currents are especially strong
    C. fault lines extend out from the coast
    D. tidal forces are unusual

    5._____

6. A tombolo is a variety of

    A. concretion   B. lake   C. sand bar   D. volcano

    6._____

7. The Humboldt current is located in the

    A. south pacific
    B. north pacific
    C. south atlantic
    D. north atlantic

    7._____

1

8. Where two valley glaciers come together, deposition may result in the formation of
   A. terminal moraine
   B. esker
   C. lateral moraine
   D. medial moraine

9. Of the following forms of ice, which one had a terrestrial origin although it is found in sea waters?
   A. Pack ice
   B. Ice floes
   C. Icebergs
   D. Ice foot

10. Of the following evidences, which one does NOT indicate the general direction of movement of a glacier?
    A. Striae
    B. Direction of flow of post-glacial streams
    C. Roche moutonnees
    D. U-shaped valleys

11. The total relief of the earth is closest, in miles, to which one of the following?
    A. 5
    B. 7
    C. 12
    D. 17

12. Of the following, the rock most rapidly eroded by ground water is
    A. breccia
    B. sandstone
    C. shale
    D. limestone

13. Elongated ridges of till, usually in clusters, and oval in shape are known as
    A. kames
    B. eskers
    C. drumlins
    D. outliers

14. Of the following, a mineral that will effervesce with warm dilute hydrochloric acid is
    A. selenite
    B. dolomite
    C. fluorite
    D. biotite

15. The "moho" refers to
    A. a deep in the Pacific Ocean
    B. the boundary between the crust and the mantle
    C. a type of drilling machine
    D. a fault in the crust of the earth

16. Of the following, the drainage pattern typical of a dome mountain region is
    A. dendritic
    B. radial and annular
    C. rectangular
    D. trellis

17. Of the following, the agent of erosion that produces ventifacts is the
    A. driving force of wind blown sand
    B. milling action of sub-glacial streams
    C. chemical action of ground water
    D. pounding force of waves

18. To be of most use to the geologist, the organism in an index fossil should have existed over a
    A. widespread area for a relatively short period of time
    B. widespread area for a relatively long period of time

C. relatively narrow range of area for a short period of time
D. relatively narrow range of area for a long period of time

19. Of the following, the earliest event in the development of a folded mountain range is

    A. folding and metamorphism of sediments
    B. formation of a geosyncline
    C. extrusive and intrusive volcanic activity
    D. deposition of sediments

20. The divide between two stream systems shifts in the direction of the system

    A. having the steeper gradients
    B. having the gentler gradients
    C. eroding more resistant rocks
    D. receiving the greater volume of precipitation

21. The concept of isostasy has been used to explain the

    A. original formation of continents and ocean basins
    B. occurrence of earthquakes and volcanic activity along the shores of the Pacific Ocean
    C. origin of flat-topped submarine mountains in the Pacific Ocean
    D. alternation of glacial and inter-glacial stages in the Pleistocene epoch

22. When a river that is in its old age stage is rejuvenated, which one of the following is most likely to form?

    A. Levee
    B. Flood plain
    C. Intrenched meander
    D. Alluvial cone

23. The Cambrian period is characterized by

    A. the advent of man
    B. widespread vulcanism
    C. the first abundant fossils
    D. the first appearance of glaciers

24. Of the following, the Ewing-Donn hypothesis attempts to explain the

    A. origin and development of folded mountains
    B. origin and formation of submarine canyons
    C. cause and distribution of earthquakes
    D. onset and succession of glacial stages in the Northern hemisphere

25. The most recent age determinations of rocks by radioactive methods indicate that the length of geologic time is

    A. approximately 1 1/2 billion years
    B. between 2 and 2 1/2 billion years
    C. in excess of 3 billion years
    D. approximately 5 billion years

26. Of the following events which occur in mountain-building, the LAST in the sequence is

   A. lithification of sediments
   B. folding of sedimentary rocks
   C. invasion of roots by magma
   D. elevation of sedimentary rocks

27. Clay varves are useful to geologists in their study of

   A. climates of the past   B. fossils
   C. ripple marks   D. weathering

28. Of the following, the measurement of the interfacial angles of a crystal is accomplished by the use of the instrument known as a

   A. spectrometer   B. clinometer
   C. goniometer   D. refractometer

29. Of the following, the most likely source of heat energy necessary to keep magma in a molten condition is

   A. residual heat within the earth's crust
   B. bombardment of the earth by cosmic rays
   C. energy released by radio-active disintegration within the earth's crust
   D. infra-red radiation from the sun

30. Guyots are

   A. steep-cliff mountains
   B. deep-sea trenches
   C. flat-topped mountains rising from the sea floor
   D. submarine valleys

31. The most recent of the following processes responsible for the hilly topography of northern Manhattan and the Bronx is

   A. synclinal folding   B. anticlinal folding
   C. volcanic intrusions   D. differential erosion

32. Of the following, the concept of magmatic differentiation is useful in explaining the

   A. diversity of composition of igneous rocks
   B. difference between intrusive and extrusive igneous rocks
   C. difference between the various phases of volcanic activity
   D. diversity of igneous structures

33. In the history of mountain formation from isostatic readjustment, the first step would be

   A. formation of a geosyncline
   B. synclinal folding
   C. anticlinal folding
   D. vulcanism

34. A cyclothem is a repetitive series of sedimentary rocks deposited under the condition of alternating cycles of

    A. glacial and interglacial deposition
    B. dry and wet climatic intervals
    C. marine transgression and regression
    D. fresh water and salt water inudation

34.____

35. Phyllite is formed by metamorphism of

    A. sandstone   B. shale   C. limestone   D. granite

35.____

36. Most of the surface bedrock of New York State was formed from sand, mud or limestone deposited in seas and lakes during which one of the following eras?

    A. Cenozoic   B. Mesozoic
    C. Paleozoic   D. Proterozoic

36.____

37. The magma which erupts as extensive basaltic lava flows, probably originates in

    A. sialic crust   B. simatic crust
    C. earth's mantle   D. earth's core

37.____

38. Columnar jointing, a characteristic of igneous rocks, is the result of

    A. expansion due to heating
    B. contraction due to cooling
    C. contact metamorphism
    D. mineral displacement

38.____

39. The white bands in gneiss consist principally of which one of the following pairs?

    A. Quartz and muscovite   B. Biotite and feldspar
    C. Quartz and feldspar   D. Biotite and amphiboles

39.____

40. Calcite deposits around mineral springs are called

    A. gypsum   B. onyx   C. sphalerite   D. travertine

40.____

41. Of the following, a physical property common to granite, basalt and obsidian is

    A. overall hardness greater than 5
    B. predominantly dark color
    C. specific gravity of 2.7 or less
    D. uniform size of the mineral grains

41.____

42. Of the following, a rock which *CANNOT* be classified on the basis of its mineral content is

    A. basalt   B. shale   C. obsidian   D. marble

42.____

43. Our best estimate of the age of the earth is derived from

    A. the amount of salt in the sea
    B. the study of erosion
    C. the total thickness of sedimentary rock layers
    D. radioactive decay products in rocks

43.____

44. Of the following, the one which represents a sequence of increasing metamorphism in rock formation is 44.____

    A. shale, phyllite, slate, schist
    B. shale, slate, phyllite, schist
    C. shale, schist, slate, phyllite
    D. shale, slate, schist, phyllite

45. On the Mohs' scale of hardness, quartz is closest to which one of the following? 45.____

    A. 2   B. 4   C. 7   D. 9

46. Which one of the following BEST describes the mineral composition of a granite? 46.____

    A. Biotite, orthoclase, quartz
    B. Quartz, calcite, talc
    C. Mica, hornblende, olivine
    D. Calcite, feldspar, magnetite

47. Of the following, the type of cloud most likely to produce a halo around the moon is 47.____

    A. cumulonimbus   B. altocumulus
    C. cirrocumulus   D. cirrostratus

48. The wave length of an ocean wave represents the distance from the 48.____

    A. crest of one wave to the trough of the next wave
    B. crest of wave to the trough of the same wave
    C. trough of one wave to the trough of the next wave
    D. crest of one wave to the crest of the next wave divided by 2

49. A great deal of seaweed accumulates in the Sargasso Sea largely because 49.____

    A. of warm Equatorial air
    B. of unusual quantities of sunshine
    C. there is little current in the central part of an ocean
    D. in that area there are too few fish to consume the plants

50. If iron were left on the surface of the moon, it would probably 50.____

    A. remain chemically unchanged
    B. change to Fe_2O_3 more quickly than on earth
    C. change to FeS
    D. change to Fe_2O_3 at a rate approximately 1/7 of the rate of iron's corrosion on earth

KEY (CORRECT ANSWERS)

1. A	11. C	21. B	31. D	41. A
2. B	12. D	22. C	32. A	42. C
3. A	13. C	23. C	33. A	43. D
4. B	14. B	24. D	34. C	44. B
5. A	15. B	25. C	35. B	45. C
6. C	16. B	26. D	36. C	46. A
7. A	17. A	27. A	37. B	47. D
8. D	18. A	28. C	38. B	48. C
9. C	19. B	29. C	39. C	49. C
10. B	20. B	30. C	40. D	50. A

TEST 2

DIRECTIONS: Each question or incomplete statement is followed by several suggested answers or completions. Select the one that BEST answers the question or completes the statement. PRINT THE LETTER OF THE CORRECT ANSWER IN THE SPACE AT THE RIGHT.

1. Of the following, which rock is the extrusive equivalent of gabbro?   1.___
    A. Andesite   B. Basalt   C. Dacite   D. Rhyolite

2. Relatively quiet bodies of water between offshore bars and the mainland are called   2.___
    A. lagoons   B. fjords   C. shoals   D. tidal races

3. According to most recent scientific estimates based on radioactivity, the earth's age, in years, is closest to which one of the following?   3.___
    A. 40 million   B. 400 million   C. 4 billion   D. 40 billion

4. Calcium carbonate deposited from ground water is called   4.___
    A. geyserite   B. ocher   C. travertine   D. gypsum

5. Which one of the following metals is usually extracted commercially from sea water?   5.___
    A. Iron   B. Aluminum   C. Magnesium   D. Titanium

6. Which one of the following is a mineral that is isomorphic with magnesite?   6.___
    A. Siderite   B. Selenite   C. Albite   D. Biotite

7. The large crystals in a porphyry are called   7.___
    A. aphanites   B. metacrysts   C. phenocrysts   D. porphyrites

8. Dinosaurs were the dominant form of life in which one of the following periods?   8.___
    A. Cambrian   B. Jurassic   C. Permian   D. Carboniferous

9. An obsequent stream would be found   9.___
    A. on the inface of a cuesta
    B. on the backslope of a hogback
    C. in a belt of weak rock parallel to the coastline
    D. in the direction of the consequent streams

10. Of the following, which one is a narrow block of rock uplifted between two normal faults?   10.___
    A. Flatiron   B. Horst   C. Polje   D. Stack

11. Of the following statements concerning bodies of water, the one which is correct is: 11.___
    A. The Caspian Sea is a fresh water lake.
    B. Lake Ronkonkoma is of glacial origin.
    C. Lake Champlain has been a fresh water lake since its formation.
    D. Lake Mead was formed by impounding river water behind the Grand Coulee Dam.

12. The Badlands of South Dakota are cut up by numerous small gullies. These features were formed mainly by   12.____

    A. waves B. glacial action
    C. winds D. running water

13. "Chimney rocks" or "stacks" are largely the result of   13.____

    A. wind erosion B. weathering
    C. glaciation   D. wave erosion

14. Of the following, the mineral which is NOT a sulfide is   14.____

    A. chalcocite B. sphalerite
    C. galena   D. cassiterite

15. Which one of the following is an example of block mountains?   15.____

    A. Sierra Nevadas B. Black Hills
    C. Andes   D. Appalachians

16. Loess is a result of deposition by   16.____

    A. gravity   B. wind
    C. ground water   D. ocean currents

17. During a long period of drought, deep rooted plants may obtain a limited water supply from immediately above the water table. This water is obtained from ground water and moves upward through the soil because of   17.____

    A. cohesive forces
    B. viscous flow
    C. its seeking its own level
    D. capillary action

18. A barchan is a variety of   18.____

    A. cave   B. concretion   C. monadnock   D. dune

19. Which one of the following is a physiographic feature that requires a rise of land or a fall in sea level for its development?   19.____

    A. Alluvial fan   B. Intrenched meander
    C. Oxbow lake   D. Sea cave

20. In the field of earth science, a pediment may be defined as a(n)   20.____

    A. unattached sand bar at the mouth of a bay
    B. smooth sloping rock surface fringing a desert mountain range
    C. lava flow that has dammed a river to form a lake
    D. monadnock in an old plateau region

21. Of the following rocks, the kind in which fossils are most likely to be found is   21.____

    A. granite   B. basalt   C. pumice   D. sandstone

22. The fractional scale 1:24,000 represents a map scale of 1 inch to

   A. 1/2 mile
   B. 1,200 meters
   C. 800 yards
   D. 2,000 feet

23. Of the following, which one is a correct description of the Catskills?

   A. Complex mountains
   B. Domed mountains
   C. Folded mountains
   D. Dissected plateaus

24. The presence of which one of the following causes the red coloring of many rocks and soils?

   A. Hematite
   B. Sphalerite
   C. Cinnabar
   D. Calcite

25. The average speed, in miles per second, of the primary wave set up by an earthquake is closest to which one of the following?

   A. 1
   B. 5
   C. 20
   D. 186,000

26. The most recently active volcano in the contiguous 48 states of the continental United States area is

   A. Mount Hood
   B. Mount Shasta
   C. Mount Lassen
   D. Mount Rainier

27. Our most recent continental glacier withdrew from north-central North America at a number of years ago closest to

   A. 1,000
   B. 9,000
   C. 60,000
   D. 1,000,000

28. The brightest "star" in the night time sky of either hemisphere is

   A. Venus
   B. Canopus
   C. Betelgeuse
   D. Sirius

29. Mechanical disintegration due to temperature changes is most pronounced in the United States

   A. in arid regions and on exposed mountain summits
   B. in sandy deserts
   C. on northern slopes
   D. in regions of warm temperature and high humidity

30. The vertical displacement of a fault block is known as the

   A. heave
   B. throw
   C. dip slope
   D. strike slip

31. The auroras are believed to result from

   A. interaction of earth's magnetic field with particles emitted by the sun
   B. annihilation of electrons and positrons in upper regions of the atmosphere
   C. creation of glowing particles by interaction of cosmic rays
   D. emission of electrical particles from outer galaxies

32. A man-made earth satellite is most likely to collide with a

   A. comet
   B. planet
   C. meteor
   D. planetoid

33. To which one of the following phenomena is the blue color of the sky attributed?

    A. Differential scattering
    B. Total internal reflection
    C. Absorption
    D. Refraction

34. Of the following, which one is an effective moderator for an atomic reactor?

    A. Boron steel B. Lead
    C. Cadmium   D. Heavy water

35. To which one of the following is a Geiger counter most likely to respond?

    A. Galena   B. Limonite
    C. Pitchblende D. Pyroxene

36. The ratio of the brightness of a star of the first magnitude to that of a star of the second magnitude is

    A. 2:1   B. 2.5:1   C. 4:1   D. 8:1

37. The "Bad Lands" of South Dakota is an example of which one of the following kinds of sculpture?

    A. Wind   B. Wave
    C. Glacier D. Stream and rain

38. Topographic maps utilize

    A. only one contour interval for each map
    B. the changing of a contour interval in abrupt changes from plains areas to very mountainous areas
    C. no definite contour interval
    D. depression contours to indicate submarine depths along shorelines

39. Which one of the following contributed most to the development of the air mass theory of weather?

    A. Ferrel   B. Guys-Ballot
    C. Petterssen D. Bergeron

40. The man named below most likely to be associated with the Cosmogonists is

    A. William Smith   B. Seneca
    C. René Descartes   D. Cuvier

41. The Polar-front theory to explain the origin of cyclones and anticyclones originated with

    A. Brunt   B. Shaw   C. Murphy   D. Bjerknes

42. The igneous activity which produced the rock of the Palisades of the Hudson River occurred principally during the geologic period called

    A. Triassic   B. Jurassic
    C. Cretaceous D. Eocene

43. It is not possible to correlate reliably Precambrian rocks between different regions of the continent because of the 43._____

    A. intense deformation
    B. lack of uranium ores
    C. absence of fossils
    D. lack of sedimentary deposits

44. In which one of the geologic eras were the rocks of Manhattan and the Bronx formed? 44._____

    A. Archeozoic   B. Proterozoic
    C. Mesozoic   D. Cenozoic

45. Which one of the following actions is a factor in the formation of the basins of karst lakes? 45._____

    A. Landslide   B. Glacial
    C. Volcanic   D. Ground water

46. Which one of the following is NOT associated with unconsolidated material when it is attacked by waves? 46._____

    A. Wave-cut terrace   B. Wave-built terrace
    C. Wave-cut cliff   D. Wave-cut notch

47. Of the following, which one is NOT associated with rock phenomena originating from ground water? 47._____

    A. Geodes   B. Travertine
    C. Petrified wood   D. Arêtes

48. Great Salt Lake, together with which one of the following, constitutes much of the area once filled by ancient Lake Bonneville? 48._____

    A. Lake Sevier   B. Death Valley
    C. Lake Winnipeg   D. Salton Sea

49. Which one of the following bodies of water has no outlet? 49._____

    A. Lake Superior   B. Caspian Sea
    C. Lake Cayuga   D. Lake Huron

50. According to Gilbert's sixth power law, if the velocity of a stream is doubled, the size of the particles composing the load may be increased up to how many times? 50._____

    A. 12   B. 24   C. 32   D. 64

KEY (CORRECT ANSWERS)

1. B	11. B	21. D	31. A	41. D
2. A	12. D	22. D	32. C	42. A
3. C	13. D	23. D	33. A	43. C
4. C	14. D	24. A	34. D	44. A
5. C	15. A	25. B	35. C	45. D
6. A	16. B	26. C	36. B	46. C
7. C	17. D	27. B	37. D	47. D
8. B	18. D	28. D	38. B	48. A
9. A	19. B	29. A	39. D	49. B
10. B	20. B	30. B	40. C	50. D

TEST 3

DIRECTIONS: Each question or incomplete statement is followed by several suggested answers or completions. Select the one that BEST answers the question or completes the statement. PRINT THE LETTER OF THE CORRECT ANSWER IN THE SPACE AT THE RIGHT.

1. Which one of the following rocks is known to be most radioactive?   1.____

   A. Gabbro   B. Granite   C. Basalt   D. Sandstone

2. Which one of the following upon being subjected to contact metamorphism may develop into two different rocks?   2.____

   A. Conglomerate   B. Sandstone
   C. Shale   D. Limestone

3. Columnar jointing is associated with the cooling of   3.____

   A. diorite   B. syenite   C. diabase   D. granite

4. Which one of the following is NOT a sedimentary rock?   4.____

   A. Conglomerate   B. Chert
   C. Sandstone   D. Gabbro

5. Which one of the following rocks is formed when talus materials are cemented together?   5.____

   A. Tuff   B. Breccia
   C. Consolidated gravel   D. Conglomerate

6. Residual mantle rock   6.____

   A. may be found below a mantle of transported rock
   B. is never found below a mantle rock
   C. is found in desert areas only
   D. does not resemble the bedrock below it

7. Which one of the following rocks is classified as metamorphic?   7.____

   A. Syenite   B. Rhyolite
   C. Quartzite   D. Marl

8. Which one of the following pairs associates a characteristic of diorite with one of granite?   8.____

   A. Little visible quartz and oligoclase feldspar
   B. Large crystals of quartz and plagioclase feldspar
   C. Large crystals of quartz and oligoclase feldspar
   D. Little visible quartz and a predominance of plagioclase feldspar

9. Which one of the following is NOT an intrusive igneous rock?   9.____

   A. Stocks   B. Tufa bed
   C. Laccoliths D. Batholith

10. The schistose texture of metamorphic rocks is best described by which one of the following?   10.____

    A. Roughly foliated, alternating parallel bands of light and dark colored minerals
    B. Well foliated, consisting dominantly of mica minerals large enough to be recognized
    C. Foliated, but with no recognizable minerals
    D. Nonfoliated, mineral grains interlocked

11. Which one of the following groups describes orthoclase feldspar?   11.____

    A. 2 cleavage planes meeting at right angles, hardness of 6
    B. 2 cleavage planes meeting at 56° and 124° angles, hardness of 5 to 6
    C. 3 cleavage planes not at right angles to each other, hardness of 3
    D. No cleavage planes, hardness of 7

12. Which one of the following is the formula for magnetite?   12.____

    A. Fe_2O_3 B. Fe_3O_4
    C. $Fe_2O_3 \cdot H_2O$ D. $Fe_2O_3 \cdot 3H_2O$

13. Which one of the following minerals is used as an electrical insulator?   13.____

    A. Muscovite   B. Chlorite
    C. Plagioclase   D. Albite

14. In which one of the following forms are the atoms in a diamond arranged?   14.____

    A. Rings of six   B. A cube
    C. A rhomboid   D. A tetrahedron

15. Which one of the following pairs characterizes halite?   15.____

    A. Colorless, hardness of 2.5
    B. Purple color, hardness of 4
    C. Lead gray, hardness of 2.5
    D. Brassy yellow color, hardness of 6

16. Few surface streams are found in Yucatan because the underlying rock is   16.____

    A. sandstone   B. limestone
    C. conglomerate   D. shale

17. Deep, black color in limestone cave deposits indicates the presence of   17.____

    A. ferric oxide   B. manganese dioxide
    C. carbon   D. graphite

18. Which one of the following minerals exhibits the nearly perfect cleavage?   18.____

    A. Mica   B. Gypsum   C. Calcite   D. Feldspar

19. To which one of the following crystal systems does garnet belong?   19.____

    A. Tetragonal   B. Isometric
    C. Triclinic   D. Hexagonal

20. The coalescence of several high mountain glaciers results in the formation of a(n) 20.____

    A. cirque   B. esker
    C. piedmont glacier   D. plateau glacier

21. Werner's Theory stated that 21.____

    A. basalt originated by volcanic action
    B. all rocks of the earth were precipitated from a universal ocean
    C. dense, fine-grained basalt was associated with scoria
    D. fused basalt produces a glassy rock

22. If the hanging wall in a fault has been forced upward relative to the foot wall, the resulting formation is described as which one of the following faults? 22.____

    A. normal   B. reverse   C. horizontal   D. tensional

23. When an upthrown block of the earth's crust is bounded on two sides by faults, it is called a(n) 23.____

    A. graben   B. overthrust block
    C. lateral thrust block   D. horst

24. Which one of the following terms is NOT associated with the concept of weathering? 24.____

    A. Frost heaving   B. Growing roots of trees
    C. Burrowing rodents   D. Mass wasting

25. The dry adiabatic lapse rate is CLOSEST to which one of the following? 25.____

    A. $1.5°$ F per 1000 feet   B. $5.5°$ F per 1000 feet
    C. $6.5°$ F per 500 feet   D. $9.5°$ F per 500 feet

26. Felsenmeer result primarily from 26.____

    A. frost action   B. wind erosion
    C. faulting   D. carbonation

27. The chemical weathering of orthoclase may result in the formation of which one of the following groups? 27.____

    A. Clay, carbon dioxide, potassium sulfate
    B. Clay, silica, potassium carbonate
    C. Bauxite, limonite and carbon dioxide
    D. Calcium bicarbonate, silica, potassium carbonate

28. Which one of the following conditions will favor the growth of coral? 28.____

    A. Salt water, 240 ft. deep at $58°$
    B. Salt water, 120 ft. deep at $68°$ F
    C. Salt water, 120 ft. deep at $58°$ F
    D. Fresh water, 120 ft. deep at $68°$ F

29. Which one of the following combinations will produce the highest tides?

    A. Moon at apogee, sun at perihelion, low barometric pressure, wind with the tide
    B. Moon at perigee, sun at perihelion, high barometric pressure, wind with the tide
    C. Moon at perigee, sun at perihelion, high barometric pressure, wind against the tide
    D. Moon at perigee, sun at perihelion, low barometric pressure, wind with the tide

30. Tsunamis are *MOST CLOSELY* associated with

    A. meteorological disturbance
    B. seismological disturbance
    C. solar gravitational attraction
    D. lunar gravitational attraction

31. Of which one of the following shorelines is the Chesapeake Bay region an example?

    A. Neutral   B. Ria   C. Fiord   D. Delta

32. If it is high tide at 3:00 p.m., the next high tide will occur at a time *CLOSEST* to which one of the following?

    A. 3:52 p.m.   B. 9:13 p.m.
    C. 3:26 a.m.   D. 9:13 a.m.

33. According to the theory of isostasy, the bedrock of the oceanic basins consists essentially of

    A. sandstone   B. basalt   C. granite   D. limestone

34. Which one of the following currents occurs when large waves cause water to pile up on the shore area?

    A. Tidal   B. Rip   C. Longshore   D. Surf

35. Which one of the following statements is *NOT* a true description of ocean wave phenomena?

    A. Water particles in waves move along at the same velocity as the wave.
    B. Waves originate by the frictional action of wind on water.
    C. Energy is imparted to waves by winds.
    D. Wave height is the vertical distance between crest and trough.

36. Uparchings many miles wide and hundreds of miles long are known as

    A. anticlines   B. domes
    C. laccoliths   D. geanticlines

37. Tuff originates from action of

    A. rivers   B. volcanoes   C. glaciers   D. geysers

38. Which one of the following stages of concentration of carbon is *NOT* represented in the production of hard-coal?

    A. Lignite   B. Bituminous   C. Peat   D. Graphite

39. With which one of the following groups may the Adirondacks be classified?

    A. Laurentian Upland, Younger Appalachian, Southern Rockies
    B. Laurentian Upland, New England, Southern Rockies
    C. New England, Older Appalachians, Younger Appalachians
    D. New England, Younger Appalachians, Southern Appalachians

40. In which one of the following states is the largest single block of faulted mountain area located?

    A. Utah B. California C. Oregon D. Nevada

41. Which one of the following metamorphic rocks has concretionary lumps through it?

    A. Schist
    B. Banded gneiss
    C. Augen gneiss
    D. Foliated gneiss

42. In the principle of superposition it was recognized that

    A. the bed of sedimentary rock at the lowest level must be the oldest
    B. the bed of sedimentary rock at the lowest level must be the youngest
    C. the beds of sedimentary rocks do not follow an orderly succession toward the top
    D. the correlation of sedimentary rocks can be well utilized

43. Which one of the following minerals is LEAST likely to be found in a light colored, course-grained granite?

    A. Orthoclase
    B. Olivine
    C. Plagioclase
    D. Quartz

44. Which one of the following groups does NOT consist of plateaus having a common origin?

    A. Allegheny, Catskill, Colorado
    B. Cumberland, Allegheny, Catskill
    C. Cumberland, Colorado, Columbia
    D. Cumberland, Colorado, Allegheny

45. Classic examples of breached anticlines and synclines may be found in which one of the following physiographic areas?

    A. Cascade Mountains
    B. Adirondack Mountains
    C. Younger Appalachian Mountains
    D. Older Appalachian Mountains

46. Assume that an airplane takes off from New York City (longitude 75° W.) at 10 a.m. Eastern Standard Time and heads toward London (longitude 0°). If the flying time is 5 hours, the London standard time at which the plane will reach its destination is

    A. 2 a.m. the next day
    B. 3 p.m. the same day
    C. 8 p.m. the same day
    D. 10 p.m. the same day

47. In successful drilling for oil from the surface downward in anticlinical structures, one would probably encounter the indicated three substances in which one of the following orders?

    A. Oil, water, gas
    B. Water, gas, oil
    C. Gas, water, oil
    D. Gas, oil, water

48. With which one of the following is a peneplane very closely associated?

    A. Dried up lake bottom
    B. Outwash planes
    C. Monadnocks
    D. Young Mountains

49. Which one of the following types of springs will result when the surface of the land intersects the water table?

    A. Artesian
    B. Contact
    C. Tubular
    D. Oases and tubular

50. Which one of the following physiographic features is MOST characteristic of the north shore of Long Island?

    A. Karst topography
    B. Outwash plains
    C. Terminal moraine
    D. Barrier beaches

KEY (CORRECT ANSWERS)

1. B	11. A	21. B	31. B	41. C
2. C	12. B	22. B	32. C	42. A
3. C	13. A	23. D	33. B	43. B
4. D	14. D	24. D	34. B	44. C
5. B	15. A	25. B	35. A	45. C
6. A	16. B	26. A	36. D	46. C
7. C	17. B	27. B	37. B	47. D
8. D	18. A	28. B	38. D	48. C
9. B	19. B	29. D	39. B	49. B
10. B	20. C	30. B	40. B	50. C

TEST 4

DIRECTIONS: Each question or incomplete statement is followed by several suggested answers or completions. Select the one that BEST answers the question or completes the statement. PRINT THE LETTER OF THE CORRECT ANSWER IN THE SPACE AT THE RIGHT.

1. When surface air at a temperature of 80° F rises 2000 feet without reaching its dew point, its temperature becomes

   A. 65° F   B. 69° F   C. 73° F   D. 74.5° F

   1._____

2. The upper portion of a body of water warms up more slowly than an adjacent sandy beach for all of the following reasons EXCEPT:

   A. The water surface reflects more sunlight than the sand.
   B. Water is a poorer absorber of insolation than sand.
   C. Sunlight penetrates to greater depths in water than into sand.
   D. The specific heat of water is less than that of sand.

   2._____

3. A west coast region over which the horse latitudes and the prevailing westerlies alternate would have

   A. dry summers and dry winters
   B. dry summers and rainy winters
   C. wet summers and dry winters
   D. wet summers and rainy winters

   3._____

4. Which one of the following minerals gives a red flame test?

   A. Rhodonite   B. Rhodochrosite
   C. Celestite   D. Zincite

   4._____

5. Which one of the following pairs of elements is found in the mineral gypsum?

   A. Magnesium and sodium   B. Calcium and sulphur
   C. Calcium and sodium   D. Magnesium and sulphur

   5._____

6. Which one of the following minerals can scratch glass?

   A. Galena   B. Fluorite   C. Dolomite   D. Pyrite

   6._____

7. Which one of the following minerals has the HIGHEST specific gravity?

   A. Garnet   B. Hornblende
   C. Barite   D. Albite

   7._____

8. Of the following, an example of a mineral with perfect octahedral cleavage is

   A. sphalerite   B. diamond
   C. magnetite   D. corundum

   8._____

9. Of the following, the MOST IMPORTANT ore of zinc is

   A. hematite   B. cinnabar
   C. zincite   D. sphalerite

   9._____

10. Sapphire is a gem variety of the mineral,

    A. beryl   B. kyanite   C. corundum   D. sodalite

11. A feature of sedimentary rocks which can be used to distinguish the top from the bottom of beds is a(n)

    A. chalk deposit
    B. even lamination
    C. oscillation ripple mark
    D. torrential cross bedding

12. The most definite evidence of a continental (subaerial) deposit is the formation of

    A. torrential cross-bedding
    B. ripple marks
    C. arkose sandstone
    D. graded bedding

13. A young river is characterized by

    A. natural levees
    B. flood plains
    C. slight meandering
    D. rapids

14. Which one of the following depressions is most commonly found in a region underlaid with limestone?

    A. Deflation hollows
    B. Sink holes
    C. Plunge basins
    D. Craters

15. When estuaries are restricted to one section of a coast line, it means that there was a

    A. rise of the coast line
    B. lowering of sea level
    C. subsidence of the coast line
    D. rise of sea level

16. Bronx, New York, lies in the physiographic province known as the

    A. New England Upland
    B. Coastal Plain
    C. Triassic Lowland
    D. Piedmont

17. Which one of the following is properly classified as an erosional process?

    A. Exfoliation on a cliff
    B. Fire spalling
    C. Sand blast action in a desert
    D. Wedgework of ice

18. Annular drainage is characteristic of areas in which the dominant rock structure is

    A. domed   B. faulted   C. folded   D. isoclinal

19. Barchanes are wind deposits that have

    A. crescent shapes with steep leeward slopes
    B. crescent shapes with steep windward slopes
    C. crescent shapes with the cusps pointing into the wind
    D. circular shapes with even slopes

20. Which one of the following is NOT an epeiric sea?
    A. Salton Sea
    B. Hudson Bay
    C. White Sea
    D. Baltic Sea

21. The topography of northern Long Island is characterized by MANY
    A. drumlins
    B. eskers
    C. knobs and kettles
    D. outwash plains

22. In which one of the following national parks is Half Dome, an example of exfoliation, located?
    A. Bryce
    B. Yellowstone
    C. Yosemite
    D. Zion

23. The type of stream which will form on a newly-uplifted coastal plain is
    A. consequent
    B. subsequent
    C. obsequent
    D. antecedent

24. Which one of the following is dominant when a stream is in the stage of maturity?
    A. Downward erosion
    B. Headward erosion
    C. Lateral erosion
    D. Hydraulic erosion

25. The Colorado River at the Grand Canyon is an example of a
    A. young river
    B. mature river
    C. late mature river
    D. old river

26. It has been concluded that the speed of the "L" (Long) waves of seismic disturbances probably indicates that
    B. continents consist of granite and the ocean basins of basalt
    C. continents consist of basalt and the ocean basins of granite
    D. continents and ocean basins consist of granite
    E. continents and ocean basins consist of granite and basalt

27. As one approaches the pole, the number of miles representing one degree of longitude
    A. increases
    C. decreases
    B. remains the same
    D. varies irregularly

28. Which one of the following did NOT result from metamorphism?
    A. Foliation
    C. Slaty cleavage
    B. Schistosity
    D. Stratification

29. Which one of the following types of metamorphism results from the weight of overlying rock layers?
    A. Contact
    C. Dynamic
    B. Kinetic
    D. Load

30. Which one of the following map scales corresponds to a scale of 1 inch to the mile?
    A. 1/5280
    B. 1/31680
    C. 1/63,360
    D. 1/126,720

31. Which one of the following conditions is a deterrent to the growth of coral polyps?

    A. Depth of 50 feet
    B. Temperature of 75° F
    C. Salt water currents
    D. Muddy water

32. On the average, the continental shelf terminates at a depth CLOSEST to which one of the following?

    A. 100 feet
    B. 500 feet
    C. 1,000 feet
    D. 2,000 feet

33. Wind gaps are the result of the work of

    A. glaciers
    B. wind
    C. streams
    D. ocean waves

34. A sea cave at an altitude of 100 feet above sea level indicates a(n)

    A. great tidal range
    B. land submergence
    C. recent severe storms along the coast
    D. uplift of the land

35. The shortest distance on the earth's surface between New York and London is measured along

    A. a great circle
    B. an isogonic line
    C. a parallel
    D. a rhumb line

36. Oscillatory waves at sea upon breaking become

    A. undertow
    B. tsunamis
    C. tidal waves
    D. waves of translation

37. An important east-west fault on Manhattan Island is located along which one of the following?

    A. 86th Street
    B. 125th Street
    C. 155th Street
    D. Third Avenue

38. The YOUNGEST of the following mountain ranges is the

    A. Adirondacks of New York
    B. Blue Ridge Mountains of Virginia
    C. Green Mountains of Vermont
    D. Sierra Nevada Mountains of California

39. The maximum number of degrees of latitude possible for any place on earth is

    A. 90   B. 180   C. 270   D. 360

40. The materials of glacial moraines are best described by which one of the following?

    A. Unassorted, unstratified, rounded
    B. Unassorted, stratified, striated
    C. Unassorted, unstratified, striated
    D. Assorted, stratified, angular

41. Of the following areas the one NOT famous for its combination of hot springs and geysers is

    A. North Island of New Zealand
    B. Iceland
    C. Yellowstone
    D. Yosemite

42. The percentage by weight of the earth's atmosphere that lies below an altitude of 18,000 feet is CLOSEST to which one of the following?

    A. 25%   B. 50%   C. 75%   D. 90%

43. Of the following months, the one in which hurricanes are most likely to strike northeastern United States is

    A. March   B. May   C. August   D. November

44. The gas produced by the reaction of yeast on glucose is also produced by the reaction between

    A. washing soda and limewater
    B. baking soda and water
    C. caustic soda and muriatic acid
    D. baking soda and sour milk

45. Of the following types of clouds, the one MOST LIKELY to cause a solar halo is

    A. cumulonimbus   B. cumulus
    C. cirrostratus   D. stratocumulus

46. The direction of the Northern Hemisphere middle latitude jet stream is principally

    A. eastward   B. northward   C. southward   D. westward

47. If ten milliliters of hydrogen and ten milliliters of chlorine are placed in a eudiometer and exploded, the volume of gas that remains after the reaction is completed is

    A. 2.5 ml.   B. 5 ml.   C. 10 ml.   D. 20 ml.

48. Of the following National Parks, which one is located wholly within the area of an exposed batholith?

    A. Yellowstone   B. Grand Canyon
    C. Yosemite   D. Mt. Rainier

49. Residual soil is derived from the weathering of

    A. flood plain deposits
    B. the underlying bedrock
    C. glacial drift
    D. sand dunes

50. Of the following, the one which is a limestone principally composed of microscopic shells and shell fragments cemented together is

    A. chalk
    B. travertine
    C. coquina
    D. diatomaceous earth

KEY (CORRECT ANSWERS)

1. B	11. C	21. C	31. D	41. D
2. D	12. A	22. C	32. B	42. B
3. B	13. D	23. A	33. C	43. C
4. C	14. B	24. C	34. D	44. D
5. B	15. C	25. A	35. A	45. C
6. D	16. A	26. A	36. D	46. A
7. C	17. C	27. B	37. B	47. D
8. B	18. A	28. D	38. D	48. C
9. D	19. A	29. D	39. A	49. B
10. C	20. A	30. C	40. C	50. A

EXAMINATION SECTION
TEST 1

DIRECTIONS: Each question or incomplete statement is followed by several suggested answers or completions. Select the one that BEST answers the question or completes the statement. PRINT THE LETTER OF THE CORRECT ANSWER IN THE SPACE AT THE RIGHT.

1. Rock fragments at the base of a steep slope form 1.____
    A. talus B. moraines C. kames D. geodes

2. The most important activity of a mature river is 2.____
    A. downcutting B. headward erosion
    C. deposition D. widening its valley

3. Among the following, the one which is a common mineral that replaces organic substances in fossil formation is 3.____
    A. $CaSO_4$ B. Na_2CO_3 C. SiO_2 D. SiO_3

4. The most common mineral in the earth's crust is 4.____
    A. mica B. feldspar C. hornblende D. calcite

5. Niagara Falls has a limestone cap underlaid by 5.____
    A. shale B. granite C. basalt D. schist

6. The theory that mountains and plains maintain a state of balance by slow vertical adjustment is known as 6.____
    A. isostasy B. isomerism
    C. isomorphism D. isotopism

7. The Devil's Tower in Wyoming is an example of a(n) 7.____
    A. erratic B. stock
    C. monadnock D. volcanic neck

8. Of the following, a volcano that BEST illustrates a composite cone is 8.____
    A. Mauna Loa B. Paricutin
    C. Vesuvius D. Kilauea

9. The feature below that is most useful in indicating the direction of movement of a continental glacier is the 9.____
    A. arete B. cirque C. kettle hole D. drumlin

10. Sinkhole lakes would be found most readily in which one of the following states? 10.____
    A. New York B. Florida
    C. Minnesota D. Massachusetts

27

11. The Sierra Nevada mountains were produced primarily by   11.____

    A. folding   B. igneous intrusion
    C. volcanic eruptions   D. faulting

12. Of the following agents of erosion, the one that produces limestone caves is   12.____

    A. ocean waves   B. wind
    C. ground water   D. surface streams

13. The most recent covering of New England by continental glaciers ended at a time closest   13.____
    to which one of the following?

    A. 10,000 B.C.   B. 100,000 B.C.
    C. 200,000 B.C.   D. 400,000 B.C.

14. The earliest deposits of graphite left by simple forms of life resulted from such life in   14.____
    which one of the following eras?

    A. Cenozoic   B. Archeozoic
    C. Mesozoic   D. Paleozoic

15. The study of radioactive minerals shows the earth to have a minimum age, in years, clos-   15.____
    est to which one of the following?

    A. 50,000   B. 500,000
    C. 5,000,000   D. 5,000,000,000

16. The texture of an igneous rock is determined primarily by   16.____

    A. chemical composition   B. rate of cooling
    C. age   D. density

17. Shale may metamorphose into   17.____

    A. quartzite   B. marble
    C. anthracite coal   D. slate

18. Of the following, the mineral most resistant to both chemical and mechanical weathering   18.____
    is

    A. calcite   B. mica   C. quartz   D. feldspar

19. Which one of the following is NOT a star classification?   19.____

    A. White dwarfs   B. Red giants
    C. Green giants   D. Red variables

20. Which one of the following is the minimum average monthly temperature required for a   20.____
    zone to be considered tropical?

    A. 54° F   B. 64° F   C. 74° F   D. 84° F

21. Which one of the following is the name given to lines on a weather map connecting   21.____
    points of equal barometric pressure?

    A. Isobars   B. Isomers C. Isotopes   D. Isotherms

22. Which arrangement below is typical of a lunar eclipse?　　22._____

    A. Moon between earth and sun
    B. Earth between moon and sun
    C. Sun between moon and earth
    D. Dense clouds between earth and moon

23. Of the following, which statement about auroras is *LEAST* accurate?　　23._____

    A. They occur near the poles only.
    B. They are caused by ionization of oxygen and nitrogen in the upper air.
    C. They are at their brightest during maximum sunspot activity.
    D. They are at their brightest during full moon.

24. Of the following, which one is closest to the distance, in miles, from the earth to the moon?　　24._____

    A. 2.5×10^3　　　　　　　　B. 2.5×10^4
    C. 2.5×10^5　　　　　　　　D. 2.5×10^6

25. When flying along which one of the following is a plane on a great circle route?　　25._____

    A. The Tropic of Capricorn　　　B. Any rhumb line
    C. A meridian　　　　　　　　　　D. The Arctic Circle

26. Of the following, which lunar feature is *NOT* truly described by its name?　　26._____

    A. Mountain　　B. Sea　　C. Crater　　D. Valley

27. Boothbay Maine is characterized by its　　27._____

    A. barrier beaches　　　　　　　B. lagoons
    C. long narrow bays　　　　　　D. regular coastline

28. Streams tend to swerve to the right in the northern hemisphere in accordance with Ferrel's law. This deflecting force would be greatest at which one of the following latitudes?　　28._____

    A. the equator　　　　　　　　　B. 30 degrees N.
    C. 60 degrees N.　　　　　　　　D. 80 degrees N.

29. Of the following volcanoes, the one known in the 20th century for its most violently explosive type of eruption is　　29._____

    A. Mt. Lassen, Cal.　　　　　　　B. Mt. Pelee, Martinique
    C. Mt. Vesuvius, Italy　　　　　　D. Paricutin, Mexico

30. The star nearest to the sun is in the constellation,　　30._____

    A. Capricornus　　　　　　　　　B. Centaurus
    C. Sagittarius　　　　　　　　　　D. Ursa Major

31. When it is 3 P.M. standard time in New York City, the city, among the following, in which it is 8 P.M. standard time is　　31._____

    A. Honolulu, Hawaii　　　　　　B. London, England
    C. Nome, Alaska　　　　　　　　D. Moscow, Russia

32. At the summer solstice, the vertical rays of the sun at noon are on the 32.____
    A. equator B. parallel of 15 north
    C. Tropic of Cancer D. Tropic of Capricorn

33. The reason why the period of the Earth's rotation has been increasing is that 33.____
    A. the moon's orbit has been increasing
    B. frictional heat is produced in the atmosphere
    C. tides produce a drag
    D. the Earth has been cooling down

34. Of the following, the cloud formation that consists entirely of ice crystals is 34.____
    A. cumulus B. nimbus C. stratus D. cirrus

35. When a glaciated valley is undercut below sea level, it is called a 35.____
    A. tidal race B. tidal bore
    C. fjord D. cirque

36. A pale gray, non-crystalline rock, which contains many small shells of marine animals, and which dissolves slowly in carbonic acid is probably 36.____
    A. shale B. sandstone C. limestone D. granite

37. Dendritic drainage is characteristic of which one of the following? 37.____
    A. Coastal plains in the mature stage
    B. Plains of essentially homogeneous rocks
    C. Domed areas
    D. Volcanoes

38. Extensive mud stone and silt stone deposits indicate that deposition probably occured in which one of the following areas? 38.____
    A. In low-lying land source areas
    B. In blow holes
    C. Along steep coastal areas
    D. In front of mountain ranges

39. A river meander migrates as a result of which one of the following? 39.____
    A. Retreat of cut-bank and advance of slip-off slope
    B. Retreat of cut-bank
    C. Advance of slip-off slope
    D. Retreat of cut-bank, advance of slip-off slope and downstream erosion

40. A mature river will become intrenched when the area in which it is located is which one of the following? 40.____
    A. Flooded B. Peneplaned
    C. Elevated D. Lowered

41. Fall Line cities are located where rivers flow from the rocks of 41.____
    A. newer Appalachians to those of the older Appalachians
    B. older Appalachians to those of the coastal plain
    C. coastal plain into the Atlantic Ocean
    D. Appalachian plateau to the rocks of the newer Appalachian

42. Most Cenozoic mammal fossils were preserved by 42.____
    A. burial after drowning or suffocation
    B. mummification
    C. volcanic ash
    D. trapping in caves

43. The skull of Pithecanthropus erectus differs from that of an ape in that the former presents which one of the following features? 43.____
    A. Lack of a median crest
    B. No prominent bony ridges over the eye orbits
    C. A slightly smaller brain cavity than a full-grown gorilla
    D. No brain convolutions

44. Baltic amber contains large numbers of which one of the following fossilized remains? 44.____
    A. Worms   B. Insects
    C. Cephalopods   D. Crinoids

45. Of the following, the one in which the greatest variety of species is found is 45.____
    A. cretaceous chalk   B. Cenozoic angiosperms
    C. Eocene algae   D. Cenozoic protozoa

46. Of the following, the primate which LEAST resembles man in structure is the 46.____
    A. chimpanzee   B. lemur   C. gorilla   D. gibbon

47. The triangulation point on a topographic map shows 47.____
    A. latitude and longitude   B. true elevation
    C. magnetic declination   D. true north

48. Of the following, a heavy black line on a geologic map, with the letters U and D appearing on opposite sides of the line, is the symbol for a(n) 48.____
    A. unconformity   B. plunging anticline
    C. overtuned fold   D. fault

49. On a geologic map, the symbol T 30 indicates 49.____
    A. strike N-S; dip 30° E.
    B. dip E-W; strike 30° N.
    C. strike E-W; dip 30° S.
    D. strike E-W; dip 30° N.

50. If the direction of a sight line from a fire tower to a column of smoke indicating the start of a forest fire has a magnetic compass bearing N 25° W, and if the magnetic declination of the locality is 12° E, the true direction which must be plotted on the map, in order to locate the trouble spot, is which one of the following?

50.____

A. N 13° E
C. N 37° W
B. N 13° W
D. N 37° E

KEY (CORRECT ANSWERS)

1. A	11. D	21. A	31. B	41. B
2. D	12. C	22. B	32. C	42. A
3. C	13. A	23. D	33. C	43. A
4. B	14. B	24. C	34. D	44. B
5. A	15. D	25. C	35. C	45. D
6. A	16. B	26. B	36. C	46. B
7. D	17. D	27. C	37. B	47. B
8. C	18. C	28. D	38. A	48. D
9. D	19. C	29. B	39. D	49. C
10. B	20. B	30. B	40. C	50. B

TEST 2

DIRECTIONS: Each question or incomplete statement is followed by several suggested answers or completions. Select the one that BEST answers the question or completes the statement. PRINT THE LETTER OF THE CORRECT ANSWER IN THE SPACE AT THE RIGHT.

1. The moon revolves about the earth at a speed (in miles per hour) closest to   1.____

    A. 2000 B. 7000 C. 18,000 D. 25,000

2. Through approximately how many degrees of latitude do the vertical rays of the sun move from January 1 of one year to January 1 of the next year?   2.____

    A. 23 1/2 B. 47 C. 94 D. 180

3. Which one of the following represents the highest rate of revolution, in miles per hour?   3.____

    A. The earth at perihelion
    B. The earth at aphelion
    C. The moon at perigee
    D. The moon at apogee

4. Which one of the following depositional features is characterized by a high degree of sorting of its component particles?   4.____

    A. Alluvial fan   B. Delta
    C. Ground moraine   D. Talus slope

5. A column of air that has a lapse rate of 7.5° F per 1000 feet is   5.____

    A. absolutely stable   B. conditionally unstable
    C. stable   D. unstable

6. The name given to the process whereby rocks are altered due to the exchange of ions is   6.____

    A. microscism   B. lithification
    C. metasomatism   D. metamorphism

7. The symbol mTk appears on a weather map over the southeastern United States in summer. The characteristic MOST LIKELY to be associated with it is   7.____

    A. poor visibility   B. stratiform clouds
    C. thunderstorms   D. low humidity

8. What is the approximate altitude of a plane in which a barometer reads 843 millibars when a sea level barometer reads 1013 mb.?   8.____

    A. 1000' B. 2000' C. 3000' D. 5000'

9. Aberration of starlight is regarded as evidence of the   9.____

    A. earth's revolution around the sun
    B. earth's rotation on its axis
    C. earth's spheroidal shape
    D. existence of the earth's magnetic field

10. The cyclic nature of the processes by which our planet is eroded and carved, only to be reelevated and the cycle to begin again, was first clearly presented by

    A. Aristotle
    B. Louis Agassiz
    C. James Hutton
    D. A.K. Lobeck

11. Chemical weathering is likely to be the dominant weathering process in regions having a climate that is

    A. moist, cold
    B. dry, warm
    C. moist, warm
    D. dry, cold

12. The stage of dissection of a region is determined on the basis of

    A. type of drainage pattern present
    B. kinds of rocks underlying the region
    C. amount of material removed by erosion in relation to volume present before dissection
    D. type of erosional agent responsible for the dissection

13. Where stream capture has occurred, the feature which may develop in the pirated stream course is a(n)

    A. increased volume
    B. increased velocity
    C. barbed tributaries
    D. wind gap

14. Of the following, the main feature formed by a river after it has attained its profile of equilibrium is a

    A. canyon
    B. waterfall
    C. deep channel
    D. flood plain

15. Of the following, the one that does NOT produce deposition of minerals by ground water is

    A. evaporation
    B. reduction of temperature
    C. addition of dissolved minerals
    D. increase in temperature

16. An entrenched meander occurs as a consequence of

    A. headward erosion
    B. differential weathering
    C. vertical uplift
    D. shifting of the stream bed

17. Which one of the following processes is responsible for MOST of the geologic work accomplished by ground water?

    A. Abrasion
    B. Solution
    C. Hydraulic action
    D. Oxidation

18. The artesian wells of southern Long Island are fed by water that enters the ground PRINCIPALLY in

    A. the locality of the wells
    B. northern Long Island
    C. southern Connecticut
    D. the Catskills

19. In order to yield a maximum amount of water in the minimum time, a well should be drilled in rocks which are

    A. porous and permeable
    B. porous and impermeable
    C. non-porous and permeable
    D. non-porous and impermeable

20. The coast of southern Long Island is classified as a

    A. shoreline of emergence
    B. submerged coast
    C. neutral shoreline
    D. compound shoreline

21. Sandbars are MOST LIKELY to appear in the bed of a river

    A. on the outside curve of a meander
    B. where the slope increases rapidly
    C. at a place where the river widens
    D. regions rejuvenated by uplift

22. The Niagara River Gorge is approximately 300 ft. deep, despite the fact that the falls are only about 160 ft. above the water. This seeming discrepancy is due to

    A. diastrophic action along the river course
    B. sinking of the limestone bed
    C. formation of a plungepool at the base of the falls
    D. formation of potholes from the rapids

23. Of the following, the one region with the MOST extensive plains in the world is

    A. central India
    B. Australia
    C. northern Siberia
    D. the Amazon basin

24. Of the following, the feature that CANNOT be used as evidence for faulting is

    A. slickensides
    B. displacement of beds
    C. cross-bedding
    D. dragging of beds

25. The Sierra Nevada is a mountain chain formed PRINCIPALLY by

    A. folding
    B. volcanic eruptions
    C. block faulting
    D. erosion of horizontal strata

26. Plateaus can ALWAYS be distinguished from mountains on the basis of

    A. elevation
    B. depth of valleys
    C. rock structure
    D. faulting

27. The theory of earth movements advanced by Wegener is known as the

    A. Contraction Theory
    B. Continental Drift Theory
    C. Convection Hypothesis
    D. Theory of Gravitational Sliding

27.____

28. Which one of the following topographic quadrangles would be BEST for showing water gaps?

    A. Bright Angel, Arizona
    B. Donaldsonville, Louisiana
    C. Harrisburg, Pennsylvania
    D. Niagara Gorge, New York

28.____

29. Thrust faults are the result of

    A. isostatic movements
    B. tensional forces
    C. compressional forces
    D. movements of the sea level

29.____

30. The general rule that younger rocks lie on top of older rocks is known as the law of

    A. horizontality   B. superposition
    C. consequence   D. competence

30.____

31. The slopes of surfaces of aggradation are usually steepest on

    A. flood plains   B. river bars
    C. alluvial fans   D. talus cones

31.____

32. The Catskills of New York State are classified structurally as

    A. an extension of the New England peneplane
    B. domed mountains
    C. a mature dissected plateau
    D. part of the Appalachian ridge and valley region

32.____

33. Pittsburgh, Pa., lies in the physiographic province known as the

    A. Triassic Lowland   B. Folded Appalachians
    C. Appalachian Plateau   D. Atlantic Coastal Plain

33.____

34. The rocks in the vicinity of New York, New Jersey and Connecticut which contain the remains of dinosaurs are in the

    A. Atlantic Coastal Plain   B. Jurassic Lowlands
    C. Triassic Lowlands   D. Cretaceous Lowlands

34.____

35. An unconformity is the line of contact between

    A. displaced horizontal layers
    B. rocks on both sides of a thrust fault
    C. rocks of different ages of the earth's history
    D. unconsolidated material and sedimentary rock

35.____

36. Of the following national parks, which one exhibits the *BEST* exposed evidences of past valley glaciation?   36._____

    A. Yellowstone
    B. Mt. Ranier
    C. Yosemite
    D. Crater Lake

37. The topography of the present Columbia River region in the State of Washington was formed by the dissection of a   37._____

    A. huge granite batholith
    B. thick sequence of tilted limestones
    C. wide belt of folded, metamorphic rocks
    D. series of fissure flows of basalt

38. Deep canyons are characteristic of   38._____

    A. young plateaus
    B. maturely dissected plateaus
    C. old plateaus
    D. peneplanes

39. Slaty cleavage is developed in an attitude which is most nearly   39._____

    A. parallel to the bedding
    B. vertical
    C. horizontal
    D. parallel to the axial planes of the folds

40. Since about 1860, glaciers in general around the world appear to be   40._____

    A. maintaining their size
    B. maintaining their size and position
    C. shrinking and receding
    D. advancing but maintaining their size

41. An example of a former glacial lake of large size which left a broad lake plain is   41._____

    A. Lake Bonneville
    B. Lake Agassiz
    C. Lake Pontchartrain
    D. Great Salt Lake

42. Of the following, the *BEST* evidence for the epeirogenic uplift of the Grand Canyon region of the Colorado River, which elevated its rims to a position 7500 feet above sea level, is the   42._____

    A. depth of the present Canyon, exceeding 5000 feet
    B. intense folding of the Paleozoic rocks exposed in the Canyon walls
    C. presence of marine fossils in the unfolded rim rocks (Kaibab limestone)
    D. intense metamorphism of the Pre-Cambrian rocks exposed in the walls of the Inner Gorge

43. Hanging valleys may occur where a   43._____

    A. mountain region has undergone glaciation
    B. plateau has been maturely dissected
    C. shoreline has been recently submerged
    D. stream has been rejuvenated

44. Of the following glacial deposits, the one that will show some degree of stratification is the

    A. terminal moraine
    B. esker
    C. drumlin
    D. ground moraine

45. The projection used for U.S. Geological Survey topographic maps is the

    A. Mercator
    B. Polyconic
    C. Orthographic
    D. Azimuthal Equidistant

46. Slope (in feet per mile) can be determined from a topographic map by using the

    A. contour interval and scale of miles
    B. elevation and contour interval
    C. direction and scale of miles
    D. distance between two adjacent contour lines

47. Of the following statements, the one that is NOT true of clay minerals is that a clay mineral

    A. has a characteristic space lattice
    B. is formed by weathering or alteration of a pre-existing mineral
    C. is stable under a wide range of pressures and temperatures
    D. crystallizes in distinct crystal forms

48. Petrology is a branch of geology concerned with the study of

    A. oil and gas
    B. landforms
    C. rocks
    D. fossils

49. A rock structure formed by fracturing of the rock in response to tensional forces is

    A. foliation
    B. columnar structure
    C. slaty cleavage
    D. flow structure

50. Rocks are said to be metamorphosed if they were

    A. recrystallized without melting
    B. compacted by the weight of overlying sediments
    C. cemented by crystallization in the pore spaces
    D. crystallized after melting

KEY (CORRECT ANSWERS)

1. A	11. C	21. C	31. D	41. B
2. C	12. C	22. C	32. C	42. C
3. A	13. D	23. C	33. C	43. A
4. B	14. D	24. C	34. C	44. B
5. D	15. D	25. C	35. C	45. B
6. C	16. C	26. C	36. C	46. A
7. C	17. B	27. B	37. D	47. C
8. D	18. B	28. C	38. A	48. C
9. A	19. A	29. C	39. D	49. B
10. C	20. C	30. B	40. C	50. A

TEST 3

DIRECTIONS: Each question or incomplete statement is followed by several suggested answers or completions. Select the one that BEST answers the question or completes the statement. PRINT THE LETTER OF THE CORRECT ANSWER IN THE SPACE AT THE RIGHT.

1. Coarse, crystalline textures are characteristic of igneous rocks which are

    A. formed by intrusion
    B. formed by extrusion
    C. light-colored and relatively light-weight
    D. dark-colored and relatively heavy

2. Of the following, the one mineral of hardness 3 that possesses three perfect directions of cleavage is

    A. gypsum B. fluorite C. calcite D. galena

3. Rhyolite is an extrusive igneous rock which has essentially the same mineral composition as

    A. gabbro B. syenite C. granite D. diorite

4. The contact between the Newark Series and the New York City Series of rocks is a(n)

    A. normal fault
    B. conformable sedimentary contact
    C. reverse fault
    D. unconformable sedimentary contact

5. "The present is a key to the past" is a concise statement summarizing the operation of the Law or Doctrine of

    A. Evolution   B. Uniformitarianism
    C. Neptunism   D. Catastrophism

6. "The Age of Mammals" refers to the

    A. Mesozoic   B. Cenozoic
    C. Cretaceous   D. Triassic

7. William Smith (1769-1839) made his greatest contributions to the budding science of geology in a field of study which would now be called

    A. paleontology   B. stratigraphy
    C. petrology   D. geophysics

8. The physiographic province that includes the MAJOR part of New York State is the

    A. Laurentian Uplands   B. Atlantic Coastal Plains
    C. New England Province   D. Appalachian Plateau

9. The temperature of the earth's core is, in degrees C., approximately,

    A. 1000 B. 2500 C. 25,000 D. 100,000

40

10. The main geologic activity of young rivers is   10.____

    A. deposition   B. side cutting
    C. down cutting   D. widening its flood plain

11. An alluvial fan may be produced by   11.____

    A. an increase in stream velocity
    B. stream piracy
    C. stream rejuvenation
    D. a reduction in stream velocity

12. When a stream cuts below the water table, it becomes   12.____

    A. graded   B. mature   C. permanent   D. subsequent

13. The number of times northern United States was covered by glacial ice sheets in the Pleistocene Epoch is   13.____

    A. 2   B. 3   C. 4   D. 6

14. The cause of the most recent glacial period in the earth's history is   14.____

    A. not yet established
    B. fluctuation in sunspot activity
    C. variation in inclination of the earth's axis
    D. change in elevation of large surface areas

15. The minimum number of glaciers necessary to form a matter-horn peak is   15.____

    A. 1   B. 2   C. 3   D. 4

16. Kettle holes are *MOST CLOSELY* associated with   16.____

    A. uplift of the land   B. limestone layers
    C. water falls   D. glaciation

17. Which one of the following quadrangles would be *BEST* for presenting a unit on terminal moraines?   17.____

    A. Boothbay, Maine   B. Moses Lake, Washington
    C. Whitewater, Wisconsin   D. Charleston, West Virginia

18. The average depth of the oceans is closest to   18.____

    A. 100 feet   B. 1 mile   C. 2 1/2 miles   D. 10 miles

19. Shorelines which were initially formed by uplift of the coast may be found in   19.____

    A. Florida   B. Bermuda   C. Hawaii   D. Maine

20. A type of sandbar connecting an island to the mainland is called a   20.____

    A. bay mouth bar   B. spit
    C. tombolo   D. headland beach

21. Karst regions are associated with bedrock composed of   21.____

    A. limestone   B. sandstone   C. shales   D. basalt

22. A flat-topped submarine volcanic cone is known as a

    A. guyot B. inselberg C. nappe D. tombolo

23. How many seconds long is the period of a wave that is 80 feet long traveling at 20 feet per second?

    A. 4 B. 20 C. 60 D. 80

24. Which one of the following would be the most difficult to direct students to find evidences of in New York City?

    A. Fossils B. Striae C. Potholes D. Meanders

25. The river valleys of New York City have as their bedrock

    A. sandstone B. limestone C. gneiss D. shale

26. The largest figure for the age of the solar system is obtained from the study of

    A. pre-cambrian rocks B. Canadian Shield
    C. meteorites D. Colorado Plateau

27. During which one of the following eras were the rocks of the Adirondack Mountains formed?

    A. Cenozoic B. Mesozoic
    C. Paleozoic D. Pre-Cambrian

28. In which one of the following types of rock is quartz NOT found?

    A. Basalt B. Sandstone
    C. Pegmatite D. Granite

29. A mineral that has a needle-like structure would be described as

    A. micaceous B. columnar
    C. acicular D. pisolitic

30. The products resulting from the chemical weathering of orthoclase are in which one of the following groups?

    A. Sodium carbonate and potassium hydroxide
    B. Sodium chloride and silica
    C. Potassium carbonate, silica, and clay
    D. potassium carbonate and sodium silicate

31. A mixture in which one atom takes the place of another without changing the form of crystal is termed

    A. isomorphous B. amorphous
    C. isentropic D. non-crystalline

32. "Ceiling" height is determined by all EXCEPT

    A. pibal B. ceiling balloon
    C. searchlight D. sonar

33. Which one of the following statements about the Van Allen belts is *NOT* true? 33.____

    A. They are belts of radiation.
    B. They form concentric spheres around the earth.
    C. They consist of electrically charged particles.
    D. They are 800 to 40,000 miles thick.

34. Which one of the following statements about the ionosphere is *NOT* true? 34.____

    A. It is known as the Heaviside layer after its discoverer.
    B. It consists of at least three distinct layers.
    C. It reflects all radio waves.
    D. It consists of ions produced by solar radiation.

35. Which one of the satellites below is *NOT* used for communications? 35.____

    A. Echo   B. Telstar   C. Syncom   D. Vanguard

36. The basis for the common road warning "Caution - Bridge freezes before road", is which one of the following? 36.____

    A. The freezing point of steel is below that of concrete.
    B. The bridge is cooled from both top and bottom.
    C. Steel is a better conductor of heat than concrete.
    D. Steel is smoother than concrete.

37. Of the following, which one is the *BEST* explanation for the dark appearance of a tornado? 37.____

    A. Refraction of light by the violent winds
    B. Debris sucked up into the vortex
    C. Water churned by violent winds
    D. Anomalous electrical effects

38. The average thickness of snow, in inches, which is equivalent to one inch of rain is 38.____

    A. 1   B. 5   C. 10   D. 15

39. Under which one of the following conditions will dew form most rapidly? When 39.____

    A. the air is dry and still
    B. a strong wind is blowing
    C. the air is warm and still
    D. still warm air is cooled rapidly

40. Which one of the following is *NOT* necessarily true of a cTw air mass? 40.____

    A. It is relatively uniform
    B. Its origin is continental
    C. Its origin is tropical
    D. It is warm

41. Which type of precipitation below is indicated on weather maps by three horizontal lines? 41.____

    A. Rain   B. Sleet   C. Snow   D. Fog

42. Which one of the following would NOT tend to make temperature changes in rising air adiabatic?

   A. Air is a poor conductor of heat
   B. Air is a poor absorber of heat
   C. Surface air mixes with adjacent air
   D. Expansion occurs as a result of reduced pressure

43. Which one of the following is NOT a temperature scale?

   A. Baumé   B. Celsius   C. Réamur   D. Rankine

44. To which one of the following latitudes are the vertical noontime rays of the sun closest on September 20?

   A. 0°   B. 10° N   C. 10° S   D. 23° S

45. The number of degrees of earth latitude over which the noontime vertical rays of the sun travel in a six-month period is closest to

   A. 23 1/2°   B. 47°   C. 66 1/2°   D. 90°

46. The percent of the area of India which is south of the Equator is

   A. 0%   B. 25%   C. 50%   D. 75%

47. At which one of the following meridians is Mountain Standard Time the standard time?

   A. 75° W   B. 90° W   C. 105° W   D. 120° W

48. Which one of the following changes is made when a westbound ship crosses the International Date Line at 12 noon on a Wednesday?

   A. Clocks are moved to 12 midnight on Wednesday
   B. Clocks are moved to 11 A. Wednesday
   C. Calendars are changed to Tuesday
   D. Calendars are changed to Thursday

49. Contour maps do NOT show

   A. latitude and longitude
   B. dip and strike
   C. distance between points on a map
   D. direction in which streams flow

50. Which representative fraction below is closest in equivalence to a scale of 1" per mile?

   A. 1:31,680   B. 1:62,500
   C. 1:63,360   D. 1:100000

KEY (CORRECT ANSWERS)

1. A	11. D	21. A	31. A	41. D
2. C	12. C	22. A	32. D	42. C
3. C	13. C	23. A	33. B	43. A
4. D	14. A	24. A	34. C	44. A
5. B	15. C	25. B	35. D	45. B
6. B	16. D	26. C	36. B	46. A
7. B	17. C	27. D	37. B	47. C
8. D	18. C	28. A	38. C	48. D
9. B	19. A	29. C	39. D	49. B
10. C	20. C	30. C	40. D	50. C

TEST 4

DIRECTIONS: Each question or incomplete statement is followed by several suggested answers or completions. Select the one that *BEST* answers the question or completes the statement. *PRINT THE LETTER OF THE CORRECT ANSWER IN THE SPACE AT THE RIGHT.*

1. As far as we now know, for which one of the reasons below is our moon different from other moons in our solar system?

    A. It is the largest
    B. It is the closest in size to its planet
    C. Its density is almost exactly that of its planet
    D. It is the only one with no atmosphere

2. Which instrument below is used to photograph stars by the light of a single spectral line?

    A. Coronagraph	B. Pyroheliometer
    C. Spectroheliograph	D. Sun camera

3. Which one of the constellations below is always visible on clear nights from New York City?

    A. Ursa Major	B. Ursa Minor
    C. Orion	D. Andromeda

4. Which one of the following is *NOT* a first magnitude star?

    A. Arcturus	B. Capella	C. Rigel	D. Polaris

5. How many times brighter is a first magnitude star than a third magnitude star?

    A. 2.5	B. 6.3	C. 16	D. 40

6. Which one of the major planets below has an average density less than that of water?

    A. Jupiter	B. Saturn	C. Uranus	D. Neptune

7. When the moon is in new crescent phase, in which phase will an astronaut on the moon see the earth?

    A. Full	B. New	C. Crescent	D. Gibbous

8. In which one of the following ways does the appearance of a star change when viewed with good quality telescopes of higher and higher power?

    A. Apparent size remains constant, brightness increases
    B. Apparent size increases, brightness increases
    C. Color fringes appear
    D. Twinkling decreases

9. Which feature below is *NOT* part of the solar surface?

    A. Granule	B. Corona
    C. Prominance	D. Bailey's Beads

10. Which one of the following is used to regulate the buoyancy in the Piccard bathyscaphe? 10.____

   A. Air
   B. Helium
   C. Polyurethane foam
   D. Gasoline

11. Which one of the following ocean currents flows generally southward? 11.____

   A. Bahama
   B. Gulf Stream
   C. Alaska
   D. California

12. Of the following, which condition will **prevent the growth of coral reefs**? 12.____

   A. Water temperature below 60° F
   B. Salinity less than 30 parts per thousand
   C. Water depth greater than 50 feet
   D. Lack of adequate sunlight

13. Which one of the following types of shoreline is the result of submergence? 13.____

   A. Fiord
   B. Coastal plain
   C. Outwash plain
   D. Volcanic island

14. An entrenched meander in the bed of a river indicates 14.____

   A. deepening by valley glaciers
   B. uplift of the region
   C. a limestone bedrock
   D. stream piracy

15. Stream capture may result in the formation of 15.____

   A. water gap
   B. wind gap
   C. hanging valley
   D. incised meander

16. Of the following, the river that marks a portion of the southern limit of glaciers in North America during the most recent Ice Age is the 16.____

   A. Missouri
   B. St. Lawrence
   C. Delaware
   D. Hackensack

17. Downfolds of sedimentary rock are called 17.____

   A. anticlines
   B. geodynes
   C. isoclines
   D. synclines

18. The Badlands of South Dakota have been produced *PRIMARILY* by 18.____

   A. stream erosion
   B. wind erosion
   C. glaciation
   D. vulcanism

19. Disturbed rock layers are usually associated with 19.____

   A. lacustrine plains
   B. coastal plains
   C. flood plains
   D. peneplanes

20. Which one of the following is a geologic feature *NOT* characteristic of a glaciated region? A(n) 20.____

   A. kame   B. esker   C. stack   D. drumlin

21. Dreikanters are produced by

    A. wave erosion
    B. wind erosion
    C. glaciers
    D. stream erosion

22. An outstanding feature of the Yosemite Valley in California is

    A. hanging valleys
    B. natural bridges
    C. volcanic necks
    D. crater lakes

23. Of the following, the one which is a deposit formed by wind is a(n)

    A. esker   B. barchan   C. spit   D. delta

24. Geodes are formed by

    A. volcanic action
    B. metamorphosis
    C. deposition of minerals
    D. meteorites

25. Of the following, the one which is a mineral with no natural cleavage planes is

    A. mica   B. calcite   C. feldspar   D. quartz

26. The texture of an igneous rock containing large crystals set in a background of small crystals of the same material is

    A. porphyritic
    B. granular
    C. glassy
    D. aphanitic

27. Fossils are LEAST likely to be found in

    A. sandstone   B. coquina   C. limestone   D. gneiss

28. Galena crystals have which one of the following structures?

    A. Monoclinic
    B. Cubic
    C. Hexagonal
    D. Orthorhombic

29. Granite always contains silica and which one of the following?

    A. Plagioclase feldspar
    B. Orthoclase feldspar
    C. Olivine
    D. Biotite mica

30. When feldspar decomposes it forms the mineral,

    A. quartz   B. talc   C. mica   D. kaolinite

31. Old mountains are characterized by

    A. steep slopes
    B. irregular skyline
    C. extensive earthquake activity
    D. monadnocks

32. A typical artesian formation would be characterized by a

    A. layer of clay between two layers of granite
    B. layer of quartzite between two layers of clay
    C. layer of sandstone between two layers of shale
    D. surface layer of sand resting on a layer of shale

33. Compared to granite, basalt is USUALLY

    A. lighter in color and less dense
    B. darker in color and less dense
    C. lighter in color and more dense
    D. darker in color and more dense

34. The minimum number of seismograph stations needed to locate the focus of an earthquake is

    A. one B. two C. three D. four

35. In which one of the following are seismic waves arranged in order of speed, from slowest to fastest?

    A. Long, primary and secondary
    B. Primary, secondary and long
    C. Long, secondary and primary
    D. Secondary, primary and long

36. Tectonic earthquakes are the result of

    A. crustal movements   B. volcanic activity
    C. tsunamis   D. landslides

37. As far as is now known, the greatest depth of the Earth's oceans, in feet, is closest to

    A. 10,000 B. 22,000 C. 35,000 D. 60,000

38. The geologic period for which the trilobite is an index fossil is the

    A. Cambrian   B. Jurassic
    C. Cretaceous   D. Triassic

39. The basin of Crater Lake, Oregon, is a

    A. sinkhole   B. glacial valley
    C. inland sea   D. caldera

40. Active volcanoes are usually found in areas that include

    A. dissected plateaus   B. peneplanes
    C. young mountains   D. lacustrine plains

41. The coal deposits in Pennsylvania were formed during which one of the following eras?

    A. Cenozoic   B. Pre-Cambrian
    C. Paleozoic   D. Mesozoic

42. Which one of the following is NOT a silicate mineral?

    A. Augite   B. Biotite
    C. Olivine   D. Sphalerite

43. The formula for siderite is

    A. $FeCO_3$ B. $Fe_2O_3 \cdot H_2O$ C. FeS_2 D. Fe_3O_4

44. Of the following chemicals, the one that can be used to simulate the appearance of an erupting volcano is

    A. potassium chlorate
    B. potassium nitrate
    C. ammonium chloride
    D. ammonium dichromate

45. The oldest bedrock of New York City is

    A. dolomite
    B. limestone
    C. Manhattan schist
    D. Fordham gneiss

46. Carbonado is a gray to black opaque variety of

    A. graphite
    B. lignite
    C. bone fossil
    D. diamond

47. Hydrated calcium sulfate is known as

    A. iceland spar   B. talc   C. calcite   D. gypsum

48. Of the following physical properties, which one is most useful in distinguishing between hematite and limonite?

    A. Luster   B. Streak   C. Hardness   D. Cleavage

49. Which one of the following is a sedimentary rock?

    A. Diorite   B. Dolomite   C. Rhyolite   D. Slate

50. Fire Island and Jones Beach are good examples of

    A. off shore bars
    B. barrier reefs
    C. wave built terraces
    D. outwash plains

KEY (CORRECT ANSWERS)

1. B	11. D	21. B	31. D	41. C
2. C	12. D	22. A	32. C	42. D
3. B	13. A	23. B	33. D	43. A
4. D	14. B	24. C	34. C	44. D
5. C	15. B	25. D	35. C	45. D
6. B	16. A	26. A	36. A	46. D
7. D	17. D	27. D	37. C	47. D
8. A	18. A	28. B	38. A	48. B
9. D	19. D	29. B	39. D	49. B
10. D	20. C	30. D	40. C	50. A

EXAMINATION SECTION
TEST 1

DIRECTIONS: Each question or incomplete statement is followed by several suggested answers or completions. Select the one that BEST answers the question or completes the statement. PRINT THE LETTER OF THE CORRECT ANSWER IN THE SPACE AT THE RIGHT.

1. A somewhat narrow intrusive formation of magma that cuts across prevailing rock structures is termed a   1.____
    A. batholith   B. sill   C. laccolith   D. dike

2. Which one of the following units represents the LONGEST period of geologic time?   2.____
    A. Epoch   B. Period   C. Age   D. Era

3. The MOST abundant metallic element in the earth's crust is   3.____
    A. aluminum   B. iron   C. magnesium   D. copper

4. Most of our knowledge concerning the structure and composition of the earth's interior has been gained from the study of which one of the following?   4.____
    A. Radio-active minerals in the earth's crust
    B. Deep-seated volcanic activity
    C. Earthquake waves
    D. Cosmic radiation

5. The study of layered rock and the reconstruction of its past history is known as which one of the following?   5.____
    A. Paleontology   B. Varvology
    C. Uniformitarianism   D. Stratigraphy

6. The ice advances and retreats during the Wisconsin Period have been MOST accurately timed by measuring the   6.____
    A. amount of silt deposited
    B. ratio of uranium to lead
    C. size of the terminal moraines
    D. ratio of carbon-14 in pieces of fossilized wood to ordinary carbon

7. Of the following, the LEAST reliable property in the identification of MOST minerals is   7.____
    A. color   B. hardness
    C. crystal form   D. chemical composition

8. Amethyst is a variety of which one of the following minerals?   8.____
    A. Beryl   B. Fluorite   C. Quartz   D. Rhondonite

9. Of the following, the one rock having a glassy appearance and which was cooled rapidly from the molten state is   9.____
    A. sandstone   B. shale   C. obsidian   D. hornblende

10. In a region of Karst topography, the underlying rock is USUALLY of which one of the following types?

   A. Granite   B. Limestone   C. Mica schist   D. Gneiss

11. Of the following, the MOST important agent of erosion of the earth's surface is

   A. wind   B. glaciers   C. running water   D. oceans

12. The GREATEST detail can be shown on a topographic map using a _____ scale and _____ contour interval.

   A. small ; small
   B. large ; large
   C. small ; large
   D. large ; small

13. Which one of the following types of air masses could be labeled mT?

   A. Warm and dry   B. Warm and moist
   C. Cold and dry   D. Cold and moist

14. Of the following, the zone in which the temperature of the atmosphere is PRACTICALLY constant is the

   A. mesophere   B. ionosphere   C. stratosphere   D. troposphere

15. A geological feature NOT associated with glaciers is a

   A. caldera   B. kame   C. drumlin   D. esker

16. The term podzolic refers specifically to a(n)

   A. type of metamorphic rock   B. oceanic deposit
   C. tektite   D. type of soil

17. The alternate light and dark colored deposits found in glacial lakes are called

   A. varves   B. kettles   C. terraces   D. tills

18. Hard water is likely to be encountered in an area whose bedrock is composed of which one of the following?

   A. Sandstone   B. Granite   C. Limestone   D. Schist

19. Which one of the features below is NOT typical of the old age phase of a river?

   A. Rapids   B. Yazoo streams   C. Meanders   D. Oxbow lakes

20. Bridal Veil Falls in California owes its presence to the fact that it is located

   A. along a line of fault
   B. along a joint line
   C. in the path of an old lava flow
   D. in a hanging valley

21. The boundary between the upper portion of the mantle and the lower limit of the earth's crust is known as the

    A. isostatic boundary
    B. Bergschrund
    C. Moho
    D. zone of deformation

22. Proof of the sphericity of the earth CANNOT be obtained by which one of the following?

    A. Observing a lunar eclipse
    B. Determining the magnetic declination at different localities along a meridian between the equator and the south pole
    C. Taking photographs of the earth from a satellite
    D. Making observations of the position of the North Star at different localities along a meridian between the equator and the north pole

23. The contour interval on a topographic map is 10 feet. The face of a steep sea cliff is shown by five closely spaced contour lines including the sea level contour. The elevation, in feet, at the top of the cliff is

    A. *exactly* 50
    B. *between* 50 and 60
    C. *between* 40 and 49
    D. *exactly* 40

24. On a topographic map, the GREATEST exaggeration occurs in which one of the following?

    A. Graphic scale
    B. Vertical scale
    C. Horizontal scale
    D. Representative fraction

25. Of the following, the fossil that is MOST commonly used as a guide in correlating oil producing areas on a worldwide basis is called

    A. Placenticeras
    B. Trilobites
    C. Foraminifera
    D. Cephalopods

KEY (CORRECT ANSWERS)

1. D		11. C	
2. D		12. D	
3. A		13. B	
4. C		14. C	
5. D		15. A	
6. D		16. D	
7. A		17. A	
8. C		18. C	
9. C		19. A	
10. B		20. D	

21. C
22. B
23. C
24. B
25. C

TEST 2

DIRECTIONS: Each question or incomplete statement is followed by several suggested answers or completions. Select the one that *BEST* answers the question or completes the statement. *PRINT THE LETTER OF THE CORRECT ANSWER IN THE SPACE AT THE RIGHT.*

1. Amphibians arose during which one of the following times?

    A. Mississippian
    B. Cretaceous
    C. Ordovician
    D. Silurian

2. The average interval, in years, between the times of the GREATEST number of sunspot groups is CLOSEST to which one of the following?

    A. 7
    B. 11
    C. 15
    D. 19

3. Natural levees, alluvial fans, and braided streams are indications of which one of the following conditions?

    A. Stream load exceeds capacity
    B. Stream load is equal to capacity
    C. Stream load is less than capacity
    D. The base level of stream erosion is dropping

4. Clay minerals are formed by chemical weathering of which one of the following groups?

    A. Calcite and dolomite
    B. Orthoclase and albite
    C. Varieties of quartz
    D. Gypsum and anhydrite

5. Of the following, the feature which CANNOT be used to infer the existence of a second cycle of erosion is that of

    A. entrenched meanders
    B. river terraces
    C. accordant hilltops
    D. oxbow lakes

6. An erosional landform produced by glacial action is a

    A. hogback
    B. cirque
    C. monadnock
    D. natural bridge

7. Of the following, the MOST recent glacial stage was the

    A. Nebraskan
    B. Wisconsin
    C. Sangamon
    D. Kansan

8. During their geologic history the Great Lakes NEVER drained

    A. *southward* through the Mississippi
    B. *eastward* through the Mohawk and Hudson
    C. *northward* through the Red River of the North
    D. *northeastward* through the St. Lawrence

9. The degree of inclination of the beds of rock from a horizontal surface is called the

    A. plunge
    B. dip
    C. strike
    D. hade

54

2 (#2)

10. Of the common rocks, limestone is MOST easily changed by contact metamorphian because of its

   A. density   B. porosity   C. solubility   D. hardness

11. From the study of velocity and changes in intensity of earthquake waves, we know that which one of the following statements is TRUE:
The

   A. crust of the earth is between 20 and 30 miles thick on the average
   B. mantle is composed of granite
   C. core is 1,000 miles thick
   D. magma forms in the outer portion of the core

12. MOST of the mountains on the surface of the earth today are the result of which one of the following?

   A. Doming   B. Faulting
   C. Folding   D. Volcanic entrusion

13. The doctrine of uniformitarianism states that

   A. processes at work affecting the earth today are about the same as those that operated in the past
   B. the earth is the center of the solar system
   C. sedimentary rock structures follow a fixed pattern
   D. the youngest rocks are found at the top of a rock sequence

14. The MOST important source of condensation nuclei for fog and cloud formation found in nature are

   A. silver iodide   B. pollen
   C. salt   D. fine clay particles

15. Since the pressure force is perpendicular to the isobars and the deflecting force caused by the earth's rotation is opposite to the pressure force, it follows that a wind above the friction level will blow

   A. at right angles to the isobars
   B. parallel to the isobars
   C. in the direction of the low pressure area
   D. in opposition to the Coriolis force

16. How many calories of heat energy are released when 1 kilogram of water vapor at a temperature of zero degrees C condenses and then turns to ice at zero degrees C?

   A. 54,000   B. 80,000   C. 620,000   D. 800,000

17. Radiation type ground fogs are ALWAYS accompanied by a

   A. greater than normal lapse rate
   B. moist adiabatic lapse rate
   C. marked temperature inversion
   D. pseudoadiabatic lapse rate

18. The occurrence of waterfalls in stream-valley history is a mark of

 A. youth   B. early maturity
 C. late maturity   D. old age

19. Which one of the following mountain ranges are mature?

 A. Adirondacks   B. Himalayas
 C. Sierra Nevadas   D. Rockies

20. Which one of the following terms BEST describes the Catskill mountains?

 A. Complex mountains   B. Block-fault mountains
 C. Domed mountains   D. Dissected plateau

21. Which one of the following minerals is MOST resistant to chemical weathering?

 A. Feldspar   B. Gypsum   C. Talc   D. Quartz

22. Molten rock which solidifies below the surface of the earth is called

 A. intrusive   B. extrusive   C. metamorphic   D. sedimentary

23. Which one of the following is used to designate the high land between two river systems? A

 A. terrace   B. plateau   C. tor   D. divide

24. At which one of the following periods are both ends of the earth's axis equidistant from the sun?

 A. Every day of the year
 B. Only during the summer solstice
 C. Only during the winter solstice
 D. Only during the equinoxes

25. Which one of the following is considered the MOST probable cause of the Aurora Borealis?

 A. Electrically charged particles from the sun
 B. Reflection of light rays from snowfields
 C. Dispersion of light by prismatic effects of ice crystals
 D. Refraction of moonlight

KEY (CORRECT ANSWERS)

1.	C	11.	A
2.	B	12.	C
3.	A	13.	A
4.	B	14.	C
5.	D	15.	B
6.	B	16.	C
7.	B	17.	C
8.	C	18.	A
9.	B	19.	A
10.	C	20.	D

21. D
22. A
23. D
24. D
25. A

TEST 3

DIRECTIONS: Each question or incomplete statement is followed by several suggested answers or completions. Select the one that BEST answers the question or completes the statement. PRINT THE LETTER OF THE CORRECT ANSWER IN THE SPACE AT THE RIGHT.

1. Granite is a rock that was made from which one of the following?

    A. Cooling of lava from volcanoes
    B. Cooling of lava deep beneath the earth's surface
    C. Compression of sediments
    D. Cementation of sediments

    1.____

2. Besides temperature, which one of the following factors determines the nature of a metamorphic rock?

    A. Pressure
    B. Erosion of overlying sediments
    C. Pressure and composition of fluids that permeate rocks
    D. Pressure and erosion of overlying sediments

    2.____

3. At which one of the following seasons of the northern hemisphere of the earth is the earth FARTHEST from the sun?

    A. Autumn   B. Spring   C. Summer   D. Winter

    3.____

4. With which one of the following are active volcanoes USUALLY associated?

    A. Dissected plateaus   B. Glaciated areas
    C. Peneplanes   D. Young mountains

    4.____

5. The YOUNGEST bedrock found in New York City is which one of the following?

    A. Mica schist   B. Dolomite   C. Gneiss   D. Marble

    5.____

6. If a mine foreman is brought to the surface, which is at an elevation of 300 ft. above sea level, from a mine, which is 1,250 feet below sea level, an aneroid barometer in his possession would show a(n) _____ of _____ inches.

    A. decrease ; 1 1/2
    B. decrease ; 3
    C. increase ; 1 1/2
    D. increase ; 3

    6.____

7. Columnar structure found in many volcanic necks will form according to which one of the following sets of patterns and conditions?

    A. Parallel to the lava surface, accompanied by slow cooling
    B. Parallel to the lava surface, accompanied by rapid cooling
    C. At right angles to the lava surface, accompanied by slow cooling
    D. At right angles to the lava surface, accompanied by rapid cooling

    7.____

8. Of the following, which one rock will permit the EASIEST movement of ground water?

    A. Basalt   B. Conglomerate   C. Granite   D. Quartzite

    8.____

9. Of the following, the one element MOST evenly represented in sea water, river water, and rock is

   A. silica B. chlorine C. calcium D. magnesium

10. Of the following, the mineral which can be scratched by a fingernail is

    A. feldspar B. hornblende C. mica D. quartz

11. All crystals which have three axes of the same length and at right angles to each other belong to which one of the following systems?

    A. Monoclinic B. Isometric C. Rhombic D. Orthorhombic

12. Which one of the following is MOST representative of lake deposits?

    A. Sands and talus
    B. Sands and gravels
    C. Sands and clays
    D. Clays and silts

13. In strongly meandering streams the deepest water is USUALLY found in which of the following regions? _____ along the _____ curve.

    A. *Upstream* ; outer
    B. *Upstream* ; inner
    C. *Downstream* ; outer
    D. *Downstream* ; inner

14. An esker is a deposit formed by which one of the following?

    A. Running water
    B. Shore currents
    C. Weathering
    D. Wind

15. Isoseismic lines on a map connect points that are equal in which one of the following?

    A. Intensity of earthquake shocks
    B. Variation of magnetic force
    C. Metamorphosis of rock in contact with magma
    D. Temperature

16. Of the following, which one is an instrument used to study the composition of stars?

    A. Chronometer
    B. Seismograph
    C. Sextant
    D. Spectroscope

17. Of the following rocks, which one is MOST easily weathered by freezing and thawing?

    A. Limestone
    B. Obsidian
    C. Quartzite
    D. Sandstone

18. Among the following, the one planet whose orbit has the GREATEST eccentricity is

    A. Mercury B. Jupiter C. Mars D. Pluto

19. The spectra of the more distant galaxies show spectrum lines at greater wavelengths than normal.
    The interpretation usually given to these spectrum lines is that the distance between galaxies is

    A. *decreasing* steadily
    B. *decreasing* intermittently
    C. *increasing* steadily
    D. *increasing* intermittently

20. The existence of fossil corals indicates that in addition to clean water, which one of the following sets of conditions prevailed at the time of their formation?

    A. Deep, cool, fresh water
    B. Shallow, warm, fresh water
    C. Shallow, cool, marine water
    D. Shallow, warm, marine water

21. The SMALLEST number of elements which together comprise 99% of the earth's crust is

    A. 8　　　B. 18　　　C. 80　　　D. 98

22. Of the following groups, which one represents ONLY the constructive work of ground water?

    A. Stalagmite, helictite, travertine, natural bridge
    B. Helictite, travertine, natural bridge, stalactite
    C. Travertine, natural bridge, staclactite, stalagmite
    D. Travertine, helictite, column, stalagmite

23. Which one of the following problems has been MAINLY solved in Paleontology? The

    A. stratigraphic and geographic occurrence of fossil organisms and the range in variation in fossil materials
    B. actual environment of most fossil assemblages
    C. time, place, and manner in which different animal groups developed hard parts
    D. relative age of rock units and fossils over most of the earth

24. Which one of the following sets of minerals have rhombohedral cleavage?

    A. Halite and galena
    B. Dolomite and calcite
    C. Feldspar and hornblende
    D. Sphalerite and mica

25. The SMALLEST daily temperature ranges are MOST likely to occur at which one of the following regions?

    A. Arctic circle　　　B. Equator
    C. North Pole　　　D. Tropic of Cancer

KEY (CORRECT ANSWERS)

1. B
2. C
3. C
4. D
5. A

6. A
7. C
8. B
9. D
10. C

11. B
12. D
13. C
14. A
15. A

16. D
17. D
18. D
19. C
20. D

21. A
22. D
23. D
24. B
25. C

TEST 4

DIRECTIONS: Each question or incomplete statement is followed by several suggested answers or completions. Select the one that *BEST* answers the question or completes the statement. *PRINT THE LETTER OF THE CORRECT ANSWER IN THE SPACE AT THE RIGHT.*

1. Fossil remains indicate that the course of evolution of organisms on the earth has been which one of the following? 1.____

   A. A continuous straight line evolution
   B. Advance in large and sudden jumps
   C. Development of greater complexity at a specific rate
   D. Radiation of organisms in many directions

2. At the present time MOST species are classified on the basis of 2.____

   A. genetic structures
   B. homologous compatability
   C. physiological characteristics
   D. cytological resemblances

3. Of the following, the one which is characteristic of youthful streams is that they 3.____

   A. have meanders   B. are graded
   C. have rapids   D. flow on flood plains

4. The Ewing-Donn hypothesis attempts to explain 4.____

   A. mountain building   B. the origin of the earth
   C. ice ages   D. the origin of life on earth

5. The two MOST abundant chemical elements in the earth's crust are 5.____

   A. oxygen and silicon   B. oxygen and hydrogen
   C. silicon and aluminum   D. silicon and iron

6. Taconite is a low-grade ore of 6.____

   A. nickel   B. iron   C. titanium   D. copper

7. The type of rock MOST commonly found in batholiths is 7.____

   A. basalt   B. granite   C. felsite   D. gabbro

8. The Great Salt Lake of Utah is the remnant of a much larger fresh-water lake of Pleistocene times called Lake 8.____

   A. Agassiz   B. Lahontan   C. Bonneville   D. Algonquin

9. Which one of the following minerals is ALSO a native element? 9.____

   A. Galena   B. Gypsum   C. Graphite   D. Garnet

10. The type of coal MOST likely to be found in strata that were deeply buried and strongly folded is

    A. bituminous coal
    B. lignite
    C. anthracite
    D. peat

11. A common accessory mineral in the mica schist of Manhattan Island is

    A. garnet   B. magnetite   C. diopside   D. olivine

12. Of the following, the MOST likely reason for the failure of geologists to find fossils in the bed rock of Manhattan Island is that

    A. living organisms were scarce at the time of formation of the rocks
    B. any possible remains of life were obliterated by metamorphism
    C. fossil-bearing layers are deeply buried beneath alluvium and glacial deposits
    D. little search has been made for them

13. Glacial striations on exposed bedrock outcrops in New York City strike

    A. NW-SE   B. N-S   C. W-E   D. NE-SW

14. An igneous intrusion which causes doming of the overlying sedimentary rocks is known as a

    A. batholith   B. dike   C. volcanic neck   D. laccolith

15. Eskers are depositional features which have the shape of

    A. broad, flat-topped hills
    B. dome-like mounds
    C. narrow, winding ridges
    D. rectilinear escarpments

16. An erosional remnant on a peneplane is called a

    A. roche moutonee   B. monadnock   C. nunatak   D. stack

17. A rhumb line on the earth's surface is ALWAYS a(the)

    A. line of constant bearing
    B. segment of a great circle
    C. segment of a small circle
    D. shortest distance between two points

18. Of the following, the form of vegetation MOST typical of the tundra is the

    A. dwarf pine   B. cactus   C. moss   D. sagebrush

19. The first IMPORTANT record of fossil land plants is found in rocks of which one of the following periods?

    A. Devonian   B. Triassic   C. Cambrian   D. Cretaceous

20. Of the following, the type of soil which absorbs water MOST slowly is

    A. loam   B. sand   C. humus   D. clay

21. Of the following, the one which is an example of an alluvial plain is a(n) _____ plain.   21._____
    A. lava   B. till   C. outwash   D. delta

22. Lines drawn on a map through points of equal pressure are called   22._____
    A. divides   B. isobars
    C. isotherms   D. contour lines

23. The OLDEST type of map projection is the   23._____
    A. Mercator   B. Gnomonic
    C. Lambert conformal   D. Polyconic

24. Level areas are indicated on a contour map by contour lines which   24._____
    A. are close together   B. are far apart
    C. coincide   D. are circular or oval

25. Compared with a land area, a water area heats more_____ and cools more _____.   25._____
    A. rapidly ; rapidly
    B. rapidly ; slowly
    C. slowly ; rapidly
    D. slowly ; slowly

KEY (CORRECT ANSWERS)

1. D   11. A
2. B   12. B
3. C   13. A
4. C   14. D
5. A   15. C

6. B   16. B
7. B   17. A
8. C   18. C
9. C   19. A
10. C   20. D

21. D
22. B
23. A
24. B
25. D

TEST 5

DIRECTIONS: Each question or incomplete statement is followed by several suggested answers or completions. Select the one that *BEST* answers the question or completes the statement. *PRINT THE LETTER OF THE CORRECT ANSWER IN THE SPACE AT THE RIGHT.*

1. All of the following statements concerning artesian wells are TRUE EXCEPT that 1.____

    A. they usually provide much larger quantities of water than ordinary wells
    B. their main source of water is local rainfall
    C. in general, the farther they are from their outcrops, the deeper their aquifer
    D. the water in the aquifers is under pressure

2. A speleologist is a 2.____

    A. cave explorer   B. space explorer
    C. weather forecaster   D. mountain climber

3. The use of which one of the following is the MOST accurate way of dating relatively recent fossils? 3.____

    A. Concentration of salt in the sea
    B. Rate of deposition of river sediment
    C. Half-life of radioactive carbon
    D. Uranium-lead ratio

4. Through the measurement of the fluorine and nitrogen contents of fossil bones, scientists have shown that which one of the following fossil men is a hoax? 4.____

    A. Pithecanthropus   B. Sinanthropus
    C. Piltdown   D. Australopithecus

5. The rugged, deeply embayed shoreline of New England was formed by 5.____

    A. volcanic activity accompanied by regional faulting
    B. the uplift of a submerged peneplane
    C. the subsidence of a well-dissected region
    D. wave attack upon glacial and glacio-fluvial deposits

6. An animal thought to have become extinct some 60 million years ago has been discovered still living in the ocean off the coast of Madagascar. It belongs to the group known as 6.____

    A. coelacanths   B. trilobites
    C. graptolites   D. plesiosaurs

7. The contact between the Cretaceous marine sediments and the crystalline metamorphic rocks of New York City beneath Long Island may be described as 7.____

    A. conformable   B. gradational
    C. unconformable   D. faulted

8. A rock of igneous origin occurring in New York City and vicinity is which one of the following? 8.____

    A. Muscovite schist   B. Dolomitic marble
    C. Arkose sandstone   D. Granite pegmatite

65

9. Abandoned magnetite mines in the Adirondack Mountains have been re-activated in recent years for the recovery of

   A. iron B. titanium C. copper D. lead

10. Of the following conditions, the one which would prevent the periodic eruption of a geyser is

   A. an intricate underground fracture system
   B. subterranean heat
   C. a plentiful supply of ground water
   D. contact of the ground water with molten rock below the surface

11. Which one of the following elements may be called a native element?

   A. Phosphorus B. Sulfur C. Potassium D. Chlorine

12. The much publicized *Mohole* is an undertaking designed to

   A. discover more petroleum reserves
   B. explore recently discovered mineral deposits
   C. obtain information on the conditions prevailing at the base of the earth's crust
   D. tap a reservoir of magma in the earth's crust

13. The base level of erosion is the

   A. line along which a stream becomes graded
   B. water table
   C. first resistant stratum the stream reaches
   D. limit of downward erosion by running water

14. It is INCORRECT to state that a loccolith

   A. is extrusive in origin
   B. has a flat floor
   C. is a concordant igneous intrusion
   D. has caused doming of the overlying rock layers

15. A pebble which is in part well-rounded and in part sub-angular was MOST likely abraded by the action of

   A. wind B. waves C. glaciers D. streams

16. The second MOST abundant element in the earth's crust is

   A. Al B. Ca C. Na D. Si

17. Of the following common minerals, the one which MOST successfully resists weathering is

   A. quartz B. calcite C. hornblende D. orthoclase

18. Gneiss is a(n)

    A. intrusive igneous rock exhibiting a streaky alignment of minerals
    B. stratified sedimentary rock
    C. metamorphic rock with a banded structure
    D. metamorphic rock with a massive, non-foliated structure

    18.____

19. Of the following, the rock structure which is the result of metamorphism is

    A. columnar structure   B. stratification
    C. vesicular structure   D. foliation

    19.____

20. The radioactive method which CANNOT be used to determine rock ages in excess of 50,000 years involves the radioactive decay of an isotope of which one of the following elements?

    A. Potassium   B. Carbon   C. Strontium   D. Thorium

    20.____

21. Orogenic movements in the earth's crust are responsible for the formation of which one of the following?

    A. Folded mountain ranges
    B. Geosynclines
    C. Elevated marine terraces
    D. Submerged shorelines

    21.____

22. Accepted inferences concerning the layered structure of the earth's interior are LARGELY based on

    A. calculations of the average density of the earth
    B. gravimetric measurements from submarines
    C. measurements of the earth's magnetic field
    D. sharp changes in travel time of earthquake waves at certain depths

    22.____

23. A meandering stream flows MOST rapidly

    A. near the undercut bank   B. near the slip-off slope
    C. near the center   D. at the bottom

    23.____

24. An erosional remnant produced by the action of waves along a shore is called a

    A. col   B. stack   C. roche moutonnee   D. kame

    24.____

25. Of the following, which structure CANNOT be classified as a fold?

    A. Homocline   B. Anticline   C. Monocline   D. Syncline

    25.____

KEY (CORRECT ANSWERS)

1. B
2. A
3. C
4. C
5. C

6. A
7. C
8. D
9. B
10. D

11. B
12. C
13. D
14. A
15. C

16. D
17. A
18. C
19. D
20. B

21. A
22. D
23. A
24. B
25. A

EXAMINATION SECTION
TEST 1

DIRECTIONS: Each question or incomplete statement is followed by several suggested answers or completions. Select the one that *BEST* answers the question or completes the statement. *PRINT THE LETTER OF THE CORRECT ANSWER IN THE SPACE AT THE RIGHT.*

1. Generally speaking, MOST of the world's volcanoes   1.____
   A. lie in belts which are almost identical with the two great earthquake belts
   B. are roughly at right angles to the earthquake belts
   C. are in the equatorial regions
   D. form no particular geographic pattern

2. The point in the bedrock at which an earthquake seems to center is known as its   2.____
   A. anticline   B. epicenter   C. focus   D. fault

3. Of the following groups, the one which contains ONLY metamorphic rocks is   3.____
   A. basalt, diorite, dolomite, shale
   B. conglomerate, granite, serpentine, marble
   C. diabase, schist, obsidian, serpentine
   D. quartzite, gneiss, slate, marble

4. Diatrophism refers to which one of the following? The   4.____
   A. rising and sinking of the earth's surface
   B. formation of geysers
   C. erosion caused by wind
   D. movement of clouds

5. The fraction of the solid part of the earth that lies beneath water and ice is   5.____
   A. 1/3   B. 1/2   C. 3/4   D. 5/6

6. The surface of the solid part of the earth consists essentially of huge blocks of rock which sometimes break away and rise or sink.   6.____
   This action is called
   A. volcanic action   B. folding
   C. faulting   D. weathering

7. Of the following groups of materials found in the earth's crust, the group in which the items range progressively from softest to hardest is   7.____
   A. talc, fluorite, quartz, diamond
   B. feldspar, gypsum, topaz, corundum
   C. gypsum, quartz, apatite, diamond
   D. calcite, quartz, diamond, corundum

8. Which one of the following groups contains the four MOST abundant elements in the earth's crust?

   A. Oxygen, nitrogen, hydrogen, iron
   B. Nitrogen, iron, sodium, oxygen
   C. Potassium, silicon, aluminum, iron
   D. Oxygen, silicon, aluminum, iron

9. All but one of the following statements about artesian wells are true. The EXCEPTION is:

   A. Artesian well water is usually much colder than ordinary well water.
   B. The water in artesian wells is drawn from aquifers below an impervious layer.
   C. Artesian well water is usually harder than ordinary well water.
   D. The source of the water supply in an artesian well may be hundreds of miles from the well.

10. When oil spouts from a well as a gusher, it USUALLY does so because

    A. of the pressure of water beneath the oil or of gas above the oil
    B. air is pumped into the well
    C. of the release of great heat
    D. of the tremendous pressure of subsurface rock layers on the oil

11. The volcano which was formed in Mexico in 1943 was named

    A. Popocatepetl   B. Mauna Loa
    C. Paricutin   D. Krakatoa

12. A narrow V-shaped valley is considered by geologists to be

    A. young   B. old
    C. mature   D. between mature and old

13. As compared with a valley made by a stream, a glacial valley is

    A. rounded and smooth   B. irregular and rough
    C. irregular and smooth D. rounded and rough

14. The branch of geology dealing with the origin of land forms is called

    A. geomorphology   B. geopolitics
    C. geomology   D. geotology

15. The farthest south in what is now the continental United States of America that the LAST glacier reached was

    A. Maine   B. New York   C. Kentucky   D. Alabama

16. Of the following mountain ranges, the one estimated to be the YOUNGEST is the

    A. Alps   B. Rockies   C. Adirondacks   D. Himalayas

17. About 100,000,000 years ago, North America

    A. had approximately the same form as today except that a land bridge connected Alaska and Siberia
    B. was connected by land to Asia, South America and Europe
    C. was divided into two parts by a great inland sea
    D. was connected by a land bridge to Africa

17.____

18. Of the following epochs the one which is NOT associated with the Mesozoic Era is

    A. Cretaceous
    B. Jurassic
    C. Triassic
    D. Permian

18.____

19. The Moh Scale measures the

    A. acidity of the soil
    B. hardness of rocks
    C. bacterial content of the soil
    D. proportion of nitrogen to potash

19.____

20. A line on a weather map indicating that warm air has been lifted from the earth's surface by the action of opposing wedges of cold air is called a(n) _____ front.

    A. cold   B. warm   C. occluded   D. stationary

20.____

21. Points of equal pressure on weather maps are connected by lines called

    A. isotherms   B. isobars   C. isotopes   D. millibars

21.____

22. When contour lines on a topographical map are wide apart, it means that the area between the contour lines represents a(n)

    A. extensive lake
    B. steep rise
    C. comparitively level area
    D. desert

22.____

23. On a United States Geological Survey topographical map, the point at which contour lines meet represents a

    A. valley   B. hill   C. cliff   D. plain

23.____

24. The instrument among those named below which is used to determine latitude is the

    A. barometer
    B. chronometer
    C. sextant
    D. anemometer

24.____

25. The condition of *nine months of winter and three months of bad weather* in eastern Newfoundland is caused CHIEFLY by the

    A. Gulf Stream
    B. Brazil Current
    C. Labrador Current
    D. Sargasso Sea

25.____

KEY (CORRECT ANSWERS)

1.	A	11.	C
2.	C	12.	A
3.	D	13.	A
4.	A	14.	A
5.	C	15.	C
6.	C	16.	B
7.	A	17.	C
8.	D	18.	D
9.	A	19.	B
10.	A	20.	C

21. B
22. C
23. C
24. C
25. C

TEST 2

DIRECTIONS: Each question or incomplete statement is followed by several suggested answers or completions. Select the one that BEST answers the question or completes the statement. PRINT THE LETTER OF THE CORRECT ANSWER IN THE SPACE AT THE RIGHT.

1. The MOST common cause of hard water is the presence of compounds of

    A. fluorine
    B. calcium
    C. iron
    D. sulfur

2. All of the following metals are extracted from the minerals with which they are associated below EXCEPT

    A. iron from hematite
    B. uranium from pitchblende
    C. tin from sphalerite
    D. lead from galena

3. Iron pyrites, sometimes know as fool's gold, is mined CHIEFLY for use in the manufacture of

    A. costume jewelry
    B. sulfuric acid
    C. procelain and china
    D. paint

4. Of the following acids, the one MOST often used to test for calcite is cold dilute _____ acid.

    A. hydrochloric   B. carbonic   C. sulfuric   D. nitric

5. The destructive distillation of soft coal produces

    A. coal gas, bitumen, water gas and tar
    B. ammonia, coal gas, water gas and coke
    C. coal tar, coal gas, ammonia and coke
    D. coal tar, coke, ammonia and charcoal

6. Which one of the following alloys contains copper?

    A. Solder
    B. Sterling silver
    C. Gold Amalgam
    D. Stainless steel

7. At the beginning of a community succession, the FIRST of the following living things to get a foothold on bare rocks, other things being equal, are

    A. mosses   B. ferns   C. algae   D. lichens

8. The Adirondack Mountains of New York are a well-known example of a _____ region.

    A. domed mountain
    B. black mountain
    C. mature plateau
    D. folded mountain

9. The Palisades of New Jersey are an example of a

    A. laccolith
    B. lava dike
    C. lava sill
    D. lava flow

10. A MAJOR belt of volcanoes encircles which of the following oceans?

    A. Arctic   B. Atlantic   C. Indian   D. Pacific

11. The GREAT majority of earthquakes
    A. are caused by volcanic eruptions
    B. are caused by sudden earth movements
    C. are of the deep focus type
    D. occur along the borders of the Atlantic Ocean basin

12. The glacial epoch in which the MOST recent Ice Age occurred is known as the
    A. Eocene   B. Miocene   C. Pliocene   D. Pleistocene

13. The process responsible for the formation of coal is
    A. decomposition   B. distillation
    C. petrification   D. replacement

14. The undercutting at the base of Niagara Falls is the result of stream action upon relatively weak beds of
    A. shale   B. limestone   C. sandstone   D. dolomite

15. A variety of rock classified as igneous is
    A. anthracite B. conglomerate C. granite   D. quartzite

16. A mineral soft enough to be scratched by a fingernail is
    A. orthoclase B. calcite   C. talc   D. gypsum

17. In the following series, the rock which is metamorphic is
    A. marble   B. sandstone   C. limestone   D. basalt

18. An ore of iron which is growing in importance is
    A. limonite   B. magnetite   C. taconite   D. siderite

19. The physical property which is LEAST reliable in the identification of minerals is
    A. luster   B. color   C. hardness   D. crystal form

20. The kind of coal MOST likely to be found in strata that were deeply buried, but not folded, is
    A. lignite   B. bituminous C. anthracite D. peat

21. The percentage of the earth's surface from which a total lunar eclipse is theoretically visible is about
    A. 1   B. 10   C. 50   D. 100

22. The APPROXIMATE average height of the snow-line on equatorial mountains is _____ miles.
    A. 1 1/2   B. 2 1/2   C. 3 1/2   D. 4 1/2

23. We are able to date many archaeological finds by measuring the decay of radioactive
    A. uranium 235   B. potassium 40
    C. strontium 90   D. carbon 14

24. The latest of the geological eras is called the   24.____
    A. cenozoic   B. paleozoic   C. proterozoic   D. mesozoic

25. All of the following are present in pig iron as impurities, EXCEPT   25.____
    A. silicon   B. phosphorus   C. molybdenum   D. sulfur

KEY (CORRECT ANSWERS)

1.	B	11.	B
2.	C	12.	D
3.	B	13.	B
4.	A	14.	A
5.	C	15.	C
6.	B	16.	C
7.	D	17.	A
8.	A	18.	C
9.	C	19.	B
10.	D	20.	B

21. C
22. C
23. D
24. A
25. C

TEST 3

DIRECTIONS: Each question or incomplete statement is followed by several suggested answers or completions. Select the one that BEST answers the question or completes the statement. PRINT THE LETTER OF THE CORRECT ANSWER IK THE SPACE AT THE RIGHT.

1. A rock composed of angular fragments cemented together into a coherent mass is a   1.____

   A. breccia   B. tufa   C. conglomerate   D. dacite

2. In Moh's scale of mineral hardness, quartz is number   2.____

   A. 5   B. 6   C. 7   D. 8

3. A rock which shows foliated structure is   3.____

   A. marble   B. serpentine   C. schist   D. quartzite

4. A river is NOT classified as mature when it includes a   4.____

   A. chain of lakes in its course   B. gorge
   C. series of meanders   D. series of rapids

5. An esker is a   5.____

   A. winding, roughly stratified glacial ridge
   B. linear, unstratified glacial ridge
   C. roughly circular glacial mound
   D. series of glacial elevations and depressions

6. An example of an active volcano of the *quiet* type is   6.____

   A. Krakatoa   B. Mauna Loa   C. Mt. Lassen   D. Mt. Vesuvius

7. Stone Mt., Georgia, is classified as a(n)   7.____

   A. butte   B. mesa   C. monadnock   D. volcanic neck

8. An outstanding example of a glacial trough is the   8.____

   A. Grand Canyon of the Colorado
   B. Yellowstone Canyon in Yellowstone National Park
   C. Yosemite Valley in Yosemite National Park
   D. Zion Canyon in Zion National Park

9. The Keewatin Glacier of the Pleistocene ice age was centered in   9.____

   A. north central Canada   B. Labrador
   C. Alaska   D. Greenland

10. Lost rivers or underground streams are MOST likely to occur in regions whose bedrock is   10.____

    A. limestone   B. slate
    C. granite   D. conglomerate

11. The Royal Gorge of the Arkansas River represents a river valley which is   11.____

    A. young   B. mature   C. old   D. subdued

12. Sink holes are the result of the work of 12.____
    A. earthquakes B. underground water
    C. streams D. glaciers

13. The mineral which is LEAST susceptible to chemical weathering is 13.____
    A. feldspar B. hornblende C. augite D. quartz

14. Of the following, the mountains of GREATEST geologic age are the 14.____
    A. Appalachians B. Rockies
    C. Sierra Nevadas D. Cascades

15. Laccoliths are found in 15.____
    A. domed mountains B. block mountains
    C. folded mountains D. volcanoes

16. A shoreline formed as a result of submergence is a _____ shoreline. 16.____
    A. coastal plain B. delta C. fiord D. volcano

17. Spring tides occur at 17.____
    A. full moon only B. new moon only
    C. both full and new moon D. first and last quarter phases

18. An annular eclipse of the Sun takes place at the phase of the Moon called 18.____
    A. new moon B. new gibbous
    C. new crescent D. full moon

19. The Palisades of New Jersey originated as an igneous intrusion during the period known as 19.____
    A. Eocene B. Cretaceous C. Permian D. Triassic

20. A region whose warmest monthly temperature average is 80° F., while its coldest monthly temperature average is 77° F., MUST have a climate typified as 20.____
    A. marine west coast B. Mediterranean
    C. tropical desert D. tropical rain-forest

21. A necessary condition for the formation of sleet is a 21.____
    A. cold front B. strong pressure gradient
    C. steep lapse rate D. temperature inversion

22. The dry adiabatic lapse rate per 1000 feet is 22.____
    A. 2.5° F B. 3.5° F C. 4.5° F D. 5.5° F

23. The prevailing wind at 40° S latitude is 23.____
    A. northwesterly B. northeasterly
    C. southwesterly D. southeasterly

24. At perigee, our Moon's distance, expressed in miles, from the earth is about 24._____
    A. 205,000　　　B. 220,000　　　C. 235,000　　　D. 245,000

25. Stalactites and stalagmites found in limestone caverns are composed of 25._____
    A. geyserite　　　B. travertine　　　C. silica　　　D. ice

KEY (CORRECT ANSWERS)

1. A
2. C
3. C
4. D
5. A

6. B
7. C
8. C
9. A
10. A

11. A
12. B
13. D
14. A
15. A

16. C
17. C
18. A
19. D
20. D

21. D
22. D
23. A
24. B
25. B

TEST 4

DIRECTIONS: Each question or incomplete statement is followed by several suggested answers or completions. Select the one that *BEST* answers the question or completes the statement. *PRINT THE LETTER OF THE CORRECT ANSWER IN THE SPACE AT THE RIGHT.*

1. Stream piracy occurs when 1.____

    A. the headwaters of one stream are diverted by another
    B. the bed of the river is filled by deposition
    C. a dam is built on the river
    D. the river water is used for irrigation

2. The rivers that mark the southern limit of the Ice Sheet in North America are the Missouri and the 2.____

    A. St. Lawrence B. Arkansas
    C. Ohio D. Mississippi

3. The severe earthquakes that sometimes occur in California are believed to result from 3.____

    A. faulting B. volcanic action
    C. folding D. landslides

4. Horizontal rock structure and high relief are characteristic of 4.____

    A. plains B. peneplanes C. mountains D. plateaus

5. Regular shorelines form as a result of 5.____

    A. emergence of the continental shelf
    B. outwash of glaciers
    C. sinking of a mountainous coast
    D. submergence of a coastal plain

6. Fossils are found MOST commonly in rocks known as 6.____

    A. prismatic B. sedimentary
    C. igneous D. conchoidal

7. Three of the following fossil forms are considered contemporary of prehistoric man. The one that is NOT is 7.____

    A. archaeoptery B. great cave bear
    C. mammoth D. sabre-tooth tiger

8. The HIGHEST mountain peak in the United States is 8.____

    A. Long's Peak, Colorado B. Mt. Mitchell, North Carolina
    C. Mt. Ranier, Washington D. Mt. Whitney, California

9. Manhattan belongs to the physiographic region known as the 9.____

    A. Appalachian Plateau B. Atlantic Coastal Plain
    C. New England Province D. Triassic Lowland

10. Shorelines of submergence are characterized by their

    A. bays
    B. coastal plains
    C. coral reefs
    D. offshore bars

11. Coral stolls are USUALLY ring-shaped islands that have grown up from the

    A. continental shelf
    B. deep sea floor
    C. slopes of sunken volcanoes
    D. surface of sand bars

12. Gently sloping lava cones are typical of the volcanoes of

    A. Hawaii
    B. the West Indies
    C. the East Indies
    D. the Philippine Islands

13. A type of fossil man that was proven to be a hoax was

    A. Java
    B. Piltdown
    C. Cro-magnon
    D. Neanderthal

14. Statocysts and statoliths are MOST directly concerned with

    A. circulation
    B. equilibrium
    C. heredity
    D. rock formations

15. Eohippus was an early form of

    A. horse   B. elephant   C. camel   D. giraffe

16. The dinosaurs were prehistoric

    A. amphibia   B. birds   C. mammals   D. reptiles

17. The MOST abundant metal in the earth's crust is

    A. aluminum   B. iron   C. calcium   D. copper

18. Of the following, the mountain that has the HIGHEST snow line is Mt.

    A. Hood in Oregon
    B. Kenya in equatorial Africa
    C. McKinley in Alaska
    D. Orizaba in Mexico

19. The physiographic feature believed to have been formed in the bed of a subglacial stream is a(n)

    A. esker   B. drumlin   C. kame   D. moraine

20. Glacial valleys are ALWAYS characterized by

    A. uniform slope from source to mouth
    B. V-shaped cross-sections
    C. U-shaped cross-sections
    D. absence of tributary valleys

21. A characteristic of a mature river is

    A. little or no flood plain
    B. no rapids or water falls
    C. straight course
    D. new tributaries

22. A wind gap is a(n)

    A. abandoned water gap
    B. cave formed by windblown sand
    C. mountain pass made by wind erosion
    D. natural bridge

22.____

23. The pair of terms that includes a metamorphic rock and the rock from which it was derived is

    A. granite, limestone
    B. marble, obsidian
    C. quartzite, sandstone
    D. slate, gneiss

23.____

24. All of the stars visible to the naked eye in our sky are members of

    A. the Andromeda galaxy
    B. the Milky Way galaxy
    C. the solar system
    D. a number of different galaxies

24.____

25. Asbestos is a substance of _____ origin.

    A. animal   B. mineral   C. plant   D. synthetic

25.____

KEY (CORRECT ANSWERS)

1.	A	11.	C
2.	C	12.	A
3.	A	13.	B
4.	D	14.	B
5.	A	15.	A
6.	B	16.	D
7.	A	17.	A
8.	D	18.	B
9.	C	19.	A
10.	A	20.	C

21. B
22. A
23. C
24. B
25. B

TEST 5

DIRECTIONS: Each question or incomplete statement is followed by several suggested answers or completions. Select the one that *BEST* answers the question or completes the statement. *PRINT THE LETTER OF THE CORRECT ANSWER IN THE SPACE AT THE RIGHT.*

1. The mineral from which aluminum is extracted commercially is 1.____

   A. alumite B. bauxite C. corundum
   D. cryolite E. calcite

2. A mineral from which uranium is extracted commercially is 2.____

   A. chrysocolla B. olivine C. pitchblende
   D. sphalerite E. gneiss

3. A rock used in the manufacture of cement is 3.____

   A. basalt B. granite C. limestone
   D. schist E. shale

4. A metal that occurs in placer deposits is 4.____

   A. gold B. iron C. magnesium
   D. zinc E. corundum

5. In chemical composition, diamonds are MOST like 5.____

   A. rhinestone B. quartz C. granite D. coal

6. Which of the following formations or deposits can be explained MOST satisfactorily by the assumption that a glacier has passed over the region? 6.____

   A. A thick layer of rich, black soil
   B. Large boulders of a different kind of stone from the rock under the soil in the area
   C. A large number of small, rounded stones in the bed of a mountain stream
   D. A deep, narrow gorge with perpendicular walls

7. A fossil is a(n) 7.____

   A. small rock that was moved by a glacier during the ice age
   B. tool used by prehistoric man
   C. small ditch used in irrigation
   D. remnant or trace of an animal or a plant that lived in a past age

8. The area from which a river draws its water is called a 8.____

   A. water table B. water shed
   C. artesian wall D. tarn

9. If mineral A is harder than mineral B, it means that 9.____

   A. B breaks more easily than A
   B. A can scratch B

C. B is more easily cleaved than A
D. A is stronger than B

10. An igneous rock with a coarse texture suggests that the rock was formed

   A. on the surface and cooled rapidly
   B. on the surface and cooled slowly
   C. under high pressure and cooled rapidly
   D. under high pressure and cooled slowly

11. Shale is related to slate as limestone is related to

   A. calcite   B. marble   C. quartz   D. travertine

12. The deep waters of the ocean are

   A. *rich* in both carbon dioxide and oxygen
   B. *poor* in both carbon dioxide and oxygen
   C. *poor* in carbon dioxide, rich in oxygen
   D. *rich* in carbon dioxide, poor in oxygen

13. Stalactites my form in caverns where the ground water has passed through regions of

   A. lava   B. limestone   C. quartzite   D. sandstone

14. The statement *The present can be used as a key to the past* summarizes the principle of

   A. isostasy   B. diatrophism
   C. superposition   D. uniformitarianism

15. Ox-bow lakes are MOST closely related to

   A. glaciers   B. meanders
   C. sinkholes   D. waterfalls

16. A type of fine dust-like wind-deposited soil that forms steep vertical cliffs is called

   A. a barchane   B. drift   C. a dune   D. loess

17. As one travels along an isogonic line from the magnetic equator to the North Magnetic Pole, declination

   A. increases   B. decreases
   C. remains constant D. fluctuates

18. The number of miles in a degree of latitude is CLOSEST, in miles, to which one of the following?

   A. 5   B. 70   C. 90   D. 1,000

19. The Mohorovicio Discontinuity (MOHO) represents an interface between the

   A. core and the mantle   B. inner core and outer core
   C. lithosphere and hydrosphere   D. mantle and crust

20. The apparent fit of the continents is BEST explained by the theory of

   A. continental drift
   B. diastrophism
   C. isostasy
   D. volcanism

21. Monadnocks are found

   A. in volcanic regions
   B. on peneplanes
   C. near fault-block mountains
   D. on the continental shelf

22. The downfolds of sedimentary rock are called

   A. anticlines
   B. geoclines
   C. isoclines
   D. synclines

23. The Mesozoic Era was dominated on land by

   A. amphibia
   B. dinosaurs
   C. small mammals
   D. ammonites

24. On a hot summer day, sea breezes occur because of relatively

   A. high temperature of the water
   B. lower temperature of the land
   C. lower pressure over land
   D. lower pressure over water

25. A type of cloud composed PRINCIPALLY of ice crystals is

   A. cirrus
   B. cumulus
   C. nimbus
   D. stratus

KEY (CORRECT ANSWERS)

1.	B	11.	B
2.	C	12.	D
3.	C	13.	B
4.	A	14.	D
5.	D	15.	B
6.	B	16.	D
7.	D	17.	C
8.	B	18.	B
9.	B	19.	D
10.	D	20.	A
21.	B		
22.	D		
23.	B		
24.	C		
25.	A		

EXAMINATION SECTION
TEST 1

DIRECTIONS: Each question or incomplete statement is followed by several suggested answers or completions. Select the one that BEST answers the question or completes the statement. *PRINT THE LETTER OF THE CORRECT ANSWER IN THE SPACE AT THE RIGHT.*

1. The Kansan, Nebraskan, Illinoisan, and Wisconsin epochs were noted for which one of the following?   1____

    A. Widespread volcanic activity
    B. Spread of vast ice sheets
    C. Unusual deposition in geosynclines
    D. Mountain building on a huge scale

2. Barchons are defined as   2____

    A. tracks produced by prehistoric animals
    B. large deposits of glacial till
    C. sand dunes shaped like a crescent
    D. fragments of igneous rock

3. The presence of trilobite fossils dates rocks as belonging to which one of the following eras?   3____

    A. Precambrian   B. Paleozoic
    C. Mesozoic   D. Cenozoic

4. The color of the streak that results when pyrite is rubbed across a porcelain plate is   4____

    A. yellow   B. brown   C. green   D. black

5. Which one of the following would be POOREST for showing cleavage?   5____

    A. Mica   B. Calcite   C. Feldspar   D. Obsidian

6. Natural cement is composed MAINLY of which one of the following?   6____

    A. Sandstone   B. Silica
    C. Calcium carbonate   D. Loess

7. Of the following, the rock whose mineral content MOST strongly resembles that of granite is   7____

    A. obsidian   B. rhyolite   C. andesite   D. limestone

8. Of the following, which series presents transporting agents in the order of their carrying power?   8____

    A. Running water - oscillating water - wind - ice
    B. Ice - running water - oscillating water - wind
    C. Oscillating water - running water - wind - ice
    D. Wind - ice - running water - oscillating water

9. Rock masses which were produced when the magma solidified below the surface are called which one of the following?

   A. Plutons
   B. Basalts
   C. Lateral moraines
   D. Erratics

10. Stalactites and stalagmites are forms of which one of the following?

    A. Travertine
    B. Calcium bicarbonate
    C. Gypsum
    D. Silica

11. Fossils are rarely found in the bedrock of New York City because

    A. the rocks pre-date the period of skeletal life forms
    B. repeated glacial invasion has removed all traces
    C. metamorphism has destroyed any evidence of life
    D. the rocks are all igneous

12. Which one of the following is the cause of the red coloring in many sedimentary rocks?

    A. Calcite   B. Hematite   C. Pyrite   D. Silica

13. Recent studies of the sea floor indicate the widespread prevalence of cannon-ball shaped nodules of

    A. zinc   B. antimony   C. manganese   D. zirconium

14. Of the following, a factor that does NOT directly affect the direction of ocean currents is

    A. prevailing winds
    B. rotation of the earth
    C. temperature of the water
    D. outline of continents

15. A flat-topped submarine mountain whose summit has been planed away to the surface of the ocean is called a(n)

    A. offlap   B. guyot   C. nummulite   D. reef

16. Of the following, the one that is NOT an ore of copper is

    A. chalcopyrite
    B. malachite
    C. azurite
    D. sphalerite

17. Which one of the following is a speleologist?

    A. Mountain climber
    B. Deep sea diver
    C. Archeologist
    D. Cave explorer

18. In which one of the following places is the movement of a valley glacier GREATEST? Its

    A. bottom
    B. valley walls
    C. top and center
    D. large crevasses

19. To which one of the following does the process of cavitation in geology refer?

    A. Filling of cavities by groundwater
    B. Slope erosion
    C. Pothole migration
    D. Collapse of vapor bubbles in water

20. Geosynclinal deposits that reach a thickness of 50,000 ft. have, in most cases, been deposited in marine waters having a depth CLOSEST to which one of the following? _____ feet.

    A. 1,000   B. 10,000   C. 30,000   D. 50,000

21. The northernmost boundary of the zone of Middle Latitude Climate is marked by the

    A. January Average Isotherm of 50°F
    B. July Average Isotherm of 50°F
    C. Annual Average Isotherm of 50°F
    D. Annual Average Isotherm of 60°F

22. In desert regions, pebbles found there which are scoured into flat-sided, sharp-edged forms are called

    A. dreikanters   B. playas   C. aretes   D. barchanes

23. The complexity of formulas of the silicates is BEST explained in terms of

    A. excess of negative ions in a tetrahedron crystal lattice
    B. excess of positive ions in a tetrahedron crystal lattice
    C. the unfilled spaces in its rhombohedron structure
    D. a fluctuating valence among its ions

24. The dip of a rock structure refers to which one of the following?

    A. The angle of junction of two deformed and adjacent rock layers
    B. The direction of the line of intersection of the layer with the horizontal plane
    C. The angle that the rock layer makes with a north-south line
    D. Inclination of the stratum from the horizontal plane

25. In the chemical weathering of orthoclase, which one of the following takes place?

    A. Only clay is produced.
    B. Clay and finely divided quartz are produced.
    C. Clay and calcite are produced.
    D. Calcite and quartz are produced.

KEY (CORRECT ANSWERS)

1.	B	11.	C
2.	C	12.	B
3.	B	13.	C
4.	D	14.	C
5.	D	15.	B
6.	C	16.	D
7.	B	17.	D
8.	B	18.	C
9.	A	19.	D
10.	A	20.	A

21. B
22. A
23. A
24. D
25. B

TEST 2

DIRECTIONS: Each question or incomplete statement is followed by several suggested answers or completions. Select the one that BEST answers the question or completes the statement. *PRINT THE LETTER OF THE CORRECT ANSWER IN THE SPACE AT THE RIGHT.*

1. In which one of the following pairs do the two rocks MOST closely resemble each other in appearance?   1____

    A. Basalt and granite
    B. Granite and pegmatite
    C. Conglomerate and sandstone
    D. Felsite and scoria

2. A goniometer is used to measure   2____

    A. crystal angles
    B. crystal displacement
    C. glacial movement
    D. upper wind velocities

3. The bedrock on Manhattan Island is, for the MOST part,   3____

    A. granite   B. schist   C. sandstone   D. gneiss

4. Geodes are MOST commonly found in which one of the following?   4____

    A. Granite   B. Limestone   C. Sandstone   D. Shale

5. Foliation is associated with the class of rocks known as   5____

    A. igneous
    B. sedimentary
    C. metamorphic
    D. fossiliferous

6. The cap rock of Niagara Falls is a massive layer of   6____

    A. basalt   B. limestone   C. sandstone   D. shale

7. Loess is a fine-grained sedimentary rock deposited by   7____

    A. precipitation from water solutions
    B. continental glaciers
    C. slow-flowing streams
    D. wind action

8. The Sierra Nevada Mountains were formed PRINCIPALLY by   8____

    A. folding
    B. block faulting
    C. thrust faulting
    D. glaciation

9. A shallow horseshoe-shaped lake was PROBABLY formed as a result of   9____

    A. an earthquake
    B. glaciation
    C. river action
    D. a volcanic eruption

10. Sink holes occur PRINCIPALLY in regions whose bedrock is   10____

    A. granite   B. limestone   C. schist   D. sandstone

11. Abandoned iron mines in the Adirondack Mountains of New York have recently been re-opened for the recovery of

    A. manganese   B. titanium   C. antimony   D. strontium

12. A metamorphic rock composed PRINCIPALLY of the mineral calcite is

    A. gneiss   B. marble   C. schist   D. slate

13. A pair of minerals ALWAYS found in granites is

    A. augite and magnetite
    B. calcite and mica
    C. feldspar and quartz
    D. hornblende and talc

14. Within the confines of Greater New York, rock deposited in the Age of the Dinosaurs is

    A. a sandstone on Staten Island
    B. gneiss in the Bronx
    C. marble beneath the East River
    D. schist in Central Park

15. The mineral MOST resistant to both chemical and mechanical weathering is

    A. calcite   B. hornblende   C. feldspar   D. quartz

16. At the end of 11,000 years, the percentage of carbon-14 that will be found in an artifact is CLOSEST to which one of the following?

    A. 10%   B. 18%   C. 25%   D. 50%

17. Instead of a Geiger tube, the scintillation counter contains a crystal of

    A. zinc sulphate
    B. uranium oxide
    C. sodium carbonate
    D. sodium iodide

18. Which one of the following pairs includes a metamorphic rock and the rock from which it was derived?

    A. Slate, limestone
    B. Granite, shale
    C. Obsidian, marble
    D. Sandstone, quartzite

19. When feldspar decomposes, it forms the mineral

    A. flint   B. kaolinite   C. hornblende   D. talc

20. Plaster of Paris is made from the mineral

    A. gypsum   B. anhydrite   C. aragonite   D. calcite

21. Of the following minerals, the one that has been MOST often used in the manufacture of phosphate-rich fertilizers is

    A. kaolinite   B. feldspar   C. apatite   D. fluorite

22. The chemical composition of the mineral pyrite is

    A. $FeCO_3$ B. $AuTe_2$ C. FeS_2 D. Fe_2O_3

23. The MOST porous rock among the following is 23____
    A. slate   B. quartzite   C. basalt   D. conglomerate

24. Of the following rocks, the one that will NOT effervesce in cold dilute hydrochloric acid is 24____
    A. basalt   B. marble   C. limestone   D. chalk

25. Of the following rocks, the one that cooled MOST slowly from the molten state was 25____
    A. obsidian   B. gabbro   C. basalt   D. felsite

KEY (CORRECT ANSWERS)

1. B		11. B	
2. A		12. B	
3. B		13. C	
4. B		14. A	
5. C		15. D	
6. B		16. C	
7. D		17. D	
8. B		18. D	
9. C		19. B	
10. B		20. A	

21. C
22. C
23. D
24. A
25. B

TEST 3

DIRECTIONS: Each question or incomplete statement is followed by several suggested answers or completions. Select the one that BEST answers the question or completes the statement. *PRINT THE LETTER OF THE CORRECT ANSWER IN THE SPACE AT THE RIGHT.*

1. Of the following, the bedrock of a karst region is MOST likely to be
    A. granite B. sandstone C. limestone D. shale

2. Of the following rocks, the one that contains visible crystals of feldspar is
    A. granite B. marble C. sandstone D. shale

3. The BEST evidence for a past period of arid climate is an extensive deposit of which one of the following?
    A. Limestone B. Salt C. Shale D. Glacial till

4. Among the following substances, the SOFTEST is
    A. topaz B. quartz C. feldspar D. calcite

5. Of the following, the MOST reliable estimates of the age of the earth are obtained by a study of
    A. index fossils
    B. radioactive minerals
    C. the salt content of the oceans
    D. the thickness of sedimentary rocks

6. The size of crystals of an igneous rock is determined PRIMARILY by its
    A. chemical composition   B. rate of cooling
    C. specific gravity   D. acidity

7. Among the following, the bedrock MOST rapidly destroyed by ground water is
    A. schist B. sandstone C. limestone D. gneiss

8. Wind deposits of unstratified, yellowish silt are called
    A. loess B. mantle C. talus D. creep

9. Fossils are MOST likely to be found in rocks that are classified as
    A. igneous B. sedimentary C. metamorphic D. granitic

10. On the Mohs' scale of hardness, a penny has a hardness that is CLOSEST to which one of the following?
    A. 1 B. 3 C. 5 D. 7

11. Of the following types of igneous intrusion, the one that commonly forms the core of mountain ranges is called a
    A. dike B. sill C. laccolith D. batholith

12. Of the following, the mineral group MOST resistant to weathering is

    A. feldspar   B. mica   C. quartz   D. amphibole

13. Among the following minerals, the one that will effervesce with cold dilute hydrochloric acid is

    A. selenite   B. calcite   C. fluorite   D. brotite

14. The soapstone used as the acid-resistant top of chemistry laboratory tables is made PRINCIPALLY of

    A. talc   B. andesite   C. rhyolite   D. peridotite

15. Limestone is to marble as shale is to

    A. sandstone   B. slate   C. granite   D. gneiss

16. Of the following substances, the one which BEST shows conchoidal fracture is

    A. galena   B. granite   C. mica   D. obsidian

17. Fossils are MOST likely to be found in which one of the following?

    A. Granite   B. Gneiss   C. Obsidian   D. Shale

18. Iron is obtained from which one of the following?

    A. Bauxite   B. Galena   C. Hematite   D. Chalcopyrite

19. The material commonly used for streak plates in mineral testing is

    A. glass   B. porcelain   C. slate   D. steel

20. Which one of the following characterizes scoria, basalt, pumice, and obsidian?

    A. Dark color   B. Large crystals
    C. Igneous   D. Glassy

21. The MOST common metallic element in the earth's crust is which one of the following?

    A. Silicon   B. Iron   C. Copper   D. Aluminum

22. Fossils are found MOST frequently in

    A. clay   B. sandstone   C. granite   D. basalt

23. Rocks transported and deposited elsewhere by glacial action are called

    A. striae   B. drumlins
    C. Roches mountonnées D. erratics

24. The metamorphic rock formed when pure limestone is recrystallized is

    A. gneiss   B. marble   C. schist   D. slate

25. The one of the following which is the basis for the MOST accurate method of determining the age of rocks is

    A. index fossils   B. rate of decomposition
    C. radioactivity   D. none of these

KEY (CORRECT ANSWERS)

1.	C	11.	D
2.	A	12.	C
3.	B	13.	B
4.	D	14.	A
5.	B	15.	B
6.	B	16.	D
7.	C	17.	D
8.	A	18.	C
9.	B	19.	B
10.	B	20.	C

21. D
22. B
23. D
24. B
25. C

TEST 4

DIRECTIONS: Each question or incomplete statement is followed by several suggested answers or completions. Select the one that BEST answers the question or completes the statement. *PRINT THE LETTER OF THE CORRECT ANSWER IN THE SPACE AT THE RIGHT.*

1. Of the following, the rock which is NOT affected to a great extent by chemical erosion is   1____

    A. calcite   B. marble   C. sandstone   D. limestone

2. A lobster-like invertebrate, the trilobite, was the MOST dominant form of life during the _____ era.   2____

    A. Archeozoic   B. Proterozoic
    C. Paleozoic   D. Mesozoic

3. Modern theory concerning the causes of an ice age asserts that man may inadvertently trigger another ice age by   3____

    A. breaking up the ice in the Arctic Sea
    B. seeding clouds
    C. exploding an H-bomb in the Van Allen belt
    D. none of the above

4. The *Tsunami* result from   4____

    A. earthquakes   B. hurricanes
    C. tornadoes   D. violent thunderstorms

5. The igneous intrusion composing the Palisades of the Hudson is a   5____

    A. laccolith   B. dike
    C. sill   D. none of the above

6. The Black Hills of South Dakota are examples of   6____

    A. dome mountains   B. block mountains
    C. volcanic mountains   D. none of the above

7. Caverns are LEAST likely to form in regions underlain by which one of the following?   7____

    A. Limestone   B. Gypsum   C. Rock salt   D. Sandstone

8. Of the following rock samples, the one which bubbles when treated with hydrochloric acid is   8____

    A. granite   B. sandstone   C. limestone   D. sphalerite

9. Fossils are MOST likely to be found in which one of the following?   9____

    A. Gneiss   B. Shale   C. Obsidian   D. Felsite

10. In which one of the following types of rocks is oil found in oil fields?   10____

    A. Aeolian   B. Metamorphic   C. Igneous   D. Sedimentary

11. Quartz belongs to the crystal system known as

    A. isometric   B. hexagonal   C. monoclinic   D. orthorhombic

12. Of the following minerals, the one MOST abundant in the earth's crust is

    A. feldspar   B. quartz   C. hornblende   D. mica

13. Of the following, the mineral MOST abundant in stony meteorites is

    A. calcite   B. muscovite   C. olivine   D. quartz

14. Of the following, the division of geologic time in which the MOST extensive glaciation occurred in the Southern Hemisphere is the

    A. Jurassic   B. Permian   C. Pleistocene   D. Silurian

15. Of the following, the HARDEST mineral is

    A. apatite   B. fluorite   C. quartz   D. topaz

16. Which one of the following forms of coal has been MOST changed from the original vegetation?

    A. Anthracite   B. Bituminous   C. Lignite   D. Peat

17. Which one of the following fossiliferous organisms is a plant?

    A. Crinoid   B. Diatom   C. Foraminifera   D. Radiolaria

18. Using P for Permian epoch, C for Cambrian epoch, M for Miocene epoch, E for Eocene epoch, which one of the following is the CORRECT sequence going from the oldest to the most recent epoch?

    A. P,C,M,E   B. M,E,P,C   C. C,P,E,M   D. E,M,C,P

19. Which one of the following is a mineral that separates very easily into thin elastic sheets?

    A. Mica   B. Malachite   C. Calcite   D. Quartz

20. A rock specimen, hollow on the inside and partially filled with quartz crystals, is called a

    A. geode   B. neve   C. travertine   D. gabbro

21. Cinnabar is an ore of

    A. mercury   B. tin   C. uranium   D. zinc

22. On the Mohs' scale, a steel pocketknife has a hardness CLOSEST to which one of the following?

    A. 3.5   B. 4.5   C. 5.5   D. 6.5

23. If a mineral specimen weighs 10 grams in air, and when immersed in water appears to weight 7 grams, then the specific gravity of the specimen is

    A. 7/10   B. 1 3/7   C. 2 1/3   D. 3 1/3

24. Of the following, which rock is NOT a sedimentary rock?

    A. Gneiss   B. Limestone   C. Shale   D. Sandstone

25. A geologic feature NOT characteristic of a region that was covered by alpine glaciers is a   25____

    A. hanging valley   B. v-shaped valley
    C. cirque   D. tarn

KEY (CORRECT ANSWERS)

1.	C	11.	B
2.	C	12.	A
3.	A	13.	C
4.	A	14.	B
5.	C	15.	D
6.	A	16.	A
7.	D	17.	B
8.	C	18.	C
9.	B	19.	A
10.	D	20.	A

21. A
22. C
23. D
24. A
25. B

TEST 5

DIRECTIONS: Each question or incomplete statement is followed by several suggested answers or completions. Select the one that BEST answers the question or completes the statement. *PRINT THE LETTER OF THE CORRECT ANSWER IN THE SPACE AT THE RIGHT.*

1. Of the following ratios, the one which would NOT be useful as the basis for a method of dating igenous rocks over 1,000,000 years old is   1___

    A. Uranium 238 / Lead 206
    B. Rubidium 87 / Strontium 87
    C. Carbon 14 / Carbon 12
    D. Potassium 40 / Argon 40

2. Fossil evidence has indisputably shown that the origin of the camel was in which one of the following regions?   2___

    A. Indo-China   B. Egypt
    C. Australia   D. North America

3. Carbonized fossils MOST frequently represent evidence of which one of the following forms of life?   3___

    A. Plants   B. Trilobites   C. Brachiopods   D. Corals

4. Of the following, the CHIEF product of chemical weathering is   4___

    A. clay   B. feldspar   C. mica   D. slate

5. Of the following, the ONLY group that includes one igneous rock, one sedimentary rock, and one metamorphic rock is   5___

    A. arkose, gabbro, quartzite
    B. andesite, basalt, conglomerate
    C. gneiss, marble, shale
    D. limestone, phyllite, schist

6. Of the following, the mineral that is the MOST likely source of kaolin, after weathering, is   6___

    A. calcite   B. feldspar   C. magnetite   D. quartz

7. Of the following, which one is a light spongy rock?   7___

    A. Obsidian   B. Basalt   C. Talus   D. Pumice

8. Which one of the following terms is NOT a process involving chemical decomposition in rocks?   8___

    A. Exfoliation   B. Hydrolysis
    C. Hydration   D. Oxidation

9. Which one of the following will react with dilute hydrochloric acid?   9___

    A. Travertine   B. Kaolin   C. Garnet   D. Gypsum

10. Which one of the following rocks is MOST easily weathered by freezing and thawing?   10_____

    A. Sandstone   B. Obsidian   C. Pegmatite   D. Basalt

11. The bedrock which is MOST widespread in New York City is   11_____

    A. mica schist   B. gneiss   C. dolomite   D. granite

12. In which one of the following regions is bauxite mined?   12_____

    A. Franklin Furnace, New Jersey
    B. Little Rock, Arkansas
    C. Birmingham, Alabama
    D. Bisbee, Arizona

13. Which one of the following minerals can be scratched by a fingernail?   13_____

    A. Selenite   B. Apatite   C. Feldspar   D. Corundum

14. When water and carbon dioxide act on limestone rock to dissolve it, the soluble substance formed has the formula   14_____

    A. $CaCO_3$ B. $CaHCO_3$ C. $Ca(HCO_3)_2$ D. $CaSO_4$

15. The presence of which one of the following produces a pink variety of granite?   15_____

    A. Quartz   B. Feldspar   C. Mica   D. Hornblende

16. Sedimentary rock is forming MOST rapidly today in the   16_____

    A. St. Lawrence River Valley
    B. Pacific Coast of North America
    C. Grand Canyon
    D. Gulf of Mexico

17. The progress of scientific petrology was accelerated by microscopic inspection using   17_____

    A. better staining agents
    B. polarized light
    C. uniform sections
    D. infra-red portion of spectrum

18. Functioning artesian wells may be found when an aquifer occurs between layers of   18_____

    A. shale   B. sandstone   C. conglomerate   D. pumice

19. Which one of the following types of fossil organisms has a short life span and worldwide distribution?   19_____

    A. Fossil assemblages   B. Fossil species
    C. Index fossils   D. Historical fossils

20. In which one of the following are fossils LEAST likely to be found?   20_____

    A. Aeolian sediments   B. Marine sediments
    C. Continental sediments   D. Intrusive igneous rocks

21. Which one of the following is especially important in identifying oil horizons?

    A. Foraminifera
    B. Diatoms
    C. Radiolaria
    D. Graptolites

22. Which one of the following groups BEST describes ostraco-derms?

    A. Primitive, bony, possessing lungs
    B. Primitive, jawless, armored
    C. Ray-finned, fan-tailed
    D. Lobe-finned with only a fringe of true fin

23. The age, in years, of the oldest rocks from which records of geologic history have been decipered in considerable detail is CLOSEST to which one of the following?

    A. 200 million
    B. 500 million
    C. 1.5 billion
    D. 3.0 billion

24. The fine clay found at the top of a varve representing one year of deposition is formed during which one of the following seasons?

    A. Winter
    B. Spring
    C. Summer
    D. Autumn

25. Of the following, which one left the POOREST fossil record?

    A. Echinodermata
    B. Annelida
    C. Mollusca
    D. Brachiopoda

KEY (CORRECT ANSWERS)

1. C	11. A
2. D	12. B
3. A	13. A
4. A	14. C
5. A	15. B
6. B	16. D
7. D	17. B
8. A	18. A
9. A	19. C
10. A	20. D

21. A
22. B
23. B
24. A
25. B

EXAMINATION SECTION
TEST 1

DIRECTIONS: Each question or incomplete statement is followed by several suggested answers or completions. Select the one that BEST answers the question or completes the statement. *PRINT THE LETTER OF THE CORRECT ANSWER IN THE SPACE AT THE RIGHT.*

1. Which one of the following types of coal was formed LARGELY from windblown spores and pollen? 1.____
   A. Lignite B. Cannel C. Bituminous D. Anthracite

2. Which one of the following kinds of fuels has the HIGHEST heat value? 2.____
   A. Anthracite B. Bituminous C. Lignite D. Peat

3. Which one of the following elements in the earth's crust is the MOST abundant? 3.____
   A. Titanium B. Hydrogen C. Sulphur D. Carbon

4. In which one of the following countries are the LARGEST known reserves of mercury ore located? 4.____
   A. Spain B. United States C. Mexico D. Italy

5. The United States relies ALMOST entirely on imports for its supply of 5.____
   A. silver B. aluminum C. tin D. lead

6. Of the following, the rock MOST likely to serve as an aquifer is 6.____
   A. basalt B. granite C. quartzite D. sandstone

7. Of the following, an important ore of titanium is the mineral 7.____
   A. stibnite B. rutile C. realgar D. scheelite

8. Which one of the following countries is the LARGEST producer of nickel ore? 8.____
   A. New Caledonia B. United States
   C. Russia D. Canada

9. Of the following, which one is the PRINCIPAL factor responsible for contact metamorphism? 9.____
   A. Confining pressure
   B. Shearing stress
   C. Temperature
   D. Lack of chemical equilibrium

10. Of the following properties, the one common to chalk, diatomite, kaolin, and talc is 10.____
    A. same chemical composition
    B. overall hardness less than 2
    C. effervescence with dilute HCl
    D. their classification as minerals

11. A xenolith is a

    A. cavity in sedimentary rocks lined with crystals
    B. cavity left in lava by escaping gases
    C. form of igneous intrusion
    D. fragment of country rock enclosed in an igneous intrusion

12. Of the following, an example of a *simple oxide* occurring in nature is the mineral

    A. hematite   B. muscovite   C. labradorite   D. calcite

13. Perthite is a(n)

    A. homogeneous mineral
    B. intimate intergrowth between quartz and orthoclase
    C. intimate intergrowth between two types of feldspar
    D. type of volcanic glass

14. Of the following, the geologic measurement which can be applied ONLY to folds is

    A. strike   B. plunge   C. rake   D. dip

15. Of the following, an example of a clastic or detrital sedimentary rock is

    A. coal   B. coral limestone
    C. siltstone   D. gypsum rock

16. The expression *streak* of a mineral

    A. refers to its luster
    B. is its overall color
    C. is a measure of its brittleness
    D. refers to the color of its powder

17. Of the following rocks, the one having the LOWEST density is

    A. basalt   B. obsidian   C. pumice   D. granite

18. Of the following, the one in which fossils are NEVER found is

    A. asphalt   B. slate   C. amber   D. ice

19. Sedimentary rocks of the Cretaceous and Tertiary ages are PRINCIPALLY found in the Physiographic Province known as the

    A. Appalachian Plateau   B. Folded Appalachians
    C. New England Upland   D. Atlantic Coastal Plain

20. Of the following, the example of an epoch in the geologic time scale is the

    A. Mesozoic   B. Permian   C. Mississippian   D. Pliocene

21. Which of the following events marks the beginning of geologic time?

    A. Formation of the first igneous rock
    B. Formation of the first sedimentary rock
    C. Preservation of the first fossils
    D. First appearance of man on earth

22. Archaeopteryx, a flying animal of the Mesozoic world, belonged to the phylum   22._____

    A. Reptilia   B. Amphibia   C. Aves   D. Mammalia

23. The approximate percentage of geologic time represented by the Pre-Cambrian Era is   23._____

    A. 20%   B. 40%   C. 60%   D. 80%

24. The use of igneous rocks in establishing the geologic time scale depends upon the fact that they   24._____

    A. have a great diversity of composition
    B. usually contain fossils
    C. have invaded earlier rocks of known age
    D. often contain appreciable quantities of radioactive minerals

25. Foraminifera are primitive   25._____

    A. single-celled plants
    B. multi-celled invertebrates
    C. single-celled invertebrates
    D. vertebrates

KEY (CORRECT ANSWERS)

1. B
2. A
3. A
4. A
5. C

6. D
7. B
8. D
9. C
10. B

11. D
12. A
13. C
14. B
15. C

16. D
17. C
18. B
19. D
20. D

21. B
22. C
23. D
24. D
25. C

TEST 2

DIRECTIONS: Each question or incomplete statement is followed by several suggested answers or completions. Select the one that BEST answers the question or completes the statement. *PRINT THE LETTER OF THE CORRECT ANSWER IN THE SPACE AT THE RIGHT.*

1. The type of solid fuel MOST likely to be found in strata which were deeply buried, but not folded, is 1.____
    - A. bituminous coal
    - B. lignite
    - C. anthracite
    - D. peat

2. Of the following, the mineral with a SINGLE perfect cleavage is 2.____
    - A. calcite
    - B. magnetite
    - C. muscovite
    - D. hornblende

3. The PRINCIPAL ore of aluminum is the mineral 3.____
    - A. bauxite
    - B. bornite
    - C. celestite
    - D. cerussite

4. A common ore of lead is 4.____
    - A. magnetite
    - B. galena
    - C. pyrite
    - D. sphalerite

5. Emerald is a gem variety of the mineral 5.____
    - A. garnet
    - B. tourmaline
    - C. beryl
    - D. corundum

6. The end-product of the chemical weathering of feldspar is likely to be 6.____
    - A. kaolin
    - B. quartz
    - C. calcite
    - D. gypsum

7. An igneous rock composed of 60% feldspar, 30% quartz, and 10% hornblende having an even-grained texture is 7.____
    - A. basalt
    - B. gabbro
    - C. granite
    - D. diorite

8. A MOST important feature of distinction between a sandstone and a conglomerate is 8.____
    - A. color
    - B. texture
    - C. hardness
    - D. composition

9. Underground streams are commonly found in regions underlain by 9.____
    - A. shale
    - B. granite
    - C. sandstone
    - D. limestone

10. Taconite is an important reserve source of 10.____
    - A. coal
    - B. copper
    - C. iron
    - D. phosphates

11. The mineral wolframite is an important source of the element 11.____
    - A. osmium
    - B. tantalum
    - C. titanium
    - D. tungsten

12. The mineral whose presence in solution is MOST frequently the cause of hardness in water is 12.____
    - A. calcite
    - B. feldspar
    - C. mica
    - D. quartz

13. Which one of the following does NOT occur as a *native element*?

    A. Carbon   B. Zinc   C. Sulfur   D. Copper

14. The mineral dolomite contains

    A. calcium and iron   B. magnesium and aluminum
    C. potassium and sodium   D. calcium and magnesium

15. An element present in orthoclase feldspars but NOT in plagioclase feldspars is

    A. Al   B. Ca   C. K   D. Na

16. The spectacular development and subsequent extinction of the dinosaurs occurred during the geologic era called

    A. Pre-Cambrian   B. Cenozoic   C. Mesozoic   D. Paleozoic

17. The MOST abundant metal in the earth's crust is

    A. aluminum   B. iron   C. lead   D. copper

18. The PRINCIPAL anthracite coal deposits of the United States occur in the

    A. Appalachian Plateau   B. Atlantic Coastal Plain
    C. Folded Appalachians   D. Piedmont Province

19. Bisbee, Arizona, is MOST famous as a mining center for

    A. copper   B. gold   C. iron   D. lead

20. The rock which MOST commonly forms the aquifer of an artesian formation is

    A. conglomerate   B. limestone   C. sandstone   D. shale

21. Cleavage is possible because of

    A. weaknesses in the atomic structure of minerals
    B. perfectly balanced valence forces
    C. kinetic metamorphism of rocks
    D. mechanical weathering of minerals

22. Of the following, the rock which cooled MOST slowly from a molten state is

    A. granite   B. pumice   C. marble   D. basalt

23. A soft, white rock composed of the calcareous shells of microscopic animals is

    A. kaolin   B. diatomaceous earth
    C. soapstone   D. chalk

24. An example of a fine-grained, clastic sedimentary rock is

    A. limestone   B. gypsum   C. shale   D. pumice

25. Ruby is a gem variety of the mineral

    A. garnet   B. quartz   C. tourmaline   D. corundum

KEY (CORRECT ANSWERS)

1. A
2. C
3. A
4. B
5. C

6. A
7. C
8. B
9. D
10. C

11. D
12. A
13. B
14. D
15. C

16. C
17. A
18. C
19. A
20. C

21. A
22. A
23. D
24. C
25. D

TEST 3

DIRECTIONS: Each question or incomplete statement is followed by several suggested answers or completions. Select the one that BEST answers the question or completes the statement. *PRINT THE LETTER OF THE CORRECT ANSWER IN THE SPACE AT THE RIGHT.*

1. A common ore of zinc is the mineral 1.____
   A. ilmenite B. sphalerite C. pyrite D. carnotite

2. Dense or aphanitic textures are characteristic of igneous rocks which are 2.____
   A. intrusive
   B. light-colored and relatively lightweight
   C. extrusive
   D. dark-colored and relatively heavy

3. The contraction theory was formulated to explain the origin of forces which caused the 3.____
   A. rise of the sea level following the last Ice Age
   B. steady rise of the north shore of the Baltic Sea
   C. folding of the rocks in New York City
   D. elevation of marine terraces along the coast of California

4. Of the following, the one that is NOT a uranium ore is 4.____
   A. autunite B. carnotite C. gummite D. bornite

5. One variety of talc is known as 5.____
   A. enargite B. pitchstone C. selenite D. soapstone

6. A variety of sandstone that is flexible is 6.____
   A. alunite B. itacolumite C. kyanite D. specularite

7. The rock whose mineral content MOST strongly resembles that of granite is 7.____
   A. andesite B. rhyolite C. periodotite D. trachyte

8. A common variety of pyroxene is the mineral 8.____
   A. augite B. beryl C. albite D. olivine

9. The iron ores of the Lake Superior region of the United States occur in rocks whose age is dated as 9.____
   A. Cenozoic B. Mesozoic C. Paleozoic D. Proterozoic

10. The physiographic plateau which leads in the production of uranium ore in the United States is the 10.____
    A. Appalachian B. Colorado C. Columbia D. Ozark

11. The oldest rock which outcrops in New York City and vicinity is 11.____
    A. Manhattan schist   B. Inwood marble
    C. Fordham gneiss   D. Palisades diabase

12. The olivine zone in the Palisades resulted from   12.____

    A. the intrusion of a sill within a sill
    B. metamorphism of part of the sill
    C. gravitational settling of early crystals
    D. slower cooling in the center of the sill

13. The contact between the Newark series and the New York City rocks beneath the Hudson River is a(n)   13.____

    A. normal fault
    B. conformable sedimentary contact
    C. reverse fault
    D. unconformable sedimentary contact

14. The MOST plausible explanation for our failure to find fossils in the rocks underlying the Boroughs of Manhattan and the Bronx is that   14.____

    A. there are too few exposures of these rocks to permit adequate study
    B. the glaciers of the last Ice Age removed the fossil-bearing strata
    C. little or no organic life existed at the time of their formation
    D. metamorphism has obscured or destroyed probable fossil evidence in sedimentary rocks

15. Baluchitherium is the name given by paleontologists to the   15.____

    A. carnivorous flying dinosaur
    B. prehistoric apeman discovered in Tibet
    C. giant shark of Devonian time
    D. largest land mammal ever known

16. Salt deposits in central New York State near Syracuse were formed during the geologic period called the   16.____

    A. Cambrian   B. Miocene   C. Silurian   D. Triassic

17. The LARGEST subdivision of the geologic time scale in terms of elapsed years is a(n)   17.____

    A. epoch   B. period   C. era   D. age

18. Crossopterygians are notable in earth history as   18.____

    A. an early species of dinosaur
    B. primitive seed plants of Mississippian time
    C. ancestors of the first amphibians
    D. a link between reptiles and mammals

19. Of the following, the mountains of GREATEST geologic age are the   19.____

    A. Appalachians   B. Rockies
    C. Sierra Nevadas   D. Cascades

20. Laccoliths are found in   20.____

    A. domed mountains   B. block mountains
    C. folded mountains   D. volcanoes

21. The normal percentage of dissolved mineral matter in sea water (by weight) is APPROXIMATELY   21.____

    A. 1.5   B. 2.5   C. 3.5   D. 4.5

22. A shoreline formed as a result of submergence is a shoreline   22.____

    A. coastal plain   B. delta
    C. fiord   D. volcano

23. The Palisades of New Jersey originated as an igneous intrusion during the period known as   23.____

    A. Eocene   B. Cretaceous   C. Permian   D. Triassic

24. An outstanding example of a glacial trough is the   24.____

    A. Grand Canyon of the Colorado
    B. Yellowstone Canyon in Yellowstone National Park
    C. Yosemite Valley in Yosemite National Park
    D. Zion Canyon in Zion National Park

25. A xenolith is a   25.____

    A. cavity in sedimentary rocks lined with crystals
    B. cavity left in lava by escaping gases
    C. form of igneous intrusion
    D. fragment of country rock enclosed in an igneous intrusion

---

KEY (CORRECT ANSWERS)

1. B		11. C	
2. C		12. C	
3. C		13. D	
4. D		14. D	
5. D		15. D	
6. B		16. C	
7. B		17. C	
8. A		18. C	
9. D		19. A	
10. B		20. A	

21. C
22. C
23. D
24. C
25. D

TEST 4

DIRECTIONS: Each question or incomplete statement is followed by several suggested answers or completions. Select the one that BEST answers the question or completes the statement. *PRINT THE LETTER OF THE CORRECT ANSWER IN THE SPACE AT THE RIGHT.*

1. The Keewatin Glacier of the Pleistocene ice age was centered in
    A. north central Canada
    B. Labrador
    C. Alaska
    D. Greenland

2. The Royal Gorge of the Arkansas River represents a river valley which is
    A. young   B. mature   C. old   D. subdued

3. Sink holes are the result of the work of
    A. earthquakes
    B. underground water
    C. streams
    D. glaciers

4. A river is classified as mature when it includes a
    A. chain of lakes in its course
    B. gorge
    C. series of meanders
    D. series of rapids

5. An esker is a
    A. winding, roughly stratified glacial ridge
    B. linear, unstratified glacial ridge
    C. roughly circular glacial mound
    D. series of glacial elevations and depressions

6. An example of an active volcano of the *quiet* type is
    A. Krakatoa
    B. Mauna Loa
    C. Mt. Lassen
    D. Mt. Vesuvius

7. Stone Mt., Georgia, is classified as a
    A. butte
    B. mesa
    C. monadnock
    D. volcanic neck

8. A rock composed of angular fragments cemented together into a coherent mass is a
    A. breccia   B. tufa   C. conglomerate   D. dacite

9. In Moh's scale of mineral hardness, quartz is number
    A. 5   B. 6   C. 7   D. 8

10. A rock which shows foliated structure is
    A. marble   B. serpentine   C. schist   D. quartzite

110

11. The LATEST of the geological eras is called the 11._____
    A. cenozoic   B. paleozoic   C. proterozoic   D. mesozoic

12. The mineral which is LEAST susceptible to chemical weathering is 12._____
    A. feldspar   B. hornblends   C. augite   D. quartz

13. An animal that is PROBABLY a link between the fish and amphibia is the 13._____
    A. archeopteryx   B. coelacanth
    C. trilobite   D. lamprey

14. Lost rivers or underground streams are MOST likely to occur in regions whose bedrock is 14._____
    A. limestone   B. slate   C. granite   D. conglomerate

15. The commonest cause of hard water is the presence of compounds of 15._____
    A. fluorine   B. calcium   C. iron   D. sulfur

16. All of the following metals are extracted from the minerals with which they are associated below EXCEPT 16._____
    A. iron from hematite   B. uranium from pitchblende
    C. tin from sphalerite   D. lead from galena

17. Iron pyrites, sometimes known as fool's gold, is mined CHIEFLY for use in the manufacture of 17._____
    A. costume jewelry   B. sulfuric acid
    C. porcelain and china   D. paint

18. Of the following groups, the one which contains ONLY metamorphic rocks is 18._____
    A. basalt, diorite, dolomite, shale
    B. conglomerate, granite, serpentine, marble
    C. diabase, schist, obsidian, serpentine
    D. quartzite, gneiss, slate, marble

19. Of the following groups of materials found in the earth's crust, the group in which the items range progressively from softest to hardest is 19._____
    A. talc, fluorite, quartz, diamond
    B. feldspar, gypsum, topaz, corundum
    C. gypsum, quartz, apatite, diamond
    D. calcite, quartz, diamond, corundum

20. Of the following acids, the one MOST often used to test for calcite is cold dilute _____ acid. 20._____
    A. hydrochloric   B. carbonic
    C. sulfuric   D. nitric

21. The destructive distillation of soft coal produces 21._____
    A. coal gas, bitumen, water gas, and tar
    B. ammonia, coal gas, water gas, and coke

C. coal tar, coal gas, ammonia, and coke
D. coal tar, coke, ammonia, and charcoal

22. The bedrock of a large part of New York County is the rock called   22._____
    A. granite   B. quartzite   C. schist   D. trap

23. When in New York City (which is at longitude 75°W), it is 9:00 A.M., real time February 22. In Calcutta (90°E longitude), the real time is which one of the following?   23._____
    A. 8:00 P.M., February 22   B. 8:00 A.M., February 21
    C. 8:00 P.M., February 23   D. 8:00 A.M., February 22

24. The length, in miles, of a degree of longitude at a latitude of 60° is CLOSEST to which one of the following?   24._____
    A. 18   B. 27   C. 35   D. 60

25. Which one of the following is a natural water softener frequently used in the laboratory?   25._____
    A. Activated charcoal   B. Sodium Zeolite
    C. Sodium silicate   D. Alum

KEY (CORRECT ANSWERS)

1. A   11. A
2. A   12. D
3. B   13. B
4. D   14. A
5. A   15. B

6. B   16. C
7. C   17. B
8. A   18. D
9. C   19. A
10. C   20. A

21. C
22. C
23. A
24. C
25. B

EXAMINATION SECTION
TEST 1

DIRECTIONS: Each question or incomplete statement is followed by several suggested answers or completions. Select the one that BEST answers the question or completes the statement. *PRINT THE LETTER OF THE CORRECT ANSWER IN THE SPACE AT THE RIGHT.*

1. Which of the following is a dating technique that can be used to date rocks older than Cenozoic in age?

   A. Radiocarbon (^{14}C)
   B. Dendrochronology
   C. Stable isotope fractionation
   D. Potassium-argon
   E. Amino acid racemization

1.____

Questions 2-4.

DIRECTIONS: Questions 2 through 4 consist of five lettered headings followed by a list of numbered sentences. For each numbered sentence, select the one heading that is MOST closely related to it. One heading may be used once, more than once, or not at all.

   A. Aragonite-calcite
   B. Calcite-dolomite
   C. Magnetite-hematite
   D. Hematite-goethite
   E. Pyrite-marcasite

2. The two minerals are usually found together in modern sediments, but are rarely found together in ancient sediments.

2.____

3. The difference between the two minerals is in the oxidation state of the metallic ion.

3.____

4. The difference between the two minerals is in the state of hydration.

4.____

5.

5.____

The map shows a mid-oceanic ridge offset by a transform fault A-B.
According to the concept of sea-floor spreading, what is the relative motion between the north and south sides of the fault for the segment between A and B?

113

A. The north side of the fault is moving west relative to the south side.
B. The north side of the fault is moving east relative to the south side.
C. The north side of the fault is moving up relative to the south side.
D. The north side of the fault is moving down relative to the south side.
E. There is no relative movement between the north and south sides of the fault.

6. Which of the following represents the MOST definitive evidence for the existence of a fluid core in the Earth?

    A. The presence of strong compressional waves transmitted through the core
    B. A shadow zone for P waves at angular distances greater than 105°
    C. The absence of S waves at angular distances greater than 105°
    D. A greater period of the Chandler motion than would be observed for a rigid Earth
    E. A marked increase in electrical conductivity at a depth of about 2,900 km

7. An exploration geologist making a search for an abundant source of niobium, rare earths, titanium, and apatite should look for areas that contain

    A. carbonatites in alkalic provinces
    B. marble in Precambrian basements
    C. anorthosites in lopoliths
    D. schists of high-grade facies
    E. graywackes in eugeosynclines

Questions 8-9.

DIRECTIONS: Questions 8 and 9 are to be answered on the basis of the following phase diagram of a binary mineral system XY.

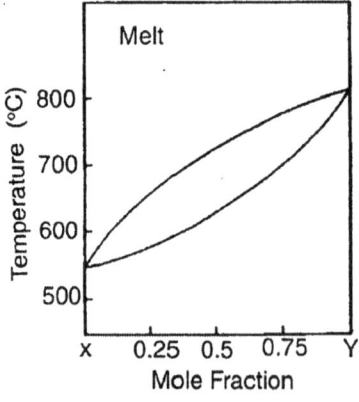

8. Mineral species X and Y exhibit _____ solid solution and _____ crystal structures.

    A. slight; differing
    B. no; isomorphous
    C. no; differing
    D. complete; differing
    E. complete; isomorphous

9. From the diagram, one can conclude that in a mineral system of this type, which of the following is TRUE?

   A. Addition of one component to the other always lowers the melting temperature
   B. The first melt to form from a solid of composition $X_{0.5}Y_{0.5}$ is more enriched in the low melting component than in the original solid
   C. The final stages of crystallization produce a eutectic mixture of X and Y
   D. There is a high heat of mixing of X and Y in the solid state
   E. None of the above

10. Which of the following mineral assemblages is MOST characteristic of the contact metamorphism of a siliceous dolomitic limestone that contains clay as an impurity?

    A. Beryl, garnet, tourmaline, diopside, corundum
    B. Amblygonite, magnetite, tremolite, barite, quartz
    C. Sphene, lepidolite, idocrase, quartz, natrolite
    D. Wollastonite, tremolite, diopside, spinel, garnet
    E. Garnet, serpentine, apatite, rutile, fluorite

11. What marine invertebrate group, whose fossils are known from rocks as old as Devonian, was a common element of Mesozoic marine faunas but became extinct at the close of the Cretaceous?

    A. Crinoids   B. Brachiopods   C. Corals
    D. Bryozoans   E. Ammonoids

12. Ancient glacial and periglacial deposits commonly contain all of the following EXCEPT

    A. dropstone-bearing laminated pebbly mudstone sequences
    B. varve sequences
    C. striated pavement
    D. striated pebbles in diamictite
    E. hummocky cross-beds

13.

The three drill holes shown above are on an east-west line and they have the same surface elevation with respect to sea level. The distance between adjacent holes is 20 kilometers.
The MOST probable explanation for the varying depth of the base of the conglomerate is that

- A. there has been folding following the deposition of the conglomerate
- B. there is an unconformity at the base of the conglomerate
- C. the compaction of sediment below the conglomerate in drill hole III has caused subsidence
- D. there is a facies change between the marine shale and the conglomerate
- E. the conglomerates are the same distance below the limestone-containing corals

14. When three adjacent piezometers are emplaced at different depths, it is observed that hydraulic head increases with depth. This implies that

    - A. a confined aquifer has been encountered
    - B. a downward component of flow exists
    - C. lateral flow is occurring
    - D. an upward component of flow exists
    - E. the piezometers are in a perched aquifer

15.

    Notes on sample localities:
    - 2. Fusulines in limestone
    - 3. Basalt
    - 5. Dinosaur tracks in sandstone
    - 7. Trilobites in calcareous shale
    - 10. Tabulate corals in limestone
    - 11. Andesite

    The rocks on the geologic map above are sedimentary unless otherwise indicated. The oldest possible age of any rock on the map is

    - A. Precambrian
    - B. Cambro-Ordovician
    - C. Siluro-Devonian
    - D. Permo-Carboniferous
    - E. Early Mesozoic

16. The development of which of the following features was MOST critical in completely freeing vertebrates from an aquatic environment?

    - A. Lungs
    - B. Bony brain case
    - C. Tetrapod limb
    - D. Differentiated dentition
    - E. Amniote egg

17. Which of the following groups of terms refers either to features associated *only* with continental glaciation or to features associated *only* with mountain glaciation?

A. Horns, outwash plains, erratics, end moraines, striated surfaces
B. Horns, cols, cirques, medial moraines
C. Striated surfaces, pitted outwash plains, cirques
D. Crevasse fillings, kames, erratics, hanging valleys, recessional moraines
E. Drumlins, eskers, striated surfaces, cirques, valley trains

18. Which of the following factors is LEAST important in governing organic productivity in the oceans?

    A. Water density
    B. Rate of upwelling
    C. Thickness of the thermocline
    D. Quantity of nutrients
    E. Seasons

19.

    All of the carnotite in the cross-section above is determined to be 3.5×10^7 years old. Which of the following is the MOST reasonable interpretation of the sequence of events resulting in the deposit and of the ages of the components?
    The

    A. shale is Cretaceous, the sandstone is Cretaceous, and the carnotite came in by groundwater in the Early Tertiary
    B. shale, the sandstone, the dinosaur bone, and the carnotite were all deposited within a few weeks of each other
    C. dinosaur bone was eroded from Cretaceous sediments but deposited in the channel sandstone during the Tertiary; afterwards the carnotite was deposited by groundwater
    D. channel sandstone was deposited by an Eocene river that had eroded carnotite-cemented sandstone containing the dinosaur bone
    E. dinosaur bone and the carnotite cement were both deposited in Cretaceous times

20. The base of the Earth's crust (Mohorovičić discontinuity) is defined by

    A. a contrast in seismic velocity
    B. an abrupt change in density
    C. the boundary between mafic and ultramafic rocks
    D. a phase boundary between basalt and eclogite
    E. the depth of isostatic compensation

21. High confining pressure has which of the following effects on a rock? It

    A. decreases the elastic range of deformation
    B. decreases the strength
    C. produces the same effect as an increase in temperature
    D. increases the permeability
    E. increases the ductility

Questions 22-23.

DIRECTIONS: Questions 22 and 23 are to be answered on the basis of the diagram below.

22. When did the folding of D take place?

    A. Before the formation of E
    B. At the time of the faulting at B
    C. After the faulting at B
    D. Before the formation of F
    E. Before the formation of C

23. When did the folding of H on the right side of the block take place?

    A. After the faulting at B
    B. At the time of the faulting at B
    C. Before the deposition of D
    D. Before the intrusion of G
    E. Before the faulting at A

24. Assume that a mountain range with an average height of 3,000 meters is supported isostatically by a *mountain root*. The average density of the range and its root is 2.7 and that of the substratum is 3.3 grams per cubic centimeter.
    If the mountain range lost an average thickness of 600 meters by erosion, approximately how much would it have to rise to restore isostatic equilibrium?
    _____ m.

    A. 160   B. 490   C. 600   D. 640   E. 730

25. The difference in elevation between the base and the top of a formation in a vertical cliff 25.____
is 100 meters. The formation dips 40 to the east.
What is the true thickness of the formation? (Data for aid in computation: sin 40° = 0.64; cos 40° = 0.76; tan 40° = 0.84; cot 40° = 1.19)
_____ m.

A. 25 B. 64 C. 76 D. 84 E. 90

KEY (CORRECT ANSWERS)

1. D   11. E
2. A   12. E
3. C   13. B
4. D   14. D
5. B   15. B

6. C   16. E
7. A   17. B
8. E   18. A
9. B   19. A
10. D   20. A

21. E
22. A
23. A
24. B
25. C

EXAMINATION SECTION
TEST 1

DIRECTIONS: Each question or incomplete statement is followed by several suggested answers or completions. Select the one that BEST answers the question or completes the statement. *PRINT THE LETTER OF THE CORRECT ANSWER IN THE SPACE AT THE RIGHT.*

1. Water that is associated with the formation of rocks is classified as

   A. metamorphic
   B. magmatic
   C. volcanic
   D. plutonic

2. Which of the following sources of groundwater contamination would be classified as a *Category 5* source?

   A. Construction excavation
   B. Irrigation practices
   C. De-icing salts application
   D. Hazardous waste, land application

3. *Artesian* water is water that comes from

   A. underground springs
   B. a confined source
   C. just below the water table
   D. glacial outwash

4. Which of the following types of sedimentary rock has the HIGHEST porosity?

   A. Sandstone   B. Limestone   C. Shale   D. Siltstone

5. Contaminant withdrawal designed *specifically* for the removal of volatile compounds from the unsaturated zone is effected by use of

   A. pumping
   B. interceptor systems
   C. soil venting
   D. excavation

6. In a porous medium, heat is transported by each of the following processes EXCEPT

   A. conduction
   B. advection
   C. radiation
   D. convection

7. Pressure recovery in a borehole after the withdrawal of a known volume of water is termed _____ testing.

   A. time-drawdown
   B. drillstem
   C. slug injection
   D. borehole-dilution

8. Which of the following is NOT a fundamental purpose for the artificial recharge of a water source?

   A. Prevention or retardation of saltwater intrusion
   B. Replenishment of depleted supplies
   C. Maintenance of normal seismic conditions
   D. Underground storage to supplement inadequate surface-storage facilities

9. The method of hydraulic testing used to determine the seepage velocity of a groundwater resource is called

   A. borehole-dilution
   B. distance-drawdown
   C. drill stem
   D. slug injection

10. Mass transport caused by flow of water in which the mass is dissolved is termed

    A. dispersion
    B. dissolution
    C. vectorization
    D. advection

11. Water below the zone of saturation is classified as _____ water.

    A. subsurface
    B. internal
    C. gravitational
    D. interstitial

12. Each of the following is a factor in determining safe yield of a groundwater resource EXCEPT

    A. permissible cost of pumping
    B. average annual recharge
    C. advection rate
    D. water table level

13. Which of the following methods of hydraulic testing requires both a pumping well and an observation well?

    A. Drillstem
    B. Slug injection
    C. Borehole-dilution
    D. Time-drawdown

14. Which of the following contaminants is classified as a volatile?

    A. Arsenic   B. Phenol   C. Toluene   D. Chlordane

15. The DOMINANT nutrient contaminant in groundwater supplies is

    A. iron   B. nitrate   C. ammonium   D. phosphorus

16. Which of the following substances is NOT used in the age-dating of groundwater?

    A. Carbon-14   B. Tritium   C. Chlorine-36   D. Strontium

17. Natural material that stores water and transmits enough water to be significant in regional migration studies, but not enough to supply individual wells, is called

    A. aquiclude   B. aquifer   C. aquitard   D. aquifuge

18. The use of seeded bacteria to transform organic compounds into less hazardous compounds is an example of

    A. bioremediation
    B. slug injection
    C. an interceptor system
    D. artificial recharge

19. Contaminants described as light non-aqueous phase liquids (LNAPLs) are MOST often found

    A. at the top of the capillary fringe
    B. in the saturated zone
    C. at the water table
    D. in soil water

20. Each of the following is a major source of trace metal contamination in groundwater EXCEPT   20.____

    A. agricultural wastes   B. urban runoff
    C. subsurface percolation   D. fossil fuels

21. Another term for *permeability* is   21.____

    A. transmissivity   B. hydraulic conductivity
    C. flux   D. porosity

22. Which of the following materials would be found at the HIGHEST point in an alluvial fan deposit?   22.____

    A. Sand   B. Mud   C. Clay   D. Gravel

23. Water that is in or derived from a magma at a depth of several kilometers is classified as   23.____

    A. metamorphic   B. magmatic
    C. volcanic   D. plutonic

24. Which of the following factors would DIRECTLY influence the shape of a contaminant solute plume?   24.____

    A. Presence of sources or sinks
    B. Configuration of water table
    C. Hydraulic conductivity distribution within the flow field
    D. Shape of flow domain

25. Water returns through the atmosphere through each of the following processes EXCEPT   25.____

    A. volatilization   B. transpiration
    C. evaporation   D. sublimation

KEY (CORRECT ANSWERS)

1. A
2. A
3. B
4. D
5. C

6. B
7. C
8. C
9. A
10. D

11. B
12. C
13. D
14. C
15. B

16. D
17. C
18. A
19. A
20. C

21. B
22. D
23. D
24. C
25. A

TEST 2

DIRECTIONS: Each question or incomplete statement is followed by several suggested answers or completions. Select the one that BEST answers the question or completes the statement. *PRINT THE LETTER OF THE CORRECT ANSWER IN THE SPACE AT THE RIGHT.*

1. _____ flow is NOT a component part of a hydrograph.   1._____

   A. Overland   B. Sub   C. Inter   D. Base

2. Which of the following is NOT an essential feature in determining the response of a basin to pumping?   2._____

   A. Distance to recharge area
   B. Configuration of cone of depression
   C. Character of recharge
   D. Distance to area of natural discharge

3. In a spreading basin, the hydraulic response to a recharge well MOST often takes the form of a   3._____

   A. mound   B. cone of impression
   C. cone of recharge   D. cone of depression

4. Which of the following is NOT an example of *point-source* contamination?   4._____

   A. Disposal pond
   B. Leaking storage tank
   C. Nitrate effluents form household disposal
   D. Sanitary landfill leachate

5. Which of the following sediments has the LOWEST porosity?   5._____

   A. Gravel   B. Clay   C. Silt   D. Sand

6. The MOST economical method of water sampling for near-surface investigations in non-cohesive sand or silts is the _____ method.   6._____

   A. conventional standpipe nest
   B. movable packer arrangement
   C. multilevel, single borehole
   D. single level, single borehole

7. The rate of flow of water at a prevailing temperature through a vertical strip of aquifer extending the full saturated thickness of the aquifer is a measure known as   7._____

   A. head   B. transmissivity
   C. hydraulic potential   D. conductivity

8. Each of the following is an advantage associated with the use of piezometer nests for water sampling procedures, as opposed to single-borehole methods, EXCEPT   8._____

   A. relative durability   B. lower cost
   C. ease in measuring water level   D. less difficulty in seal installation

125

9. Which of the following materials has the HIGHEST permeability?

   A. Sandstone
   B. Silt
   C. Fractured crystalline rock
   D. Well-sorted gravel

10. Of the following sources of groundwater contamination, a(n) _____ be classified as a *Category 4* source.

    A. open dump
    C. mine drainage
    B. saltwater intrusion
    D. septic tank

11. Which of the following materials would have the HIGHEST specific yield?

    A. Dune sand
    C. Sandstone
    B. Peat
    D. Limestone

12. The specific _____ of a water resource is expressed as a ratio of the volume of water that drains by gravity to the total volume of rock in the aquifer.

    A. yield   B. capacity   C. retention   D. storage

13. If an aquifer is bounded by a stream that provides recharge, the effect will be

    A. the production of another constant-head boundary
    B. a decrease in specific yield
    C. a decrease in well drawdown
    D. an increase in well drawdown

14. The saturated zone is separated from soil water by the _____ zone.

    A. intermediate
    C. phreatic
    B. vadose
    D. interstitial

15. Which of the following is an isotope that does NOT naturally appear in water?

    A. H_2 B. H_3 C. O_{14} D. O_{17}

16. Each of the following is a factor determining the vertical stress associated with basin loading EXCEPT

    A. hydraulic gradient
    B. depth
    C. density of saturated rock
    D. acceleration due to gravity

17. What is the term for subsurface rock which stores water but does not transmit significant amounts?

    A. Aquiclude   B. Aquifer   C. Aquitard   D. Aquifuge

18. Water that has never been in contact with the hydrosphere is classified as

    A. juvenile
    B. metamorphic
    C. connate
    D. plutonic

19. Mass is spread beyond the region it normally would occupy, due to lateral flow, through the process of

    A. volatilization
    B. dispersion
    C. dissolution
    D. advection

20. Which of the following is NOT an example of organic priority pollutants?

    A. Trace metals
    B. Volatiles
    C. Acid extractables
    D. Pesticides

21. In any region bound in part by a constant head, the flow must be directed

    A. at 45-degree angles from or toward the boundary
    B. upward or downward at angles not exceeding 60 degrees
    C. in lines parallel to the boundary lines
    D. at right angles from or toward the boundary

22. Which type of rock fractures are normal to each other, and not related to a single stress state?

    A. Conjugate
    B. Schematic
    C. Regional
    D. Orthogonal

23. The method of contaminant withdrawal used *specifically* to collect contaminant close to the water table is

    A. pumping
    B. interceptor systems
    C. soil venting
    D. excavation

24. Regions where the flow of water is directed *downward* with respect to the water table are classified as _____ areas.

    A. influent   B. recharge   C. effluent   D. discharge

25. Streams that lose water to a groundwater reservoir are classified as

    A. effluent   B. base   C. influent   D. runoff

KEY (CORRECT ANSWERS)

1. B
2. B
3. A
4. C
5. A

6. C
7. B
8. B
9. D
10. C

11. B
12. A
13. C
14. A
15. C

16. A
17. A
18. A
19. B
20. A

21. D
22. D
23. B
24. B
25. C

———

270 BASIC PRINCIPLES OF PHYSICS, CHEMISTRY, AND GEOLOGY

CONTENTS

	Page
PRINCIPLES OF PHYSICS	1
I. General Properties of Energy and Matter	1
II. Mechanics of Solids	1
III. Mechanics of Liquids	2
IV. Mechanics of Gases	2
V. Heat	3
VI. Sound	4
VII. Light	5
VIII. Magnetism	6
IX. Static Electricity	5
X. Current Electricity	6
XI. Atomic Energy and Radiation	6
PRINCIPLES OF CHEMISTRY	8
I. Chemical Nature of Water	8
II. Structure of Matter	9
III. Solutions and Colloids	10
IV. Ions in Solution-Electrolytes	10
V. Carbon and Organic Chemistry	11
PRINCIPLES OF GEOLOGY	12
I. Diastrophism and Vulcanism	12
II. Degradation	

270 BASIC PRINCIPLES OF PHYSICS, CHEMISTRY AND GEOLOGY

I. **GENERAL PROPERTIES OF ENERGY AND MATTER**
   1. Energy can be changed from one form to another, or to matter, with exact equivalence.
   2. Fluids have no elastic limit for compression.
   3. The distortion of an elastic body is proportional to the force applied provided the elastic limit is not exceeded.
   4. All liquids are compressible but only to a slight degree.
   5. Gases may be converted into liquid by reducing the speed of their molecules.
   6. If the vapor pressure of the water of hydration is greater than that of the moisture of the air, crystals will gradually yield up water to the air, and vice versa.
   7. The free surface of a liquid contracts to the smallest possible area due to surface tension.
   8. A liquid will rise in a capillary tube if the contact angle between the liquid and the side of the tube is less than 90° and will be depressed if the contact angle is greater than 90°.
   9. The height to which a liquid rises in a capillary tube is directly proportional to the surface tension of the liquid and inversely proportional to the density of the liquid and to the radius of the tube.

II. **MECHANICS OF SOLIDS**
   10. When forces act in the same direction, the resultant is their algebraic sum.
   11. When two forces act upon the same object, the resultant is the diagonal of a parallelogram whose sides represent the direction and magnitude of the two forces. A single force represented by the diagonal may be resolved into two forces represented by the sides of the parallelogram.
   12. When the resultant of all the forces acting on a body is zero, the body will stay at rest if at rest, or it will keep in uniform motion in a straight line if it is in motion.
   13. A spinning body offers resistance to any force which changes the direction of the axis about which the body rotates.
   14. Any two bodies attract one another with a force which is directly proportional to the attracting masses and inversely proportional to the square of the distance between their centers of mass.
   15. Movements of all bodies in the solar system are due to gravitational attraction and inertia.
   16. The period of a pendulum swinging through short arcs is independent of the weight of the bob but varies directly as the square root of the length and inversely as the square root of the acceleration of gravity.
   17. The speed gained by a body with constant acceleration is equal to the product of the acceleration and the time.
   18. The acceleration of a body is proportional to the resultant force acting on that body and is in the direction of that force.
   19. The distance a body travels, starting from rest with a constant acceleration, is one-half the acceleration times the square of the time.
   20. At any point on the earth's surface all bodies fall with a constant acceleration which is independent of the mass or size of the body if air resistance be neglected.
   21. The amount of momentum possessed by an object is proportional to its mass and to its velocity.

22. When one body exerts a force on a second body, the second body exerts an equal and opposite force on the first.
23. Bodies in rotation tend to fly out in a straight line which is tangent to the arc of rotation.
24. Centrifugal force is directly proportional to the square of the velocity, to the mass, and inversely proportional to the radius of rotation.
25. The energy which a body possesses on account of its motion is called kinetic energy and is proportional to its mass and the square of its velocity.
26. The energy which a body possesses on account of its position or form is called potential energy and is measured by the work that was done in order to bring it into the specified condition.
27. The work obtained from a simple machine is always equal to the work put into it less the work expended in overcoming friction.
28. When there is a gain in mechanical advantage by using a simple machine, there is a loss in speed and vice versa.
29. In the lever, the force times its distance from the fulcrum equals the weight times its distance from the fulcrum.
30. In the inclined plane, weight times height equals acting force times length, providing friction is neglected and the force is parallel to the plane.
31. Sliding friction is dependent upon the nature and condition of the rubbing surfaces, proportional to the force pressing the surfaces together, and independent of area of contact.
32. The amount of heat developed in doing work against friction is proportional to the amount of work thus expended.

III. MECHANICS OF LIQUIDS

33. Any homogeneous body of liquid free to take its own position will seek a position in which all exposed surfaces lie on the same horizontal plane.
34. The pressure in a fluid in the open is equal to the weight of the fluid above a unit area including the point at which the pressure is taken; it therefore varies as the depth and average density of the fluid.
35. The pressure at a point in any fluid is the same in all directions.
36. When pressure is applied to any area of a liquid in a closed container, it is transmitted in exactly the same intensity to every area of the container in contact with the liquid.
37. As the velocity of flow through a constricted area increases, the pressure diminishes.
38. A body immersed or floating in a fluid is buoyed up by a force equal to the weight of the fluid displaced.
39. The rate of osmosis is directly proportional to the difference in concentration on opposite sides of the membrane.

IV. MECHANICS OF GASES

40. The atmospheric pressure decreases as the altitude increases.
41. The atmospheric pressure decreases with increasing water vapor content, other things being equal.
42. A fluid has a tendency to move from a region of higher pressure to one of lower pressure; the greater the difference, the faster the movement.
43. In the northern hemisphere great volumes of air revolve in a counterclockwise direction, and in the southern hemisphere, they revolve in a clockwise direction.
44. In moving air, wind pressure increases as the square of the velocity.

45. The volume of an ideal gas varies inversely with the pressure upon it, providing the temperature remains constant.
46. If the same pressure is maintained, the volume of a gas is varied directly as the absolute temperature.
47. If the volume of a confined body of gas is kept constant, the pressure is proportional to the absolute temperature.
48. When a mixture of gases is confined, each exerts its own pressure without reference to the pressure exerted by others.
49. Diffusible substances tend to scatter from the point of greatest concentration until all points are at equal concentration.
50. A gas always tends to expand throughout the whole space available.
51. The speed of diffusion of gases varies inversely with the square root of their densities.

V. HEAT

52. The average speed of molecules increases with the temperature and pressure.
53. Most bodies expand on heating and contract on cooling; the amount of change depending upon the change in temperature.
54. The total change in length of a metal bar is equal to its coefficient of linear expansion times the original length times the change of temperature in degrees Centigrade.
55. A change in state of a substance from gas to liquid, liquid to solid, or vice versa, is usually accompanied by a change in volume.
56. Substances which expand upon solidifying have their melting points lowered by pressure; those which contract upon solidifying have their melting points raised by pressure.
57. Heat is liberated when a gas is compressed, and is absorbed when a gas expands.
58. Heat is conducted by the transfer of kinetic energy from molecule to molecule.
59. When two bodies of different temperature are in contact, there is a continuous transference of heat energy, the rate of which is directly proportional to the difference of temperature.
60. Heat is transferred by convection, in currents of gases or liquids, the rate of transfer decreasing with an increase in the viscosity of the circulating fluid.
61. The principal cause of wind and weather changes is the unequal heating of different portions of the earth's surface by the sun; thus all winds are convection currents caused by unequal heating of different portions of the earth's atmosphere, and they blow from places of high atmospheric pressure to places of low atmospheric pressure.
62. Radiant energy travels in waves along straight lines, its intensity at any distance from a point source is inversely proportional to the square of the distance from the source.
63. The more nearly vertical the rays of radiant energy, the greater the number that will fall upon a given horizontal area, and the greater is the amount of energy that will be received by that area.
64. The lower the temperature of a body, the less the amount of energy it radiates; the higher the temperature, the greater is the amount of energy radiated.
65. Dark, rough, or unpolished surfaces absorb or radiate energy more effectively than light, smooth, or polished surfaces.
66. Bodies of land heat up and cool off more rapidly and more readily than bodies of water.
67. The atmosphere of the earth tends to prevent the heat of the earth's surface from escaping, and the earth begins to cool only when the amount of heat lost during the night exceeds that gained during the day.

68. Solids are liquefied and liquids are vaporized by heat; the amount of heat used in this process, for a given mass and a given substance, is specific and equals that given off in the reverse process.
69. The amount of heat which a constant mass of liquid or solid acquires when its temperature rises a given amount is identical with the amount it gives off when its temperature falls by that amount.
70. Every pure liquid has its own specific boiling and freezing point.
71. The presence of a dissolved substance will cause the resulting solution to boil at a higher temperature and to freeze at a lower temperature than pure water.
72. Freezing point depression and boiling point elevation are proportional to the concentration of the solution.
73. The boiling point of any solution becomes lower as the pressure is decreased and higher as the pressure is increased.
74. The rate of evaporation of a liquid varies with temperature, area of exposed surface, and saturation and circulation of the gas in contact with the liquid.
75. The rate of vaporization decreases with an increase of concentration of the vapor in the gas in contact with the liquid, the temperature remaining constant.
76. Condensation will occur when a vapor is at its saturation point if centers of condensation are available and if heat is withdrawn.
77. When a gas expands, heat energy is converted into mechanical energy.
78. The higher the temperature of the air, the greater the amount of moisture required to saturate it.
79. The pressure of a saturated vapor is constant at a given temperature, and increases with an increase of temperature.
80. Each combustible substance has a kindling temperature which varies with its condition, but may be greater or less than the kindling temperature of some other substance.

VI. SOUND

81. Sound is produced by vibrating matter and is transmitted by matter.
82. When energy is transmitted in waves, the medium which transmits the wave motion does not move along with the wave, but the energy does.
83. Each vibrating particle in a wave front of any wave motion may be considered as a secondary source of spherical wavelets which spread out from their sources with the velocity of the primary wave.
84. The velocity of sound is directly proportional to the square root of the elasticity modulus and inversely proportional to the square root of the density of the transmitting medium.
85. The speed of sound increases with an increase in temperature of the medium conducting it.
86. The velocity of a wave is equal to the product of its frequency and wave length.
87. Sound waves are reflected in a direction such that the angle of incidence is equal to the angle of reflection.
88. Musical tones are produced when a vibrating body sends out regular vibrations to the ear while only noises are produced when the vibrating body sends out irregular vibrations to the ear.
89. The loudness of a sound depends upon the energy of the sound waves and, if propagated in all directions, decreases inversely as the square of the distance from the source.
90. The higher the pitch of a note, the more rapid the vibrations of the producing body.

91. When a sounding body is moving toward or away from an observer the apparent pitch will be higher or lower, respectively, than the true pitch of the sound emitted.
92. The frequency of the vibration of a stretched string is inversely proportional to its length, diameter, and square root of its density; and directly proportional to the square root of the stretching force.
93. The quality of a musical tone is determined by the pitch and intensity of the different simple tones or harmonics into which it may be resolved.
94. Harmonious musical intervals correspond to very simple frequency ratios.
95. Two sound waves of the same or nearly the same frequency will destructively interfere with each other when the condensations of the one coincide with the rarefactions of the other provided that the directions of propagation are the same.
96. Sound waves or other energy impulses may set up vibrations in a body the amplitude of which is increased if the impulses are exactly timed to correspond to any one of the natural periods of vibration of the body.

VII. LIGHT

97. Energy is often transmitted in the form of waves.
98. Waves travel in straight lines while passing through a homogeneous or uniform medium.
99. When waves-strike an object, they may be absorbed, transmitted, or reflected.
100. Whenever an opaque object intercepts radiant energy traveling in a particular direction, a shadow is cast behind the object.
101. Light travels in straight lines in a medium of uniform optical density.
102. The speed of light in any given substance bears a constant ratio to the speed of light in air.
103. The intensity of illumination decreases as the square of distance from a point source.
104. When light rays are absorbed, some of the light energy is transformed into heat energy.
105. The darker the color of a surface, the better it absorbs light.
106. If a beam of light falls upon an irregular surface, the rays of light are scattered in all directions.
107. When light is reflected, the angle of incidence is equal to the angle of reflection.
108. All rays passing through the center of curvature of a mirror are reflected upon themselves.
109. In a plane mirror a line running from any point on the object to the image of that point is perpendicular to the mirror.
110. An image appears to be as far back of a plane mirror as the object is in front of the mirror and is reversed.
111. When light is incident upon a medium in which it will travel faster and when the angle of incidence is greater than the critical angle, it is totally reflected.
112. When parallel light strikes a concave spherical mirror, the rays, after reflection, pass directly through the principal focus only if the area of the mirror is small compared to its radius of curvature.
113. When light rays pass obliquely from a rare to a more dense medium, they are bent or refracted toward the normal and when they pass obliquely from a dense to a rarer medium, they are bent away from the normal.
114. The dispersion of white light into a spectrum by a prism is caused by unequal refraction of the different wave lengths of light.
115. Parallel light rays may be converged or focused by convex lenses or concave mirrors, diverged by concave lenses or convex mirrors.

116. The curvature of a wave front will be changed a given amount by a lens; namely, 1/F.
117. The sum of the reciprocals of the conjugate focal lengths of a lens or mirror equals the reciprocal or the principal focal length.
118. The dimensions of an image produced by a lens or a mirror are to the dimensions of the object as their respective distances from the lens or mirror are to each other.
119. The colors of objects depend upon what light rays they transmit, absorb, or reflect.
120. Incandescent solids and liquids emit all wave lengths of light and give a continuous spectrum.
121. When white light passes through a substance that absorbs some waves and not others, certain bands of color are missing with the production of an absorption spectrum.
122. Luminous vapors and gases emit only certain kinds of light producing bright-line spectra.
123. When a body which emits a bright line spectrum is moving toward or away from the observer, the lines are shifted toward the short or long wave length end of the spectrum, respectively.
124. A beam of light may become plane polarized as the result of any circumstance which results in the suppression of one of the rectilinear components of the vibration without affecting the components at right angles to it.

VIII. MAGNETISM

125. Pieces of iron, steel, cobalt, or nickel may become magnetized by induction when placed within a magnetic field.
126. A magnet always has two poles and is surrounded by a field of force.
127. Like magnetic poles always repel each other and unlike magnetic poles always attract each other.
128. The force of attraction or repulsion between two magnetic poles varies directly as the product of the pole strengths and inversely as the square of the distance between the poles.
129. Magnets depend for their properties upon the arrangement of the metallic ions of which they are made up.

IX. STATIC ELECTRICITY

130. Electrons have both a magnetic and an electric field.
131. Like electrical charges repel and unlike electrical charges attract.
132. In an uncharged body there are as many protons as electrons and the charges neutralize each other; while a deficiency of electrons produces a plus charge on a body and an excess of electrons produces a negative charge.
133. The force of attraction or repulsion between two small charged bodies varies directly as the product of the two charges and inversely as the square of the distance between the charges.
134. Electrostatic induction is the separation of charges on a conductor through the influence of a neighboring charge.
135. Charges on a conductor tend to stay on the surface and to be greatest on the sharp edges and points

X. CURRENT ELECTRICITY

136. An electric current may be produced in four ways: by rubbing or friction, by chemical action, by the use of magnets, and by induction.
137. An electric current will be produced in a closed circuit including two strips of different metals if one of the junctions is heated or cooled.

138. An electric current will flow in the external circuit when two metals of unlike chemical activity are acted upon by a conducting solution, the more active metal being charged negatively.
139. Electrons will always flow from one point to another along a conductor if this transfer releases energy.
140. Gases conduct electric currents only when ionized.
141. Electrical power is directly proportional to the product of the potential difference and the current.
142. The electrical current flowing in a conductor is directly proportional to the potential difference and inversely proportional to the resistance.
143. All materials offer some resistance to the flow of electric current, and that part of the electrical energy used in overcoming this resistance is transformed into heat energy.
144. The resistance of a metallic conductor depends on the kind of material from which the conductor is made, varies directly with the length, inversely with the cross-sectional area, and increases as the temperature increases.
145. In a parallel circuit the total current is the sum of the separate currents, the voltage loss is the same for each branch, and the total resistance is less than the resistance of any one branch.
146. In a series circuit the current is the same in all parts, the resistance of the whole is the sum of the resistance of the parts, and the voltage loss of the whole is the sum of the voltage losses of the parts.
147. An electrical charge in motion produces a magnetic field about the conductor, its direction being tangential to any circle drawn about the conductor in a plane perpendicular to it.
148. When a current-carrying wire is placed in a magnetic field, there is a force acting on the wire tending to push it at right angles to the direction of the lines of force between the magnetic poles, providing the wire is not parallel to the field.
149. In a transformer the ratio between voltages in the primary and secondary circuits is the same as that between the number of turns of wire in these circuits.
150. Positively charged ions of metals may be deposited on the cathode, as atoms, when a direct current is sent through an electrolyte.
151. The mass of any substance set free by electrolysis is proportional to the current flowing and the time of flow; if the quantity of electricity is kept constant the masses of the various substances set free are proportional to their electrochemical equivalents.
152. The amount of heat produced by an electric current is proportional to the resistance, the square of the current and the time of flow.
153. Energy in kilowatt hours is equal to the product of amperes, volts and time (in hours), divided by one thousand.
154. An e. m. f. is induced in a circuit whenever there is a change in the number of lines of magnetic force passing through the circuit.
155. An induced current always has such a direction that its magnetic field tends to oppose the motion by which the current was produced.
156. The magnitude of an induced e. m. f. is proportional to the rate at which the number of lines of magnetic force change and to the number of turns of wire in the coil.
157. Two electro-magnetic waves having the same frequency and amplitude and traveling in normally the same direction will interfere constructively or destructively, depending upon whether they are in phase or out of phase.
158. Electro-magnetic waves may produce electrical oscillation in a condenser circuit which is so adjusted as to oscillate naturally with the same frequency as that of the incoming waves.
159. Condenser capacitance varies directly with the area of the plates and inversely as the thickness of the insulation between them.

160. Alternating current charges a condenser twice during each cycle inducing opposite charges on the two plates with the result that a current appears to flow through the condenser.
161. By means of high frequency generators or vacuum-tube oscillators, sustained or continuous oscillations can be produced in a condenser circuit. Their intensity is made to vary with audio-frequency currents in a transmitter circuit to produce radio waves.
162. Whenever a high-frequency oscillating current produces in the field around it oscillating electric and magnetic fields, energy in the form of an electromagnetic wave is transmitted through space.

XI. ATOMIC ENERGY AND RADIATION

163. In a tube which contains gas at low pressure subject to an intense electric field, cathode rays, streams of electrons, move away from the negatively charged terminal at high speeds.
164. A number of substances will emit electrons and become positively charged when illuminated by light.
165. Electrons are emitted from any sufficiently hot body.
166. Electrons change energy levels emitting or absorbing energy.
167. When a stream of high speed electrons strikes a body, the atoms of that body emit X-rays.
168. The atoms of all radioactive elements are constantly disintegrating by giving off various rays (alpha, beta, and gamma) and forming helium and other elements.
169. Radioactive emission involves nuclear changes.
170. Radioactivity is independent of all physical conditions: heat; cold, pressure, and chemical state.
171. Matter may be transformed into energy and energy into matter; the sum total, matter plus energy, remains constant.
172. Elements may be changed into other elements.
173. Atoms have great subatomic energy.
174. All matter is made up of protons, neutrons, and electrons.
175. Protons and neutrons only are found in the nucleus of an atom.
176. Some elements have more than one atomic weight due to differences in the neutron content of their nuclei.
177. The mass of an atom is concentrated almost entirely in the nucleus.
178. The distances of successive electron shells from the nucleus of an atom and from each other are much greater than the dimensions of the nucleus itself.
179. Atoms may be broken down by bombarding the nucleus with high speed particles such as protons, alpha particles, and neutrons.
180. Atoms or molecules may lose electrons when struck by high speed electrons or ions.

PRINCIPLES OF CHEMISTRY

I. CHEMICAL NATURE OF WATER

181. Every pure sample of any substance, whether simple or compound, under the same conditions will show the same physical properties and the same chemical behavior.
182. A pure chemical substance may be prepared from raw materials through utilization of their physical and chemical properties.
183. Each element has its own characteristic X-ray spectrum.

184. Every chemical element when heated to incandescence in a gaseous state has a characteristic glow and a characteristic spectrum which can be used to identify very small quantities of the element and which is related to the molecular and atomic structure of the gas.
185. In every sample of any compound substance formed, the proportion by weight of the constituent elements is always the same as long as the isotopic compositions of each element is constant.
186. When different amounts of one element are found in combination with a fixed weight of another element (in a series of compounds), the different weights of the first element are related to each other by ratios which may be expressed by small whole numbers.
187. At a definite temperature and pressure, the relative combining volumes of gases and of gaseous products may be expressed approximately in small whole numbers.
188. The materials forming one or more substances, without ceasing to exist, may be changed into one or more new and measurably different substances.
189. The products of reacting substances may react with each other to form the original substances.
190. The total mass of a quantity of matter is not altered by any chemical changes occurring among the materials composing it.
191. No chemical change occurs without an accompanying energy change.
192. The heat of formation of any chemical compound equals its heat of decomposition.
193. When a chemical change takes place without the addition of heat from an external source, that substance which has the greatest heat of formation will tend to form.
194. Reactions occurring at ordinary temperatures are predominately exothermic.

II. STRUCTURE OF MATTER

195. All matter is composed of single elements or combinations of several elements and can be analyzed by chemical processes and divided into these constituents.
196. All substances are made up of small particles called molecules, which are alike in the same substance (except for variations in molecular weight due to isotopes) but different in different substances.
197. Elements are made up of small particles of matter called atoms which are alike in the same element (except for occasional differences in atomic weight, i.e., isotopes) but different in different elements.
198. The orderly arrangement of molecules, atoms, or ions in crystals gives crystals regular form.
199. Equal volumes of all gases under similar conditions of temperature and pressure contain very nearly the same number of molecules.
200. Atoms of all elements are made up of protons, neutrons, and electrons; and differences between atoms of different elements are due to the number of protons and neutrons in the nucleus and to the configuration of electrons surrounding the nucleus.
201. The electrons within an atom form shells about the nucleus, each of which contains a definite number of electrons.
202. Most atoms have the property of losing, gaining, or sharing a number of outer shell electrons.
203. The properties of the elements show periodic variations with their atomic numbers.
204. The energy shown by atoms in completing their outer shell by adding, losing, or sharing electrons determines their chemical activity.
205. The valence of an atom is determined by the number of electrons it gains, loses, or shares in chemical reactions.

206. A few elements are inert or chemically inactive because their atoms are so constructed as to be complete in themselves; i. e., their outer electron rings have no tendency to gain or lose electrons.
207. The gravimetric composition of a compound may be found by multiplying the atomic weights of the elements by their subscripts in the formula of the compound.
208. Equal amounts of heat raise equal numbers of atoms of all elements in the solid state through nearly equal intervals of temperature.
209. The specific heats of many elements are approximately inversely proportional to their atomic weights.
210. Oxidation always involves the removal or sharing of electrons from the element oxidized, while the reduction always adds or shares with the element reduced.
211. Oxidation and reduction occur simultaneously and are quantitatively equal.
212. Metals comprise a group of elements (other than hydrogen) whose atoms have a tendency to lose electrons readily and whose compounds when dissolved in polar solvents are capable of forming positive ions.
213. Non-metals comprise a group of elements whose atoms tend to gain or share electrons and whose compounds, when dissolved in polar solvents, are capable of forming negative ions.
214. Metals may be arranged in an activity series according to their tendency to pass into ionic form by losing electrons.
215. Non-metals may be arranged in an activity series according to their tendency to pass into ionic form by gaining electrons.

III. SOLUTIONS AND COLLOIDS

216. The ingredients of a solution are homogeneously distributed through each other.
217. Any substance soluble in two immiscible liquids will distribute itself between the two in proportion to its solubility in the two liquids.
218. The solubility of solutes is affected by heat, pressure, and the nature of the solute and solvent.
219. The solubility of a gas in an inert solvent varies directly with the pressure to which a gas is subjected.
220. In a saturated solution, the product of the molar concentrations of the ions is constant.
221. Suspended particles of colloids have a continuous, erratic movement due to colloidal, molecular, or ion impacts.
222. Surface reactions predominate in all non-homogeneous reactions.
223. Colloids show greater chemical activity than the solid substances in mass, since rates of reaction are proportional to the surface area of the solid, other factors being equal.
224. Colloids have the property of absorption to an unusual degree.
225. Colloidal particles may carry electrical charges.
226. Temperature changes, pressure changes, the presence of electrolytes or the presence of oppositely charged particles may cause colloids to precipitate.

IV. IONS IN SOLUTION - ELECTROLYTES

227. All chemical reactions which start with the same quantities of original substances, liberate the same amounts of energy in reaching a given final state, irrespective of the process by which the final state is reached.
228. If stress is applied to a reversible chemical system, there will be a readjustment in the system to relieve the stress.

229. The speed of chemical reaction is increased by increasing the concentration of any of the reactants; and is decreased by decreasing the concentration of any of the reactants.
230. Chemical reactions may be carried more nearly to completion by any condition that establishes an unusually low concentration of one of the products.
231. Whenever the product of the concentrations of any two ions in a mixture exceeds the value of the ion-product in a saturated solution of the compound formed by their union, this compound will be precipitated.
232. Whenever the product of the concentrations of any two ions in a mixture is less than the value of the ion-product in a saturated solution of the compound formed by their union, this compound, if present in the solid form, will be dissolved.
233. Simple ionic reactions are typically rapid reactions.
234. The rates of many reactions are affected by the presence of substances which do not enter into the completed chemical reaction.

235. Acids and bases are substances which in water solution ionize to give hydrogen and hydroxyl ions, respectively, from their constituent elements.
236. The activity of an acid or base is proportional to the degree of ionization of the compound when in solution.
237. The exchange of the negative and positive ions of acids and bases results in the formation of water and a salt.
238. Salts of strong acids and strong bases undergo negligible hydrolysis, while salts of inactive acids and inactive bases undergo more marked hydrolysis.
239. Electrolytes dissolved in water exist partially or completely as electrically charged particles called ions.
240. The properties of alloys are dependent upon the relative amounts of their components, the extent of their compound formation,8 and upon the crystalline structure of the mixture.

V. CARBON AND ORGANIC CHEMISTRY

241. Carbon atoms form a number of "type groups" of compounds which are determined by the elements present and by the structural combinations of the atoms within the molecules.
242. Unsaturated hydrocarbons are active chemically and form many compounds by addition.
243. Saturated hydrocarbons are relatively inactive chemically but form compounds by substitution.
244. The boiling point of hydrocarbons increases with an increase in molecular weight.
245. Molecules of some compounds undergo polymerization.
246. Alcohols react with acids to form esters and ethers.
247. Alcohols oxidize to aldehydes, ketones, and acids.
248. Elements and compounds to which the cells of living organisms react specifically produce physiological effects.
249. The enzymes, vitamins, and hormones are chemical regulators of the reactions that occur in living organisms.

PRINCIPLES OF GEOLOGY

I. DIASTROPHISM AND VULCANISM
250. The earth's surface may be elevated or lowered by interior forces.
251. Forces within the earth may cause breaks to appear in the earth's crust.
252. Under the high pressures which occur in the earth's interior, materials that usually are solid have the capacity to flow slowly and thus bring about equalization of pressure differences on the surface.
253. Earthquakes are produced by the sudden slipping of earth materials along faults.
254. Rocks may be folded to form mountains.
255. Strata of rooks occur in the earth's crust in the order in which they were deposited, except in the case of over thrust faults..
256. Igneous rock may be formed from materials intruded into other rocks.
257. Rocks may be formed by the cooling and solidifying of molten material.
258. Rocks may be formed by the compacting and cementing of sediments.
259. Rocks may be metamorphosed, or changed, by heat, pressure, and flexion.

II. DEGRADATION
260. Parent material for the development of soils is formed through the physical disintegration and chemical decomposition of rock particles and organic matter.
261. The natural movements of air, water, and solids on the earth are due chiefly to gravity plus rotation of the earth.
262. When elevations or depressions are created upon the surface of the earth, the elevations are usually attacked by the agents of erosion, and the materials are carried to the depressions.
263. The rate of erosion is inversely proportional to the resistance of rocks to decomposition and disintegration.
264. Continual erosion results in decreasing the average density of continental masses, and continual deposition in increasing the average density of rocks under the ocean.
265. Streams, generally, are lowering the surface of land in some places and building it up in other places.
266. The transporting power of streams varies approximately as the fifth power of the velocity.
267. Streams, potentially, have a regular cycle: youth, maturity, and old age.
268. Falls or rapids tend to develop in a stream bed wherever the stream flows over a hard stratum to a soft one.
269. Glacial abrasion occurs in proportion to the weight of the ice and the velocity of its movement.
270. Glacial conditions are as a rule approached by increasing latitudes or altitudes.

BASIC FUNDAMENTALS OF GEOLOGY, GEOPHYSICS AND EARTH SCIENCE

CONTENTS

		Page
CHAPTER- I.	THE DEVELOPMENT OF THE EARTH	1
II.	INSIDE THE EARTH	6
III.	ROCKS AND MINERALS	12
IV.	CHANGING THE FACE OF THE EARTH	17
V.	GLACIERS	21
VI.	PRESSURE INSIDE THE EARTH	25
VII.	VOLCANOES	29

BASIC FUNDAMENTALS OF GEOLOGY, GEOPHYSICS AND EARTH SCIENCE

CHAPTER I. THE DEVELOPMENT OF THE EARTH

According to recent estimates, the earth is over four billion years old. Of course, these estimates may be wrong, but we can say that probably the earth is at least four billion years old.

For millions of years the earth has been part of the solar system. What was happening here during all this time? This is the question that *historical geologists* try to answer. In this unit we will see what they have been able to learn about the early part of this planet's history. You will notice that there is no mention of man on earth until fairly recently. That is because man has been on earth only about a million years. Our actual records of people go back only a few thousand years. This is only a tiny part of the earth's history.

How Geologists Work

Most of our knowledge of the early history of the earth comes from records preserved in solid rock. From time to time some living plant or animal died and left its imprint in rock. The print was preserved for millions of years. These records of living things are called *fossils*.

In some fossils the rock has preserved many of the details of the plants or animals, such as the scales of fish or the veins in tree leaves. Some of the fossils found in hard coal, for example, show ferns that grew when the coal was first started millions of years ago.

Sometimes we find actual remains of plants and animals that have been preserved by nature for thousands of years. An insect or a leaf may get caught in the gummy resin that comes from trees. If the gum completely covers the insect or plant parts, they can be preserved intact for thousands of years in the hardened tree gum. Geologists sorietimes find the bodies of whole insects trapped in this way. But this type of fossil is usually not very old in geological terms. The geologist is interested in fossils that are millions - not just thousands - of years old. The bones of animals and the leaves of plants cannot last more than a few thousand years. But a print in rock can last indefinitely. So our oldest fossils are found in solid rock.

Sometimes, too, complete animals have been found preserved in ice for some thousands of years. About twenty-thousand years ago an animal that looked like a large elephant lived on earth. We call it the *hairy mammoth*. Several of these mammoths have been found preserved in solid ice. Only a few years ago in northern Russia one of these animals was found perfectly preserved in an ice block. But information of this sort does not help the geologist in his study of the earth's very distant past. It is not old enough.

Some of the strangest fossils ever found are the trees and plants that have "turned to stone." We say that they have been *petrified*. There are a good many of these stone trees in the United States. Actually the tree does not turn to stone. When the dead tree takes in water, it also takes in minerals in the water. The water evaporates, but the hard mineral is left as a rocky deposit. It actually takes the shape of the cells in the tree and fills them. When the cells waste away, the solid rock is left. The tree is like a mold which has been filled with rock particles dissolved in water.

The historical geologist, then, searches for fossils that will give him more information about the earth's history. He is not often lucky enough to find a whole tree or animal. Usually, he finds bits and pieces of animals and plants that must be fitted together. The geologist must know enough about plants and animals to piece these bits together and learn what the complete specimen looked like. Even when this is done, there is still the problem of deciding how old the fossil may be. This is called "dating" the fossil. It is a very difficult and complex process. The geologist uses chemical methods to date most things. He must have a good knowledge of the earth's history so that he can fit the fossils into the right time period.

The Geological Era

When we study the history of the United States, we usually begin with the first colonies and study the Colonial Period. Then we study the early history of the United States to the Civil War. It is easier to divide the whole history into periods and study the periods one at a time. Of course, history doesn't really happen that way. History moves on at a steady pace. But it helps the student to divide history into periods marked off by major changes of some sort.

To help organize their work, the geologists, too, have divided the history of the earth into different time periods. These periods are called *geologic eras,* or geologic time periods. In a regular course in geology, many such periods are studied. They are based, very broadly, upon the kind of living things found on earth at different times. The geologist must deal with four billion years of history. He cannot be as accurate as a historian who deals with a few hundred years of time.

In our study we will consider only the five largest time divisions that geologists use in their work. Each of these periods may be subdivided into many smaller periods for more accuracy. But we do not have enough time to do that in this kind of introductory study. As you study them, notice how the time periods are based upon the type of plant and animal life on earth.

You will notice that each era has certain characteristics of its own. You will also see how plant and animal life on earth grows more complicated with each passing era. In the beginning, plants and animals were very simple. Gradually they grew more and more complicated. Finally there came the age of mammals, or warm-blooded animals, and then the age of man.

The Archeozoic Era

We know far less about the early history of the earth than we would like to. Very few solid facts are known about the earth four billion years ago. No fossils were made then, because there were no living things to make fossils. Most of our beliefs about this era are only theories. They cannot be proved. All the geologist can do is try to provide a reasonable explanation of how the earth may have developed as it is now.

The earliest period of earth history shows no signs of life. It is called the *Archeozoic era*. It lasted from the beginning of the earth until some 500 millions of years later. The earth probably began life as a body of hot gas and liquid. The Archeozoic era was the cooling off period. As the hot gases cooled, they turned into hot liquids. When the hot liquids cooled, they became solid rocks. Finally, a thin crust began to form on the surface of the earth. In the beginning the crust was thin and weak. It broke often. More hot liquid spilled over the crust, like the filling from a cherry pie in a hot oven. The weight of the liquid rock pressed the crust downward. This caused the crust to rise in other areas.

All this time the earth was slowly cooling. When it became cool enough, water began to condense in the atmosphere and fall as rain. It must have rained for years and years when this process first started. Water striking the hot crust would turn to steam and move back into the atmosphere. As it cooled, it would fall once again as rain. This helped cool the earth still more. But inside the crust it remained a hot liquid.

By the end of the Archeozoic era, the crust of the earth was formed and the temperature had dropped. The oceans were formed, and the water temperature was below the boiling point.

The crust was still very thin. It probably broke often. The dry crust was hammered by wind and water for thousands and millions of years. Solid rock was ground into particles and the particles were carried off by wind and rain. Thousands of square miles of the earth's surface were shifted by the great forces at work on the earth. The top of Mount McKinley in Alaska, for example, was then below the sea. Yet this mountain top is now twenty-thousand feet above sea level.

The Proterozoic Era

The Archeozoic era ends with the beginning of life on earth. The first life probably was found in the sea. For the next billion years, plants and animals developed in the oceans. Near the end of the billion years, some plants and animals were able to live on dry land. This billion-year period is called the *Proterozoic era*. The great changes in the crust of the earth continued throughout the Proterozoic era. Some parts of the crust emerged from the sea, while some dry regions were plunged beneath the oceans. The swirling mass of hot liquid inside the earth sometimes burst the earth's crust and flooded large areas with melted rock or lava. In this very early era many of our mineral deposits were laid down. The particles of metal tended to collect in small concentrations. When the rock cooled and hardened, the metal particles remained locked in the rocks as ore.

The Paleozoic Era

The first two geologic eras bring us within 500 million years of the present. The next era begins about 500 million years ago and lasts until about 200 million years ago. It is called the *Paleozoic era*. At the beginning of this era, much of the earth was covered by water. Plant and animal life grew steadily more complicated during this time. By the end of the era, sharks and reptiles had evolved from simpler animals. A few sea animals had come partly out of the water. They lived some of the time on land and some of the time in the oceans. These land-sea animals are called *amphibians*.

Many different types of insects, too, developed during the Paleozoic era. In the plant kingdom, large ferns, trees, and mosses were very plentiful. This era produced most of the plants that went into our deposits of coal. Coal is made of the remains of dead plants. During this Paleozoic era, great numbers of ferns and plants piled up in immense heaps when they died. The pressure on the bottom layers of plants eventually produced coal. We will learn more about coal in another unit.

The Paleozoic era also produced many changes in the crust of the earth. The Appalachian Mountains in the eastern part of the United States began to rise above the surface during this era. High sheets of ice, called glaciers, formed at the North and the South Poles. The oceans dropped lower and lower as more water was caught and held in the form of ice. Wind and water continued to carve the surface of the land that was above the seas.

The Mesozoic Era

The Paleozoic era ended about 200 million years ago. It was followed by a period called the *Mesozoie era*. This period lasted until some seventy million years ago. During the Mesozoic era, most of the animals on earth changed so they had to live either in the water or on dry land. Most of the amphibians found at the beginning of the era disappeared before the end of it. Warm-blooded animals appeared toward the end of the Mesozoic era. This was a great step forward for animals. Before this time, all animals adjusted their temperature to fit their environment. (The body temperature of birds and mammals remains approximately the same at all times.) Their organs gradually became more complex and better balanced. By the end of the era, animals had developed hard bones instead of soft gristle. This also marked a great step forward. Even today the shark does not have hard bones in its body. Bony fish appeared in large nunbers during the Mesozoic era.

On land, during this era, the first cone-bearing trees appeared on earth. The Rocky Mountains began to push above the surface of the earth. The Appalachian Mountains were now lifted high into the air, and erosion was at work carving them down to size once again.

The real masters of the earth during the Mesozoic era were the reptiles. Some had wings and others lived chiefly in the water. But reptiles dominated the earth. Probably the most fearsome of all reptiles was the *Tyrannosaurus Rex.* He was probably the most terrible monster that ever lived. With his huge teeth, powerful claws, and great strength, he could handle any other living animal in his time. For some reason we do not really understand, the age of reptiles passed. The giant reptiles died out.

The Cenozoic Era

The last of our geologic eras is called the *Cenozoic era. It* has lasted about 70 million years. This era might be called the age of the mammals. Warm-blooded animals have replaced the reptiles as kings of the earth. Reptiles, like birds, are hatched from eggs. Mammals are born alive and nursed by the mother. They are the most complex animals on earth. During the Cenozoic era, the mammals tool; control of the earth. The first elephant and the first horse appeared in this late era. Steadily the animal life kept growing more complex. The changes in the earth's surface also continued as before. The Grand Canyon began to take shape about 25 million years ago.

The Last Million Years

We have covered millions of years of earth history very briefly. But we have not yet caught sight of man. He appears on the scene as one of the mammals, perhaps one million years ago. For thousands of years man progressed very slowly. Then, in the last few thousand years, the age of man has blossomed suddenly. Today man is the dominant animal on earth. No other animal stands a chance of pushing him aside.

Another remarkable feature of the last million years has been the "Ice Ages." Four times the earth has grown cold. Ice sheets have advanced from the poles toward the Equator. At times North America was covered with solid ice as far south as New York City. After each time the climate has turned warm and the ice has melted. For the past 25,000 years the climate has been steady. Scientists do not know whether a new ice age is brewing or whether the day of ice ages is past. You will learn some of the effects of these ice ages in the chapters that follow.

CHAPTER II. INSIDE THE EARTH

In our last chapter we learned about the early history of the earth and how plant and animal life developed. In this chapter we will look below the crust of the earth to see what the inside is like. We will also take a look at the crust, since this is where we make our homes and earn our living. Man has never been able to penetrate very far into the earth. The deepest mines are only about two miles deep. Below this level we have not been able to move, except with oil drilling equipment. Such drills have been able to reach a four-mile depth.

Many important questions about the interior of the earth need to be answered. Beneath the crust are there, perhaps, large mineral resources that we could use? Why does the crust move and produce earthquakes? Is the interior of the earth growing warmer or colder? These and many other questions are being investigated by modern science as quickly as possible.

A Cross Section of the Earth

An observer on the moon would see the earth as a smooth, round ball, almost as smooth as a grapefruit. To us, the earth does not seem very smooth. If we compare it with a grapefruit, a dent in the grapefruit only 1/16 of an inch deep would be the same as a canyon on earth forty miles deep. From the top of our highest mountain to the bottom of the deepest valley, the distance is only thirteen miles. This is about like 1/100 of one inch on a six-inch grapefruit. The surface of the grapefruit may appear like mountains and valleys to a germ sitting in the rind. To us the grapefruit is quite smooth. The earth would look smooth too if we could stand far back and look at it.

If the earth were sliced exactly in half, it would look like the figure below. The total diameter of the slice would be about eight thousand miles. To be more exact, it is 3,960 miles from the crust to the center. Below the crust, the earth is arranged in layers like an onion. Some of the layers are easy to distinguish. Other layers are still changing as forces within the earth exert pressure on then. The thickness of the layers also varies. In fact, some geologists believe that the layers inside the earth are constantly changing.

We live on the thin outer layer, which is called the crust, of the earth. Actually, the crust is very thin when compared to the size of the entire earth. It is like the peel on a cherry. All of our minerals and other resources are obtained from this crust.

We really live on only one-fourth of the surface of the earth's crust. The rest is covered by oceans. Below the oceans the crust of the earth is a little thinner than it is on dry land. But it is made of the same materials, and it was formed in the same way. It probably contains the same kind of resources. But the ocean floor is harder to get at than dry land. So it has not been used much as a source of raw material. It may yet become an important supply region for man.

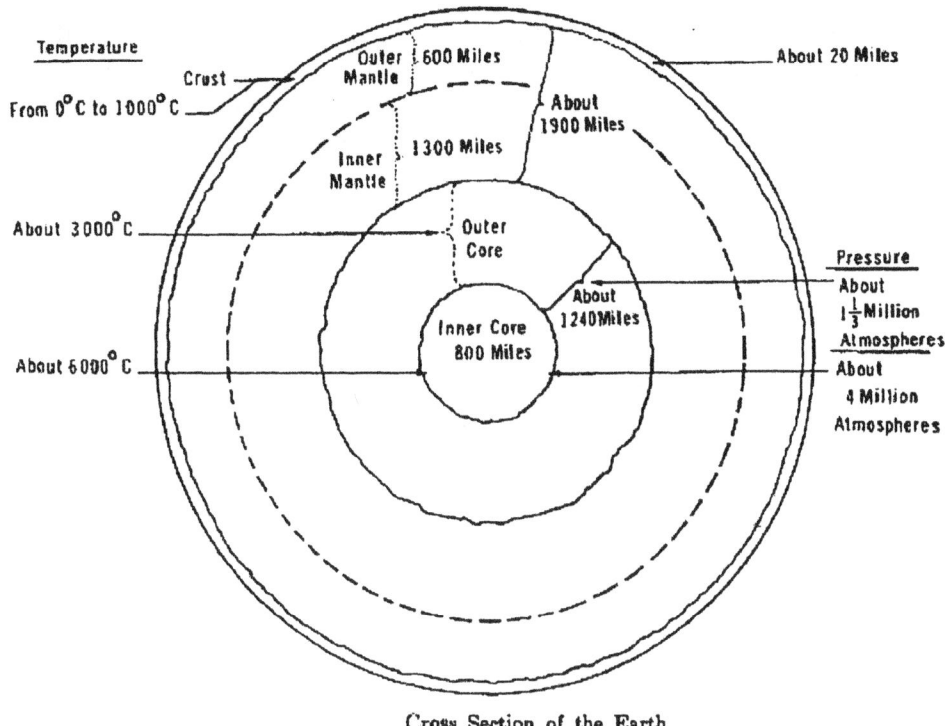

Cross Section of the Earth.

The Mantle

Below the thin crust of the earth there lies a very thick layer of rock called the *mantle*. This mantle is usually divided into two parts - the *outer mantle,* about six hundred miles thick, and the *inner mantle,* about thirteen hundred miles thick. Lying below the outer mantle, the inner one makes up most of the volume of the earth. The rock in the outer mantle is solid, but it is lighter, or less dense, than the rock in the inner mantle. The great pressure on the inner mantle forces the rock molecules together and increases the density. The outer mantle is probably made of material like the crust of the earth. The inner mantle may contain heavier elements, since it weighs more than the rock in the outer mantle.

The Core

If we compare the earth to a cherry, the thin skin of the cherry is like the earth's crust. The part of the cherry we eat is like the inner and outer mantles put together. The pit of the cherry is like the core of the earth. It is heavier and more solid than the outer parts of the earth. For a scientist, the core of the earth is a liquid. But it is not a liquid like water or oil. A scientist calls all matter a liquid if it behaves in a certain way. For example, certain kinds of earthquake shock waves that are transmitted by solids are not transmitted by liquids. The core of the earth will not transmit these waves. Therefore, the earth's core is called a liquid. But it must be a very thick, heavy liquid, under great pressure. For the material in the core of the earth weighs about five times as much as the material in the outer crust. That is, the core of the earth is very dense and heavy.

Geologists divide the core of the earth into two parts: an inner core and an outer core. The temperature in the inner core is probably about the same as the temperature on the surface of the sun, that is 6,000°C. The pressure is very high because of the weight of the upper layers of the earth. The core probably contains nickel and iron, which are very heavy. The scientists who study the core believe it may contain other material even more dense than nickel. That is why core material is five times as dense as material from the crust.

The Geologist at Work

If we cannot look inside the earth, how does the scientist learn all of these facts about the interior? The geologist must learn about the inside of the earth in the same way a doctor studies a broken arm without cutting the arm open. The doctor uses a small machine to produce x-rays. The geologist uses a natural machine of great power. He uses the waves generated by earthquakes. When an earthquake occurs, shock waves are sent out through the earth. These waves are timed and recorded by machines called *seismographs*. The record does not look like an x-ray picture. But a trained geologist can "read" the recording just as a trained doctor "reads" an x-ray. Most of our information about the interior of the earth is obtained by this method. It is called the science of *seismology*.

When some part of the earth's crust breaks apart, a great disturbance may be caused, which we call an earthquake. Earthquakes carry an immense amount of energy. If you break a stick in your hands, you can feel the shock run through your body. An earthquake produces the same effect. When great pressure causes the crust to snap, shock waves travel through the earth from the break. These waves can create great damage if they tear the surface open. A strong shock wave can tear an entire city apart in a few minutes. A large earthquake generates more power than millions of hydrogen bombs.

The geologist studies these shock waves with his seismograph. He measures the time it takes for the waves to travel through the earth. You can picture the earthquake as a transmitter. The seismograph acts as a radio receiver which receives a special type of message. By making many readings of earthquakes and comparing the results, the geologist can make a map of the interior of the earth.

The figure below shows you how seismology works. An earthquake has taken place at point A. The crust has snapped, and powerful shock waves are moving away from A through the earth. Suppose that points B, C, and D are seismographs. Each seismograph will receive a shock wave at a different time. By comparing the travel time of the waves, geologists learn about the interior. By careful checking and comparing, geologists have prepared the drawing of the earth which you see in the figure below.

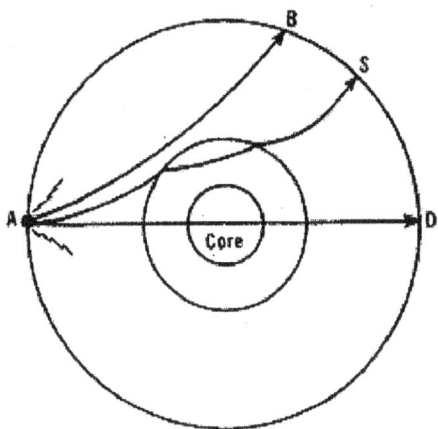

More About the Crust

Where the crust of the earth is smooth and flat, the people may have excellent farm land. Where the crust is wrinkled and torn, the land may be mountainous and of no use for farming. Where there are large mineral deposits and a supply of fuel, like coal, in the crust, the people who live there may develop a good supply of industries. Where the crust is poor in resources, the people may not be able to build large factories and machines. You can see that the condition of the crust is a matter of great importance to all of us.

There are ninety-two different natural elements found on earth, each made of a different kind of atom. All of these elements appear in the crust. But most of the crust is made of just two elements -silicon and oxygen, which are usually found tied with other elements in some compound. The most common elements are shown in the following table.

You can see that three-fourths of all the material in the crust is made of combinations of oxygen or silicon. Sand, for example, is made of silicon and oxygen; so you can see how plentiful these elements are in the crust.

The crust is made almost entirely of rock. Rocks vary in density. Some are light; others are thick and heavy. We will study the different types of rock in the next chapter. The temperature of the crust varies from freezing in some points at the top to about 1,000°C at the bottom of the crust. The pressure increases as we go down into the earth. In addition, radioactivity releases heat into the crust. In fact, some scientists believe that the earth may be growing warmer because of the amount of radioactivity in the crust.

Element	Approximate Percent of Crust	Element	Approximate Percent of Crust
Oxygen	47	Sodium	3
Silicon	28	Potassium	3
Aluminum	8	Magnesium	2
Iron	5	Others	1
Calcium	4		

Soil

A farmer with a farm made of solid rock could not grow food. Plants must have not only sunlight to grow; they must also have a supply of water, minerals, and carbon dioxide. The water and minerals cone from the earth. All living plants except those that live in the oceans are found growing in a very thin layer of rock particles and dead plant and animal material on top of the solid rock. This mixture is what we call *soil*. The layer of soil on the earth is hundreds of feet thick in some places. In other areas, there is no soil at all. The bare solid rock is exposed to the air and sun. In these bare regions few plants will grow.

Soil is produced by the action of wind and water in the process called *weathering*. Large chunks of rock are broken down into tiny rock particles. These tiny particles are mixed with bits of dead animal and vegetable matter to form soil. We will study the weathering process in another chapter. It is sometimes hard to believe that all of the loose soil on earth was once solid rock and plant life. Of course, it takes thousands or millions of years to produce these fine soil particles. But nature is in no hurry.

Conposition of Soil

Soil also contains tiny living organisms. They are called *micro-organisms* because they can be seen only with a microscope. These tiny living creatures are essential for plant life. Some micro-organisms have the ability to take nitrogen from the air and prepare it for use by the plants. A plant must have nitrogen to grow, but it cannot use nitrogen from the air. It obtains nitrogen through the work of these tiny bacteria, or micro-organisms. The bacteria take nitrogen from the air and make it into nitrates. When the nitrates dissolve in water, they can be used by plants. This is one more example of the remarkable way that the natural world is balanced.

The composition of soil is changing constantly. Plants take minerals from the soil to build their bodies. These soil minerals must be replaced before more plants will grow. If the plant dies and is buried on the same spot where it grew, some material is actually replaced in the soil. But if we take the plant away and eat it, we must do something to add the minerals which the plant used up to build its body.

Farriers return minerals to the soil by using *fertilizers.* Some fertilizers are waste materials from animals. Others are prepared commercially by chemical companies. In some cases, the farmers grow special crops and plow them back into the earth to restore the minerals to the soil and keep it fertile. Different crops use different minerals . The farmer must learn how to repair his soil scientifically. That is what is meant by *scientific farming.* The U.S. Department of Agriculture helps farmers find out exactly what a certain crop takes from the soil and what he must do to return that substance to the soil.

Erosion

Finally, the soil can be carried away by wind or water. This is called *erosion*. It is one of the great problems farmers must face. Ground that is covered with grass and trees will not blow away easily. But when the ground is plowed for farming, the soil is loosened and its protective coat is stripped away. It can then be blown away in dust storms or washed away by water. There are ways to prevent this loss of soil too. But it requires a careful conservation program. Otherwise, the topsoil needed to grow food can be lost. It is true that eventually nature will produce more soil by weathering the solid rock and breaking it into particles. But this takes a very long tine.

CHAPTER III. ROCKS AND MINERALS

We learned in the last chapter that when the crust of the earth hardened, it formed solid rock. For millions and millions of years the weather has been attacking this solid rock and breaking it down into smaller particles. Wind and rain and ice have all helped break rock up into the smaller bits by the process called *weathering*. The small rock particles, mixed with dead animal and vegetable material, called *soil*, form a thin layer. This layer covers parts of the earth and supplies the farmland that provides our food supply. When we dig down through the layer of soil, we find a layer of solid bedrock underneath. This bedrock may be very close to the surface, or it may be buried beneath many feet of loose soil. But it will always be found if we dig deep enough into the earth.

Soils

The layer of soil on top of the earth's crust can be divided into two parts. At the very top is a thin layer of fine particles, called *topsail*. This is the soil needed to grow plants. Below the topsoil is a layer of material called *subsoil*. Some subsoils are made of thick, heavy clay. Others are thin and loose and mixed with small stones or gravel. Whatever the material in the subsoil, it too is made from solid rock by weathering.

Some of the best farming land in the world was produced by a thick deposit of topsoil, carried along by wind or water. In northern China and in Argentina the wind has piled up very deep deposits of fine, rich soil. These dust deposits are called *loess*. Some of the loess deposits in China are more than a thousand feet thick. Thinner deposits of loess are found in Argentina and along the Mississippi River in the United States. Of course, the area where the wind removed the soil was stripped to make these deep, rich soil deposits.

Other rich farm areas have been produced by soil carried along by running water. The Nile River, the Mississippi River, and the Ganges River in India have all produced deep banks of rich soil at the river mouth. This type of soil deposit is called a *delta*. A delta is made of rich fine soil, carried to the mouth of the river by the current. It is excellent soil for farming.

Rocks

The earth's crust was once liquid rock. When the hot liquids on the earth cooled, a solid layer of rock was formed on the top. All our soil has been produced from this original rock surface by weathering. Since the original crust was formed, many new layers of rock have been formed. Geologists divide all rocks into three main types. Each type was made in a different way. Each rock has different characteristics.

Igneous Rock

When melted rock hardens to form a solid mass, it is called *igneous rook*. All of the original crust of the earth was made of igneous rock. This original crust has since been buried under thick layers of rock particles and vegetation.

Igneous rock is hard and durable. Two common types of igneous rock are *granite* and *basalt*. Both contain several different minerals. In granite we usually find some quartz, mica, and a mineral called feldspar. The quartz in granite is hard and glassy. The other minerals may be pink, gray, or black in color. Granite is a very tough stone which is used for heavy buildings. Basalt is a hard, dark-colored rock, which is not quite as strong as granite. After a volcano erupts, basalt is usually formed when the lava hardens. Because of its strength and availability, basalt is used for road construction and other jobs that require wearing ability and hardness.

Sedimentary Rock

When wind and water carry great piles of stone particles and store them in one place, a deep layer of material builds up. This layer is heavy, and it creates a strong pressure on the bottom of the pile. This pressure can force the particles of stone back together and fuse them into solid rock. Rocks that are formed by pressure of this sort are called *sedimentary* rocks. Sedimentary rock usually forms in layers. It looks like plywood. It is not nearly so strong as igneous rock, since sedimentary rocks are often formed from weaker minerals and the particles are not bound as strongly as those of igneous rocks, which were welded together by heat.

Three common sedimentary rocks are *limestone, shale,* and *sandstone.* Most *limestone* is formed from the bodies of tiny sea animals. Although it is mined on dry land, the deposits of limestone were originally nade beneath the oceans. This stone is whitish in color. It is used in steelmaking because it helps remove impurities from the iron.

Sandstone is made of tiny grains of sand that have been pressed together into a solid block. The sand is sometimes held together by a nixture of iron and oxygen, which we call rust. The chemist calls the mixture *iron oxide.* It is usually red, and it colors the sandstone. Because the color is attractive, sandstone is often used for building material.

Shale is a very soft rock formed in thin, weak layers. The layers are filled with airspace. Oil is found stored in the airspaces in a special type of shale.

Most of the fossils studied by geologists appear in sedimentary rocks, not in igneous rock. No fossil could survive the heat that goes into forming of igneous rock. But sedimentary rock takes a good impression when a plant or animal is trapped in it.

Metamorphic Rock

If any type of rock is heated to high enough temperatures, it will melt. Very great pressure will also cause changes in the structure of rock. Any rock that changes its form because of heat or pressure is called *metamorphic* rock. Metamorphic means *changed.* Rocks which have changed from one type to another fall into this group. Such changes may be brought about in several ways. Hot melted rock can flow up to the surface and melt the rock it touches. An earthquake can shift the rock inside the earth and allow hot liquid rock to move into a new area. The weight of a mountain range will some-tines change the rock beneath it to produce metamorphic rock.

You have probably seen a slate blackboard in a schoolroom. The color may be black or green or even gray. Usually it is black. This is a metamorphic rock. Slate was once shale rock, but it has been heated and compressed to form slate.

Marble is another common metamorphic rock. White marble is made from pure limestone. But most marble is streaked with color. This color depends upon the minerals in the original rock. Marble can easily be polished to a fine finish. It is used for decorating public buildings and for making tombstones.

Coal, Graphite, and Diamonds

Coal is often grouped as a type of metamorphic rock. There are several different types of coal. Each type is known by its hardness. Since all coal is made by the same process, all types of coal contain the same material. Hard coal, which is very important to us, is coal that has been pressed very hard.

Coal is made from dead plant and animal matter that builds up in great heaps. As the layers of material get deeper, the pressure on the bottom increases. This squeezes out some of the water. The temperature also increases, and the mixture at the bottom gradually hardens. The first stage of the process produces a soft, crumbly material called *peat.* Peat is a mixture of carbon and water and sone other minerals. It will burn, but it is very smoky and does not make good fuel.

As the peat is compressed and heated still more, it grows harder. More water is forced out. This leaves a higher percentage of carbon. By this process the next stage in coalmaking takes place. A poor grade of coal is formed, called *lignite.* It is also called *brown coal.* Brown coal also will burn, but it too makes a great deal of smoke and not much heat.

When brown coal is further compressed and heated, it is changed into *soft coal,* or *bituminous coal.* Soft coal is the most common fuel on earth. In fact, there is probably more of it in the world than of any other single material. Soft coal is a key material in many processes. When it is roasted, it forms *coke,* which is used to produce steel. When soft coal is burned, the gases can be used for many types of chemicals. Most of the electricity used in the United States is manufactured by burning soft coal, which powers electric generators. In other words, soft coal is a very important mineral. It produces electric power; and it forms the basic substance used to make dyes, plastics, and many other chemical materials.

But when coal has been compressed still more, so that nearly all the water has been driven out, we have *hard coal,* or *anthracite coal.* Hard coal is an ideal fuel for heating the house. It burns without smoke and leaves little ash. Most of the water has been removed, so that this coal is almost pure carbon. The supply of anthracite coal, however, is not large. Soft coal is far more common.

If hard coal is compressed until the last bit of water is removed, all that remains is pure carbon. A diamond is a special type of pure carbon. So is the material called *graphite.* Graphite is used for the "lead" in pencils and also as a dry lubricant in machinery.

Ores

An ore is a rock that contains minerals. In order to be an ore, a rock must contain enough minerals to be mined at a profit. Many rocks contain some minerals. But they are not ores because the minerals are not worth mining. The type of mineral in an ore may be metal or nonmetal.

The supply of ore in the world is not spread evenly in the earth's crust. Some countries, like the United States and Russia, have rich supplies of ore. Other areas have little or no ore in their part of the crust. Much of Africa and Asia seem to have little ore that can be used to build modern industry. Sometimes we find very valuable ores in small pockets. In Canada, for example, a few mines furnish a large part of the world's supply of nickel. This metal is used to harden steel. Diamonds are found chiefly in South Africa. Even coal is not found in every part of the earth. Since modern industry depends upon fuel and minerals, countries which have none cannot hope to become industrial powers without help from the outside.

Oil, or Petroleum

One of the most valuable minerals in our day is petroleum, or oil. Petroleum produces fuel for automobiles, diesel engines, and jet aircraft. It is used to make dyes and plastics. In fact, innumerable products are made from petroleum. We will study some of these products more closely in another chapter.

Oil is found in pools under the surface of the earth. We do not know what oil is made from; it probably begins as dead plant and animal matter, which seems to form in the sea, for salt water is usually found with the oil pools. There is often a supply of natural gas with the oil. When a well is tapped, the pressure of the gas can cause oil to rise through the pipes and to create a "gusher." The oil pools are usually found in layers of sandstone. This rock has many small air pockets that can contain the oil. The oil pool is often covered by a hard dome of solid rock. This holds the oil pool below the surface. A typical oil dome is shown in the figure below. The oil is found in the layer of porous rock. The hard dome above the oil pool holds in the natural gas and the oil.

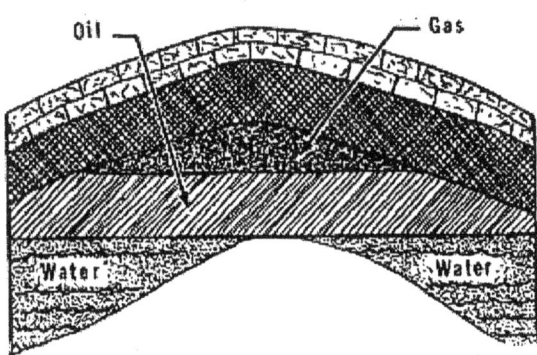

Men tap the oil dome by drilling a hole down through the rock cover. If there is enough gas pressure, the oil will bubble from the well. But most oil wells must be pumped. If carefully drilled, an oil dome can be made to produce both petroleum and natural gas. Look at the figure above. A pipe inserted at the point in the dome marked A would bring out natural gas. A pipe at point B would produce petro-leum. Both of these products are valuable. Unless the natural gas is tapped carefully, it will escape and be lost.

When petroleum comes from a well, it is a black or brown sticky liquid. Before it can be used, it must be processed. This is called *refining*. The oil coming from a well actually contains dozens of different materials. Most of them can be used and are valuable. In an oil refinery these parts of petroleum are separated. Then the different products produced from petroleum can be manufactured and prepared for marketing.

16

Geologists use the same method to search for oil that they use to study the interior of the earth. They use a seismograph, and they study the picture they get when a shock wave passes through the crust. But an oil geologist need not wait for an earthquake. He does not need such a large shock. He can set off a charge of blasting powder. This is the method usually employed. The shock from the powder is recorded by the seismograph. A skilled geologist can tell from the seismograph whether it is possible that oil may lie beneath the surface. He cannot be certain, and drilling oil wells is always an expensive gamble. But oil is a valuable product, and oil companies can afford to spend large amounts of money to locate new supplies of it.

CHAPTER IV. CHANGING THE FACE OF THE EARTH

For years the face of the earth has been changing steadily. Once the crust had formed on the earth, wind and water acted to wear it down into tiny particles. New parts of the crust have been shoved high into the air to form mountains. Then these mountains have been worn away again by wind and water. This process has been going on for millions and millions of years.

The crust of the earth, that began as solid rock, is today covered with plant life and with the particles of rock mixed with dead plant and animal matter that we call soil. Several factors go into this weathering, or breaking down of solid rock into tiny particles. The chief ones are wind, water, and sudden temperature changes. In time even the mightiest rock can be worn away by these forces.

Erosion

Weathering produces tiny particles of rock. When the solid rock is broken into smaller pieces, which are moved away from where they were forned, we call the process *erosion*. The chief causes of erosion are the same wind, water, and temperature changes that cause weathering. In fact, many people think of weathering as part of the whole process of erosion. In the end, erosion brings most of the tiny rock particles to the bottom of the sea. When the weight of them is heavy enough to cause the crust to sink, another part of the crust is thrust into the air. Then erosion begins all over again. Thus, by weathering and erosion a thick blanket of rock particles, or soil, has been built up on the face of the earth. As you already know, some of these particles become welded into solid sedimentary rock by the pressure of the particles on top of the heap.

Movements of the Earth's Crust

The ground under our feet always seems quite solid and firm. But the earth's crust is also flexible. When it is pressed down in one area, it will rise up somewhere else. When wind and water pile sediment on it until it becomes heavy, or when a large icecap forms on it, the crust sinks down to a lower level under the added weight. To compensate, or make up for this sinking, another part of the crust rises higher. This has happened over and over again. Parts of the earth that are dry today were once at the bottom of the sea.

The northern part of North America was once covered by a large, heavy glacier. This mass of ice weighed down the crust until it sank. When the glacier melted, the Great Lakes and Hudson Bay were formed. Now that the ice is gone, this area is slowly rising. Some day it nay rise high enough to cause the water to leave Hudson Bay and flow back into the ocean.

When the solid parts of the earth's crust shift, the movement is called *diastrophism*. These shifts happen quite often. Once in a while a change takes place on a very large scale. Hundreds of miles of crust are pressed into the air to form mountain ranges. Parts of a whole continent may sink beneath the sea. Of course, these changes take place very slowly. The earth does not usually move quickly. We are not likely to wake up and find a new mountain outside our window, though the earth can produce a small volcanic peak in a few weeks.

Vulcanism

When the great masses of hot melted rock move or cause changes in the earth's crust, the process is called *vulcanism*. The word has the same base as *volcanoes,* for volcanoes represent a particular kind of vulcanism. Great floods of molten rock pour across the hard crust of the earth. Some of these floods may cover thousands of square miles. Giant mountain peaks can be built by this process. The Hawaiian Islands are made almost entirely of volcanic rock thrust up from inside the earth. The flow of hot lava, or melted rock, can occur under the oceans or on dry land. Vulcanism is still going on today, for the earth is still hot inside. It can generate great pressures that can cause its crust to move.

Water Erosion

Even today a great flood can bring modern cities to a complete stop. This gives an indication of the power of running water. Even the smallest stream, if it is given time, can chew a great hole in the earth. Water is the most effective earthmover on the surface of the earth. Volcanic activity may look more spectacular and powerful. But in the long run, water does more to change the face of the earth than any other force. Every day billions of tons of water rise from the oceans and drop on the land. Each year enough water falls on earth to cover the whole surface with thirty inches of water. As it runs over dry land, it picks up particles of rock and soil and carries them along. If you ever watch a fast creek running in the spring of the year, you are likely to find the water brightly colored with earth. Given time, a trickle of water will wear away the strongest rocks. In a few thousand years, water can carve a Grand Canyon across the face of the earth.

Water that is carrying particles of rock is an even more effective eroding agent than pure water. The rock particles act like sandpaper, scraping away at the sides of the creek or river. Usually this is a slow process. But water, too, can act quickly. A sudden cloudburst can bring a torrent down a hillside, sweeping away the farmer's fields and his crops. That is why farmers are particularly concerned with water erosion. If the water carries away their topsoil, plants cannot grow.

The amount of erosion caused by running water depends upon two factors. First, since water running over solid rock will not carry away as much of the surface as water running over loose soil, *the type of surface is one factor that determines erosion.* Second, since slow moving water erodes much less soil than a fast moving stream, *the rate of travel is another and a major factor in water erosion.* In a slow stream the silt falls to the bottom and is not carried very far. When the speed of flow is doubled, the ability of the water to carry soil is increased many times. The soil particles give the water more cutting power as they strike against the banks.

Chemical Action of Water

If you place some salt in a glass of water, the water will dissolve the salt. Water has the ability to dissolve many different minerals. When water reaches the minerals in rock, it often dissolves them. This weakens the rock and makes it easier to break apart. Water also expands about 10 percent in volume when it freezes. In cold climates this expansion power of water can split very large rocks. Liquid water can enter a crack in a rock and freeze there. The expansion of the water when it forms ice acts like a wedge. Many blocks of stone are broken off the earth's crust by this process. When the solid block is removed, the face of the crust is again exposed to the erosion of wind and water.

Wind Erosion

During the 1930's, the central part of the United States was often called the Dust Bowl. There had been little rain, and the ground became a dry, thin powder. This powder was picked up by the wind and carried for hundreds of miles across the country. Millions of acres of good farmland were nearly ruined by the erosion caused by the wind. Water causes more erosion than wind; but in dry climates, where there is little water, the wind can also cut away the earth's crust.

When the wind blows hard, it picks up particles of rock and soil and carries them along. These particles give the wind a cutting edge. In fact, they make it act like a regular sandblast. The tiny particles strike against the earth and wear through solid stone very quickly. This sandblasting effect can cause odd-looking rock formations. The wind cannot raise the rock particles high in the air, so most of the cutting effect is felt close to the ground. This carves the part of the stone near the ground faster than the part high in the air.

Other Types of Erosion

When a piece of solid rock is heated and then cooled very quickly, the outer parts of the rock contract more rapidly than the inside. This places a terrific strain on the rock and can cause it to split apart. In the deserts, where the temperature falls very quickly after sundown, this type of action takes place often. Travelers in the desert may hear a loud snap like a cannon shot when a huge rock splits apart.

Plants and animals also help break down the solid crust of the earth. Plant roots work into the cracks and split the rock apart as they grow. Sometimes a large tree will grow right through the center of a solid piece of rock, splitting it apart. Waste matter from the bodies of plants and animals also produces chemicals that affect the minerals in rock. When an animal, however small, digs a hole beneath a large rock, wind and water are enabled to reach a larger surface area of the rock. This, too, increases the speed of erosion slightly. Each of these effects seems very small. But nature works steadily and slowly. Any little additional help will make some difference in the long run.

The climate can affect the speed of weathering and erosion. In a hot, wet climate erosion tends to work faster than in a cool, dry climate. In a climate that includes freezing temperatures, expanding ice helps speed the process. Some of the buildings in Egypt lasted for thousands of years in the dry climate there. When they were taken to North America or England, the dampness speedily weathered the face of the rock. In general, the amount of moisture in the air seems to be the most important single factor in weathering.

River Valleys

Most of the great valleys on earth, like the Grand Canyon, have been dug by rivers. A river needs thousands of years to dig a Grand Canyon. It can produce a smaller valley in a much shorter time. All that is needed is a good supply of water and the force of gravity. All water returns to the oceans eventually, digging a valley in the earth as it returns. Scientists have found that rivers follow a regular pattern of growth.

River Valley Development.

One heavy rainfall can begin a great river valley. Suppose a heavy rain digs a small trench in the earth. If water continues to flow through it, this little trench can become a great river valley. As the river changes, it passes through four separate stages or periods. The figure above shows a cross-section of the river in each of these stages.

The first step cuts a sharp gulley in the earth. The sides of the gulley are V-shaped, and it is cut deep into the ground. Soon a small river is formed. As the river grows, the gulley becomes deeper but not much wider. The V-shape broadens at the bottom, as the walls of the river are cut more deeply. The weight of the water on the river bottom helps speed the cutting process. When the bottom is cut down to full depth, the river valley has reached its young stage. The valley continues to broaden and smooth out. The curves of the river become more gradual. The edges of the valley become rounded off by the wind and water. In time the river moves more and more slowly. It carries a large amount of solid and rock particles. The river adds more twists and turns as it moves along. The valley becomes very broad and smooth - like a rolling dip in the landscape. The river is then in its *old age.*

The Mississippi River is in its old age at the present time. It flows in broad gentle curves, carrying a heavy load of silt. A great delta has been built up at the mouth of the Mississippi. This river carries about half a billion tons of silt into the ocean each year. The Mississippi is really an "Old Man River," though it can still break loose and cause enormous amounts of damage during a flood.

Preventing Erosion

Weathering, the breaking of solid rock into particles, is a good thing for human beings. It increases the supply of soil. But erosion, which moves these particles toward the sea, is a catastrophe. The soil is often lost for all time at the bottom of the sea. Nature has her own way of controlling this damage. A layer of strong grass and trees will reduce erosion to a minimum. But once the trees are cut and the grass is plowed, wind and water can act directly against the soft soil. Wind erosion in the 1930's carried Kansas topsoil onto the decks of ships in the middle of the Atlantic Ocean. Much of this erosion was due to careless farming.

Today farmers are aware of the need for erosion control. The U.S. Department of Agriculture and the state governments help reduce the loss of soil due to erosion. Large stands of trees have been planted to break the force of wind. Farmers have learned how to plant their crops in ways that reduce erosion. Dams have been built to control flooding. But we still lose millions of tons of topsoil every year. We must learn to take care of the land if we are going to provide for the future. It is one of our most valuable possessions.

CHAPTER V. GLACIERS

The land at the South Pole is covered by a layer of solid ice thousands of feet thick. This sheet of ice moves across the continent of Antarctica toward the sea. A moving "river" of ice is called a *glacier.* A glacier that covers a large region like Antarctica is called an *icecap.* Glaciers are found in cold climates like the North Pole and the South Pole, or high in the mountains where snow accumulates faster than it can melt.

A glacier is a moving body of very heavy solid ice. It can cause great changes in the crust of the earth. As the glacier passes over the land, its force can grind large rocks to powder and strip away all loose material. Glaciers also affect the climate of the earth and the water level in the oceans. If large glaciers should form on earth, cities like New York might find themselves hundreds of miles from the ocean because of the water taken from the ocean to form the glaciers. Or if the glaciers now on earth should melt, New York would be submerged beneath more than one hundred feet of water. Glaciers are still an important force on earth, though it appears that our glaciers are slowly melting at the present time.

Location of Glaciers

About 10 percent of the land area of the earth is covered by glaciers. One whole continent - Antarctica - is covered by a single large icecap. This Antarctic glacier alone is larger than the entire United States. It is several thousand feet thick in spots, and it contains about 85 percent of the world's ice. Another 10 percent of the glacial ice in the world is concentrated in the icecap in Greenland. The remainder is divided among the hundreds of small glaciers found in the mountains around the world. Glaciers may be a few hundred feet thick or thousands of feet thick. They may be only a few miles long or very huge like the glacier in Antarctica.

Why Glaciers Form

Glaciers form because the climate is cold enough to produce solid ice. No one knows why the climate should change enough to cause glaciers to form. We do not know why the climate changes again and causes glaciers to melt and grow smaller. But we do know that this has happened several times in the past million years. Four times the glaciers in the world have grown much larger. As much as 30 percent of the earth has been covered by glaciers at one time. That is about three times as much coverage as we have at the present time.

During the ice ages, the climate must have turned cold. The oceans were two hundred to three hundred feet lower than they are today. Great sheets of ice covered much of northern Europe and North America and northern Asia. The entire earth must have been fairly cool. Yet the earth grew warmer once again, and the glaciers began to melt.

Today the glaciers are only 1/3 as large as they were at their peak period. We do not know why this change occurred. Nor do we know if the climate may suddenly turn cold once more and the glaciers again begin to grow. We seem to be living in a period when the earth is growing warmer. But we cannot be certain that this is true.

How Glaciers Form

All glaciers begin life as falling snow. If the climate is cold, not all of the snow that falls will melt in the year. In time a thick layer of snow can pile up on the earth's crust. That is why glaciers are found near the poles or high in the mountains. Snow must remain on the ground throughout the year before a glacier can form.

When the pile of snow is thick enough, the pressure on the bottom causes the snow to change into small lumps called *buckshot ice.* The next step in the process produces a layer of solid ice on the bottom of the snow pile. The process is like the formation of sedimentary rocks. Each year the ice grows thicker and heavier.

When the weight of the ice layer reaches a certain point, the force of gravity is stronger than the friction between the ice and the ground. The ice sheet then begins to move. A glacier has been born. The energy that moves the glacier is provided by gravity acting on the weight of the ice sheet. Each year more snow falls on top of it, increasing the weight of the glacier and providing the energy for further movement. We say that the new snow "feeds" the glacier. A glacier will always move from high ground to low ground. It cannot move upward. But it can cross small hills to get to a lower area on the other side. A light glacier needs a sharp slope. But a large continental glacier can move along a very slight slope once it grows heavy enough. The glacier that once covered northern North America moved steadily across the countryside. It filled in valleys and shaved off large hills as it passed.

When a glacier reaches the sea, it shoves forward into the water. Great chunks break off the solid sheet of the glacier and float out into the ocean. We call them *icebergs.*

Why Glaciers Move

The force of gravity is centered in the core of the earth. Every object on earth will move as close to the center of the earth as possible. That is why objects fall to the ground. That is why a car will roll down a hill. The glaciers moves for the same reason. It is pulled by the gravity of the earth toward the lowest possible level. So all glaciers move toward the sea. Other forces also help move a glacier over the earth. Part of the glacier may melt and then freeze again. The expansion of water when it freezes can shove the glacier along. When it crosses a hill, it bulges and cracks on top. The cracks can fill with snow and increase the forward pressure. All of these factors combine to keep the glacier moving.

Most glaciers move very slowly. A few inches of motion each day is a good average. A few have been known to move about fifty feet in one day, but that is rare. As the glacier reaches warmer temperatures, it melts at the forward edge. If the glacier melts as rapidly as it is pushed forward from behind, it will appear to stand still. Actually, it keeps moving forward, but it loses more distance than it gains. The rate of melting changes from year to year, depending upon the climate.

Icebergs

When the front edge of a glacier reaches the ocean, it is forced out into the water by the pressure behind it. When the weight of the edge is more than the glacier can support, the chunk in the ocean breaks off. It then floats off as an iceberg. Some icebergs are very large. In Antarctica, icebergs have been seen which were several miles across and thousands of feet thick.

Fortunately, icebergs from Antarctica do not move into the world's shipping lanes. But icebergs from the Arctic Ocean are a real menace to shipping. When the oceanliner Titanic struck an iceberg in 1912, more than fifteen hundred persons were lost. This does not happen often today, but a close watch must be kept on the shipping lanes. Most of the weight of an iceberg lies below the surface. An innocent looking little iceberg has about nine times as much mass below water as it shows on the surface. We can now use sonar and other electronic equipment to locate large icebergs, even in a fog. They are less dangerous than they were before this equipment was available.

Glacial Erosion

The continent of North America shows the effect of glacial erosion better than any other area. During the ice ages the glaciers that covered the northern part of the continent made great changes in the land. The weight of the ice caused the crust to sink. But the crust has been rising steadily since the glacier melted. It will be a long time before it recovers completely.

If you run a rough file over soft wood, the surface of the wood becomes splintered and torn. A glacier has this same effect on the earth. As the glacier moves along, it picks up rocks and soil particles and holds them fast. This makes a giant rasp on the bottom of the glacier. The pressure on the bottom reaches many tons for each square foot. As the glacier slides along, it rasps off the surface of the earth right down to the bedrock. Even solid rock can be cut and torn by the weight of a moving glacier. The loose rock, stones, and soil are torn off the surface and carried away. Hills are swept clean, and valleys are filled with rock and soil. Huge boulders are carried hundreds of miles, then dropped when the glacier melts. Some of the boulders that now lie in the Ohio River Valley were carried south from Canada by the glaciers.

Once the loose soil is cleared away, the glacier goes to work on the solid rock below. It tears great blocks of stone loose and grinds large rocks to powder by its weight. After a glacier passes over the land, it looks as though a land-hungry army has been marching through. The terrain is left smooth and rounded. Tops of hills are cut off, and valleys are filled in. The topsoil has just about disappeared, carried away by the glacier. Bedrock lies exposed on the surface. Even this solid rock is scratched and torn. Areas that have been visited by a glacier may be useless for farming for thousands of years. Large parts of Canada, for example, have almost no topsoil left. It was carried away by the glaciers centuries ago.

Glacial Moraine

When a glacier stops moving, it is like a child that has stopped playing with its toys. It drops everything just where it happens to be when the movement ceases. So all glaciers leave their calling cards behind. A long line of loose rocks, boulders, and other material carried by the glacier marks the point where the movement stopped. This line of debris is called a *glacial moraine*. Glaciers cannot put anything back where they found it. They move only in one direction.

A glacier can be very generous to some parts of the world. But it is generous at the expense of some other areas. The rich farmland in the north-central United States, for example, was deposited by glacial action. The Ohio River Valley and other parts of the Midwest were made rich by such deposits. So the glacier "robs Peter to pay Paul." Millions of tons of topsoil in the United States were taken from the land in Canada. In a way, the Midwestern states are rich because large areas in Canada are very poor. In the same way, the delta at the mouth of the Mississippi River is rich because the river has stolen topsoil from large areas in central United States.

Mountain Glaciers

Glaciers that form on mountain tops are usually much smaller than the large continental glaciers. But they are formed in the same way and they move in the same way. The loose soil on the mountain is stripped away, leaving sharp clear peaks of solid rock. The Alps in Europe are covered with sharp peaks formed by glacial action. Once the glacier has done its work, only solid rock remains on the mountain. In time the erosion effect of wind and water will finish the job that the glacier started.

Glaciers also create some beautiful mountain lakes. The grinding effect of the glacier can carve out a hollow spot in the mountains. The melting glacier will fill the hollow with water. Many of these mountain lakes are famous beauty spots.

Glaciers and Erosion

You can see that the erosion effect of glaciers is tremendous. Of course, they do not affect the whole world equally. But in the areas they visit, glaciers are the most powerful forces of erosion known. Fortunately, the parts of the earth which have large populations are not troubled with glaciers at the present time. And since glaciers move very slowly, the possibility of glacial damage in the near future is small. But many of the conditions we now have are the result of glacial action. And a very large part of the world has been changed by the force of glaciers moving over the surface. If the earth should grow cold once again and if the glaciers should again begin to move across the earth, more great changes would take place.

CHAPTER VI. PRESSURE INSIDE THE EARTH

If we stretch a rubberband, it will snap back into shape again. That is, the rubberband is *elastic*. It can change its shape temporarily and then return to its original shape. But if we stretch the rubberband too far, it will not return to the original shape. The size of the rubberband can be changed permanently. When a permanent change can be made in the size or shape of material, we say it is *plastic*. Like the rubberband, the crust of the earth that we live on is both elastic and plastic. The shape of the crust can be changed temporarily, and it can be changed permanently.

Because we can see only a small part of the earth's crust at one time, it looks quite solid. But a view of the whole earth shows that the crust is changing shape all the time. Some of the changes are only temporary; others are permanent. Both types of change can occur because the earth is both elastic and plastic.

Forces at its surface change the crust of the earth. Wind, water, and glaciers erode the face of the earth. They wear down mountains and tear away the soil. In this chapter and the next, we shall learn how the crust of the earth can also be changed by forces inside the earth. The changes due to these internal causes are often far greater than those caused by erosion. Earthquakes, volcanoes, and mountains are all due to pressures inside the earth,

Diastrophism

The change in the earth's crust due to these internal pressures is called *diastrophism*. The crust may be stretched, or reshaped, or it may even be snapped apart. Heat and pressure can cause a surge of hot liquid rock to the surface of the earth. A great earthquake can shatter the crust of the earth for hundreds of miles. Hundreds of square miles of the crust can be shoved high into the air. All of these changes in the crust are examples of diastrophism. When the change is very great, it is usually permanent. Such great changes are not frequent. This is fortunate for us, since the really great changes in the surface of the earth cause immense damage to life and property. Small changes, caused by stretching of the crust, go on at all times. We do not notice them because they do not cause any effects we can see.

Causes of Diastrophism

Nothing can change in our universe without the use of energy. Where does the energy come from? Changes in the earth's crust use energy from three sources: *first,* the heat from the inside of the earth; *second,* the pressure on the crust from heavy weights like mountains or piles of sediment; *third,* the pressures caused by the rotation of the earth. The amount of energy that can be supplied by these sources is really amazing. A volcanic explosion can throw millions of tons of earth far into the atmosphere. A large earthquake uses more energy than could be produced by a thousand hydrogen bombs.

Heat Inside the Earth

If we dig into the crust of the earth, we find that the temperature rises steadily as we go below the surface. The change in temperature is not the same in all parts of the world. In some mines the temperature is only 150°F far below the surface. But in parts of the United States, the temperature rises several hundred degrees at a depth of a few hundred feet. The average change all over the earth is 1°F for every sixty feet we go below the surface. The temperature of a three-hundred-foot mine is about 5° warmer at the bottom than on the surface.

Why does the earth grow warmer inside? We do not really know the answer to this question. Many scientists believe that the earth is still cooling off from its original hot condition. But new facts show that the earth may really be growing warmer and not colder. The extra heat may come from radioactivity inside the earth. We do not really know at this time which theory is correct. We do know that the earth is very hot inside the crust. At the bottom of the crust, about thirty-five miles down, the temperature is close to 1,000°C.

The high temperatures inside the earth melt some of the rock to liquid form. This liquid is under great pressure. If the pressure becomes too great, the melted rock can open a hole in the crust and force its way to the surface. We must remember that the earth is spinning very rapidly on its axis. This spinning can put great pressure on the crust. When we think of the weight that the crust must hold, like a large mountain, and add the heat and the pressure on the crust due to rotation and heat, we can see that the crust is really under a great strain all the time. It is not surprising that it cracks, or breaks, under these forces.

Earthquakes

When these pressures cause the crust of the earth to shift or crack, an *earthquake* may occur. There are many earthquakes each year but most of them are too small to cause damage on the surface. A large earthquake can tear an entire city apart in a few minutes. The break in the crust may be a crack or split. Or we may find a large block of crust raised above the rest. Whatever the shape of the break, it is always called a *fault*. The figure below shows a typical fault.

Vertical Fault in Earth's Crust.

One section of crust has raised up above the other. You can see the layers of rock that have been broken. The fault pictured here is called a vertical fault because one part of the crust rose above the other. The crust can also slide apart and make a horizontal fault. The break separates the two parts of the crust. Sometimes, the shift of the crust is twenty or thirty feet wide on the surface. These horizontal faults usually cause more damage then vertical faults.

To summarize, then, every year there are thousands of small faults in the crust of the earth. They occur on dry land as well as under the oceans. Most of the faults are small and can be recorded only with special equipment. The earth is under a constant strain. It gives a little here and a little there to make adjustments, just as our bodies do. As you walk your bones are under a steady strain. You do not notice the strain unless it becomes too great and a bone breaks to relieve the pressure. This is like an earthquake inside the body. The earth handles small strains easily. But once in a while the pressures build up, and a really serious break takes place.

Fortunately, we do not have many serious earthquakes. They can be devastating. The great earthquake in Lisbon in 1755 lasted only five minutes, but it ruined half the city and killed thousands of people. Thousands more were drowned when a great tidal wave hit the city after the earthquake. In 1906, when a bad earthquake struck California, the city of San Francisco was ruined. The crust shifted more than twenty feet in some places. Buildings collapsed, pipes were torn apart, and the whole city went up in flames. An earthquake in 1923 destroyed almost all of the city of Tokyo and also the city of Yokohama. These earthquakes were lateral quakes. The earth shifted horizontally, that is from side to side. An earthquake that lifts part of the surface does not cause such great damage. An earthquake in 1989 interrupted the landscapes in the San Francisco - Oakland Bay area. Earthquakes may produce large tidal waves - up to a hundred feet high - that do additional damage to areas struck by the earthquake as well as other areas.

The Earthquake Belts

Some parts of the world are not bothered with earthquakes. In other places the people live in constant fear of a major eruption. There are, in fact, two large earthquake "belts" that form loops around the Middle East and the Pacific Ocean. One includes northern Africa, the Alps Mountains, and southwestern Asia. Burma lies in this area. It has many violent earthquakes. But the worst earthquake region lies around the shores of the Pacific Ocean. The western coast of North and South America and the eastern coast of Asia suffer great earthquakes. The coast of Asia produces some really bad ones. Smaller tremors seem to take place a dozen times each day in places like Japan. These two belts have more than 90 percent of all the earthquakes in the world. We know the location of the two loops, but we still do not know exactly why the earthquakes occur.

The people who live in earthquake regions can take some precautions against disaster. They can avoid building towns or cities beneath large hills or bluffs. This eliminates the danger of the large cave-in that might drop masses of rock into the city. Houses can be built of material that will bend with the earthquake. Brick and stone should not be used for houses unless a steel frame is also used. Earthquakes cannot be prevented, but danger of loss of life and property can be lessened by careful management.

Making Mountains

When the earth was first cooled enough to form a crust, it was probably flat and smooth. Since that time, the forces inside the earth have produced the tremendous mountain ranges that we now see. Different kinds of mountains are made by different processes. But all of them have been raised by the energy inside the earth.

When hot liquid rock, or *lava,* is thrown out of the earth, it cools and forms a solid mass. A layer of cooled lava builds up around the hole in the earth. As this happens over and over again, the pile of lava grows. Whole mountains have been built by this process. Mount Shasta in northern California is a volcanic mountain of this type. The mountains in Hawaii were also produced by hot lava flowing from inside the earth. A volcanic mountain usually produces a cone-shaped peak.

A second type of mountain is made by the carving away of loose material, leaving the mountain of rock standing upright. These mountains are called *residual* mountains because the mountain is what remains after erosion takes place. The Catskill Mountains in New York were formed this way.

When a great block of the earth's crust is shoved high into the air, another type of mountain is formed. The block of crust can be hundreds of miles wide, and it may be pushed two or three miles into the air. The Sierra Nevada Range in California was built this way. The range is four hundred miles long and about one hundred miles wide. The whole mass of crust was thrust several thousand feet into the air.

Fold Mountains

Most of the great mountain ranges in the world were built by still another process. If you place a piece of cloth on a table, and push the ends together, the cloth forms a set of wrinkles in the middle. Now if you raise the whole mass of wrinkles into the air, you have a complete mountain range. This process is called folding, and it is the way really large mountain ranges are formed. Of course, it is not so easy to form wrinkles in a layer of rock eight miles thick as in a piece of cloth. Try to imagine enough energy to fold together hundreds of miles of crust, several miles thick, then shove the whole wrinkled crust up into the air. All of the energy we produce on earth could not do this job. But the force inside the earth is so great that it can do it. Given time, it will produce mountains like the Alps.

A folded mountain is produced by a three-step process. First, a great weight, such as a pile of sediment, causes the crust of the earth to sag and stretch. Second, the crust around the sagging area then presses in toward the gap. This creates huge wrinkles in the crust. Third, the whole mass of wrinkles is forced high into the air by pressures from below the surface, to form the mountain range. This process takes thousands of years. It has produced the Alps Mountains in Europe, the Andes Mountains in South America, and the Rocky Mountains in the United States and Canada.

These mountain chains are thousands of miles long, hundreds of miles across, and two or three miles high. The folding process thrusts the entire mountain area far above the surface of the crust. In fact, there has been enough energy inside the earth to shove the mountains upward two or three times. Geologists have learned that the Rocky Mountains and Andes Mountains have been lifted higher into the air at least three times in the past.

Earthquakes and mountains are the result of movements in the crust of the earth. In the next chapter we shall study a third type of activity in the earth's crust - the flow of hot liquid rock. This is called volcanic activity. Of course, both mountain making and earthquakes probably require great supplies of heat energy. Volcanic actions give us a better illustration of the movement of liquid rock. All three types of activity are a reminder that our earth is far from dead and buried. Inside the crust, tremendous amounts of energy are stored. When they break loose in the form of an earthquake, or a volcano, or a mountain, man is completely helpless. All we can hope to do is to keep the damage to a minimum. Perhaps we may be able to control these forces better when we learn exactly how they work. That is what scientists hope. That is one of the reasons why we spend much of our time trying to learn how and why changes in the earth's crust take place.

CHAPTER VII. VOLCANOES

You learned that the heat inside the earth produces great pools of liquid rock. Because the pools are beneath tons of rock, the liquid is often under great pressure. When a hole appears in the crust of the earth, the liquid rock pushes up through the hole to the surface. This flowing of hot liquid rock to the surface of the earth is part of what we call *volcanic activity*. Volcanic action can produce large mountains by building up layers of hard rock. Volcanoes also are closely related to earthquakes.

The melted rock inside the earth is called *magma*. When the melted rock comes to the surface, it is usually called *lava*. When magma hardens, it forms igneous rock. Magma is a mixture of melted rock, steam, and gases. The steam and gases create the great pressure that causes the volcano to explode. Of course, many volcanoes do not explode. They allow the magma to flow out of the earth in an even stream. This reduces the pressure inside the earth and prevents an explosion. Volcanic action includes both the explosions and steady flow of magma to the surface.

The Origin of Volcanoes

How do volcanoes begin? We do not really know, since we cannot look inside the earth to see. But geologists do know that there is very hot material below the surface of the earth. They believe that this is responsible for most volcanic action. Since many volcanoes are found near mountains that have recently been formed, some scientists believe that the great weight of the mountains plays some part in volcanic action. Perhaps the pressure caused by the mountain causes the flow of magma to the surface. No matter how a volcano begins, we know that great heat and pressure are needed to produce the energy which volcanic action employs.

Types of Volcanic Action

We usually think of a volcano as a great cone spouting flame and fire and rock. But, as we have said, many volcanoes do not explode at all. Volcanoes that ooze hot lava without exploding are more common. When the liquid rock moves out of the earth, the pressure inside is reduced, and consequently the danger of explosion is also reduced. Of course, the hot liquid rock is of itself quite dangerous. But it usually moves slowly, and so there is time for people to move away from it.

There are many types of volcanic activity. The speed of the action and the size of the explosion depend upon the type of magma and the amount of pressure behind the volcano. If magma is thick and viscous, it will not flow easily. Gas pressure has time to build up behind it. Therefore, an explosion is more likely to occur when the magma is thick. If the magma is thin, it flows easily and quickly. It can move out of the earth before there is time for the pressure to build up energy enough for an explosion. The actual viscosity of magma depends upon the type and temperature of the rock. Usually, hot magma is thinner and it flows more easily than cool magma.

The amount of gas trapped inside the earth also plays an important part in volcanic action. If there is little or no gas or steam, the volcano will not build up much pressure. It will probably not explode. But when a great deal of gas and steam is trapped in the volcano, an explosion is likely to occur. A volcanic explosion is like one big puff from a steam engine. The steam and gas is released from the engine by the puff; the hot magma is blown out of the earth by the explosion.

A Volcano in Action

What do we find when we look under the surface to see how a volcano works? All volcanoes begin with a great pool of liquid rock, or magma. The hot magma may melt more rock, increasing the size of the pool. When the magma touches a pocket of water, it turns the water to steam. Since water expands about 1,700 times when it changes to steam, this produces enormous pressure on the magma pool. Other gases inside the earth add to the pressure. If the pool of magma is trapped under the earth's crust, the pressure will force the magma toward the surface. If the crust is thin and weak, the pool of magma can cause a large hump in the earth. The pressure may make a crack in the crust, allowing the magma to flow out onto the surface of the earth. If the crust is strong and heavy and the magma under very great pressure, an explosion can take place, bursting through the crust. Then we have a really large volcanic explosion.

Some of these pools of magma exist beneath the floor of the ocean. When the crust breaks, the mixture of the hot lava with water produces enormous clouds of steam. Great clouds of steam are produced by the contact of the hot magma with the water.

Volcanic Explosions

You can imagine what will happen if a large pool of magma, trapped under solid rock crust, finally builds up enough pressure to explode. Some of the most terrific explosions on earth have been due to volcanoes of this type. In 1815 a volcano in the Dutch East Indies (now Indonesia) blew forty cubic miles of material into the air. This would fill a pit two miles wide, two miles deep, and ten miles long. Some of the rocks were thrown twenty miles into the air. The whole earth was covered with ashes from the explosion. Tidal waves more than a hundred feet high were created by the blast. Thousands of persons were killed by the explosion, which was heard for several hundred miles. Thousands more drowned in the giant tidal waves. A thousand miles away, the sky was so dark that lights were needed. This was the greatest volcanic explosion ever recorded.

Volcanic Craters

When a volcanic explosion occurs, it blows an enormous hole in the crust of the earth. An explosion in Alaska opened a hole two miles wide and over three thousand feet deep, for example. These holes in the crust are called volcanic *craters*. Sometimes, a new cone will build up inside the crater left by an old volcano. Mount Vesuvius in Italy, for example, is located inside the crater caused by the explosion of another Mount Vesuvius nearly two thousand years ago. When a volcano is quiet for many years, wind and water erosion cuts away the sides of the crater.

When the center has collapsed, we call the pit a *caldera*. Cal-deras are often very beautiful. The inside of the crater fills with water. The cliffs rise straight into the air from the water's edge. Many calderas are world famous beauty spots. In Hawaii, for example, the craters of two great volcanoes have formed calderas containing lakes nearly three miles wide. The cliffs above the lakes are several thousand feet high. They rise almost straight into the air above the water.

Lava Flow

Volcanic action also includes the flow of lava through a crack in the earth's crust. This type of action is not as spectacular as a great explosion. But it can make great changes on the face of the earth. Enormous areas have been covered by liquid rock from volcanoes. In India alone, nearly 200,000 square miles of land is covered with cold lava. Some parts of the layer are over two thousand feet thick. In the northwestern part of the United States, an even larger area is covered with volcanic lava. The layer is only five hundred feet thick, but it covers almost a quarter-million square miles of surface. Of course, this flow of lava took place thousands of years ago. But we are trying to see how the crust of the earth has been changed by volcanic action. And thousands of years is not a long time in terms of the life of the earth.

Active Volcanoes

Many of the volcanoes on earth are still active. They are very dangerous to life and property, and they cannot be controlled. But we can often get an advance warning when a volcano is about to explode. Before an explosion can take place, pressure must build up inside the earth. This pressure may cause small earthquakes to occur. Cracks may appear in the volcano, and hot lava may flow out through the cracks. These signs may indicate a coming explosion. Of course, there are areas in which earthquakes occur almost every day, and no explosion follows. But a large number of small quakes is often a sign of a coming explosion.

Probably as we learn more about the way heat circulates inside the earth, we may be able to predict volcanic action better. At present we are not really certain why volcanoes erupt. We need more scientific knowledge in this area before we can control the actions of nature that cause the trouble or take steps to protect ourselves against disaster.

Other Volcanic Action

Many types of volcanic action take place entirely below the surface of the earth. We do not see the effect on the surface. The hot magma inside the earth can move from place to place because of the pressure behind it. When it finds an opening, magma flows through the opening wherever it may lead. For example, magma often flows in between the layers of the earth. This causes an effect like a blister on the finger. These blisters are filled with liquid magma. They can produce a dome-shaped swelling on the earth if they are near the surface.

When magma finds a crack in the earth, it fills it just as a plasterer fills a crack in the wall. These filled cracks are called *dikes* if they are vertical. If they are horizontal, they are called *sills*. Some of the dikes are several miles wide and hundreds of miles long. The magma may also be forced into larger zones in the earth's crust and may fill them full of liquid rock. The great pressure behind the magma acts like a grease gun in a garage. It forces magma into other rocks. When the magma cools, it forms a solid plug of rock in the earth's crust.

Hot Springs and Geysers

The hot interior of the earth heats any water trapped deep in the crust. When this hot water flows to the surface of the earth through a crack, we have a *hot spring*. The hot water dissolves many of the minerals in the rock, and hot springs are usually filled with mineral water. In Europe and in the United States, these hot springs are used as health baths. Many people believe that it is healing to bathe in the hot mineral water.

If the hot water from inside the earth is thrown out in a great jet, we have a *geyser*. The western part of the United States has many of these geysers in action. A geyser comes from a crack in the earth that fills with water. At lower levels pressure builds up inside the crack as the water is heated. When the pressure is high enough, it throws the water into the air. Then the geyser stops flowing and begins to build up pressure once again. Some geysers erupt every few minutes. Others may take several days before they raise the pressure high enough to erupt. A geyser is like a volcanic pool that is filled with water. When the pressure reaches the trigger point, the water is driven into the air, and the pressure is relieved.

Using Volcanic Power

Can we harness the tremendous energy supply locked in the earth and put it to work? The use of volcanic power is like the use of the power of the tides. It can be used, but it is more expensive than the use of coal or petroleum. Volcanic energy is used to a limited extent in some areas. Some houses in Iceland are heated by hot water from the interior of the earth. Steam generated by hot magma is also used to produce electricity. But there are many problems involved. The steam from a volcano contains acids that eat into metals. This makes it hard to use with ordinary equipment.

The problem of location is also a difficult one. A volcano in Indonesia is of no use to the people of the United States and not much use to the people of Indonesia. If the volcanoes were located near large industrial centers, some use might be made of them. Some of the acids in volcanic gases are being recovered and sold. This, however, is only a small business at the present time. Until our supply of coal and petroleum becomes much smaller, or until we discover some simple way of using volcanic power, we will probably allow the power inside the earth to go untapped.